ASPECTS OF IRISH STUDIES

Published 1990
The Institute of Irish Studies
The Queen's University of Belfast

This book has received financial assistance under the Cultural Traditions Programme which aims to encourage acceptance and understanding of cultural diversity.

Contributors and Editors

ISBN 0 85389 342 X

Printed by W.G. Baird Ltd, Antrim

Aspects of Irish Studies

EDITED BY
MYRTLE HILL AND SARAH BARBER

The Institute of Irish Studies
The Queen's University of Belfast

Contents List

Introduction by R.H. Buchanan   xi

PART I
Political perspectives

Chapter 1

Jennifer Todd
The conflict in Northern Ireland: institutional and
   constitutional dimensions   3

Chapter 2

James Loughlin
Some comparative aspects of Irish and English nationalism
   in the late nineteenth century   9

Chapter 3

Cormac Murphy
Revolution and radicalism in County Dublin, 1913-21   17

Chapter 4

Maurice Goldring
Quotas: affirmative action, reverse discrimination   25

Chapter 5

John Coakley
Typical case or deviant? Nationalism in Ireland in a
   European perspective   29

PART II
Perspectives on twentieth century culture

Chapter 6

Sophia Hillan King 'Quiet Desperation': variations on a
   theme in the writings of Daniel Corkery, Michael McLaverty
   and John McGahern   39

Chapter 7

Brian Kennedy
Irish landscape painting in a political setting, 1922-48   47

Chapter 8

Eamonn Hughes
Representation in modern Irish poetry   61

Chapter 9

Hugh Maguire
'The mirror up to nature': the theatre building as a
    socio-political cypher   65

PART III
Society in Northern Ireland

Chapter 10

Maurna Crozier
Good leaders and 'decent men': an Ulster contradiction   75

Chapter 11

Amanda Shanks
Northern Irish gentry culture: an anomaly   85

PART IV
The computer as a resource for Irish History

Chapter 12

Brenda Collins
Numbers to the alphabet of history   95

Chapter 13

Angelique Day
The computer as a resource for Irish history: an introduction
    to the Irish Ordnance Survey Memoirs database   101

Chapter 14

Kay Muhr
The Place-Name Research Project, Department of the
    Environment for Northern Ireland and the Celtic
    Department, Queen's University Belfast   109

PART V
Place and people: an historical perspective

Chapter 15

Michelle O'Riordan
A seventeenth century 'political poem'   117

Chaper 16

Rosemary Power
Irish travellers in the Norse World   127

Chapter 17

Patricia Kelly
New horizons in Hiberno-English studies   135

Notes on Contributors and Editors

SARAH BARBER was a Junior Research Fellow at the Institute of Irish Studies 1988-89. She currently lectures in the Department of Modern History, Queen's University, Belfast.

JOHN COAKLEY is a lecturer in Politics at the University of Limerick.

BRENDA COLLINS held an ESRC research award at the Institute of Irish Studies in 1986. She is currently a part-time tutor with the Open University.

MAURNA CROZIER was a Junior Research Fellow at the Institute of Irish Studies 1986-88. She is currently employed as a Development Officer for the Community Relations Council.

ANGELIQUE DAY was a Junior Research Fellow at the Institute of Irish Studies 1981–83. She is currently an Honorary Research Associate at the Institute, financed by the Department of Education.

MAURICE GOLDRING was a Senior Research Fellow at the Institute of Irish Studies in 1988. He is currently Professor of Irish Studies at the Universitie Paris VIII.

MYRTLE HILL was a Junior Research Fellow at the Institute of Irish Studies 1986-88. She currently tutors for the Modern History and Economic and Social History Departments of Queen's University Belfast.

EAMONN HUGHES is currently a tutor in the Adult Education Department at the University of Leicester and from October 1990 he will be lecturing in the School of English, Queen's University, Belfast.

PATRICIA KELLY was an Honorary Research Fellow at the Institute of Irish Studies 1987-88. She is currently Bi-Centennial Fellow at the Royal Irish Academy in Dublin.

BRIAN KENNEDY was an Honorary Research Fellow at the Institute of Irish Studies 1987-88. He is currently curator of 20th century art at the Ulster Museum, Belfast.

SOPHIA HILLAN KING was a Junior Research Fellow at the Institute of Irish Studies 1986-88. She is currently employed on the Cultural Heritage Project for teachers.

JAMES LOUGHLIN was a Research Fellow at the Institute of Irish Studies 1986-88. He is currently lecturing in the Department of History, University of Ulster, Magee College.

HUGH MAGUIRE was a Junior Research Fellow at the Institute of Irish Studies 1988-89, working on the Building Survey of Northern Ireland. He has recently worked as Books Editor on *The Dictionary of Art*.

KAY MUHR was a Junior Research Fellow in the Institute of Irish Studies 1977-79. She is currently a Research Fellow on the Place-Names Project in the Celtic Department at Queen's University, Belfast.

CORMAC MURPHY was a Junior Research Fellow at the Institute of Irish Studies 1987-89, sponsored by the Northern Ireland Postal Board. He is currently employed as an Employee Relations Adviser for Mobil Oil, London.

MICHELLE O'RIORDAN was a Junior Research Fellow at the Institute of Irish Studies 1986-88. She is currently employed as Assistant to the Chairman of *Gael Linn*.

ROSEMARY POWER was a Junior Research Fellow at the Institute of Irish Studies 1984-85. She is currently working in community education.

AMANDA SHANKS was a Junior Research Fellow at the Institute of Irish Studies 1984-85. She is currently a tutor in the Department of Social Anthroplogy at Queen's University, Belfast.

JENNIFER TODD was an Honorary Research Fellow at the Institute of Irish Studies 1987-88. She is currently lecturing in the Department of Politics, University College, Dublin.

Introduction

The collection of papers published in this volume were originally presented at a two-day conference held in the Institute of Irish Studies at Queen's University in September 1989. The occasion was an end of session gathering of a group of young scholars, most of whom had worked together at the Institute during the previous academic year. At first glance the papers appear to have little in common, for the authors come from a broad range of academic disciplines, and in their time in the Institute each has followed his or her own research interest. Yet each would acknowledge that their work has benefitted from the perspective of other disciplines; through living and working together each has gained fresh insights, developing new approaches to their subject, devising new analytical techniques, interpreting data in new ways.

The sense of a community of scholars, seeking different goals but united in the pursuit of knowledge for its own sake, is fostered at the Institute in the belief that it is basic to the idea of the university and essential for the further development of Irish Studies. In its support of the Institute, Queen's affirms its adherence to traditional academic values, despite the contemporary pressures to measure academic productivity in terms of numbers of staff publications or primary degrees. By providing the necessary finance and a good working environment, Queen's enables young scholars to develop their potential, and contribute to a greater understanding of Irish culture and history. The need for such work is self-evident. The complexities of Ireland's politics and political structures, and the range of its social and economic problems has ensured front-page headlines in the world's press for the past twenty years. And while the work of scholars rarely resolves such problems, it can increase the understanding of present decision-makers, and more particularly, help in the education of the coming generation.

The papers which follow should be seen in this context, as individual contributions of young scholars who believe passionately that their work not only has value in the academic community but can enrich the lives of their fellow countrymen and contribute to a greater understanding of Ireland's inherited culture and contemporary life. The publication owes much to the enthusiasm and hard work of Dr Sarah Barber, Dr Myrtle Hill, Dr Michelle O'Riordan and Dr Jennifer Todd; they in turn wish to acknowledge the advice and assistance they received from Dr Brian Walker, who undertook the work of publication with characteristic zeal and professionalism.

R.H. Buchanan
Director, Institute of Irish Studies

PART I
POLITICAL PERSPECTIVES

CHAPTER 1

The conflict in Northern Ireland: institutional and constitutional dimensions

by

Jennifer Todd

The Northern Ireland conflict is about power, jobs and security within Northern Ireland; it is also about the very existence of Northern Ireland itself. Observers tend to make a sharp distinction between the former level of institutional conflict and the latter level of constitutional conflict. This distinction is not made by the two main parties to the conflict. For both unionists and nationalists, the constitutional and institutional levels of conflict are intrinsically interrelated. The actors' categorisations – whether right or wrong, backward or percipient – are important because they affect the nature of the conflict and the limits of acceptable compromise for each side. What counts as a compromise on internal, institutional structures is determined by the actors' respective views on the constitutional issue.

In what follows, the logic of unionist and nationalist arguments is reconstructed, showing that institutional and constitutional issues are intimately interrelated in the thought of both unionists and nationalists. Finally, it is suggested that any proposed 'compromise' settlement is unlikely to succeed unless it takes account of the perceptions and views of the main protagonists.

I. The unionist position

It is sometimes suggested that unionists would make concessions if only nationalists would confine themselves to institutional demands. The implication is that nationalists confuse or conflate institutional demands and constitutional aspirations while unionists make this distinction clearly. In fact, unionists do not sharply distinguish between institutional and constitutional issues. Their views on questions of institutional reform are directly related to their views on the legitimacy of the state. Not only the 'extreme' but also the 'moderate' unionists share this view. As a result, what constitutes an acceptable compromise from the unionist perspective is not recognised as such by other participants and observers.

There are radically different perceptions of the unionist position. Mainstream unionists think they have already made generous concessions to nationalists and that they have nothing left to offer. Nationalists, they say, give nothing in return: their demands are too high because they do not want Northern Ireland to work.[1] Nationalists, however, think that unionists will not accept equality and that they make concessions only under pressure.[2] Observers wonder why unionists have been

3

reluctant to make a sufficiently generous offer to enable a stable settlement to be achieved.[3] The answer lies in the way in which unionists link institutional and constitutional issues.

From the unionist perspective, the partition of Ireland and the foundation of the Northern state was legitimate. Unionists had as much right to self-determination and territory as nationalists. This view has not changed in seventy years. It still forms the basis of the unionist view of the proper and necessary institutional structures in Northern Ireland.[4] This is why unionists have never found a way of integrating nationalists into Northern Ireland. They do not think that radical change in the political framework is necessary. From their perspective it is right that the majority's view should have more weight than the minority's – after all partition was to allow unionists to determine their form of government. Unionists can merely suggest reforms to make more equality for nationalists within this political framework. From the unionist perspective, twenty years of reform have addressed all the major nationalist grievances and, while a few may remain, they will gradually be remedied as political stability is achieved.

Unionists say that they claim no rights that they are not happy to share with other citizens. But their commitment to individual rights within a British framework is far from meeting nationalists' demands for full equality of the two traditions. Even in their rejection of British policies, they conceive of equality within a British framework, as their resistance to the Anglo-Irish agreement shows: it is not only integrationists who are angered by the 'colonial' treatment of Northern Ireland and demand that they are accorded the same rights as others in the United Kingdom.[5]

The effects of these basic constitutional assumptions can be seen in the reforms which unionists are willing to accept, and the concessions which they are willing to offer. Even if politicians were willing to set aside principles and bargain pragmatically, the public's perception of the limits of legitimate reform would constrain their ability to compromise.

Many unionists still favour devolved government with majority rule. Leading figures in the Official Unionist Party still oppose any strong form of executive power-sharing.[6] Other prominent unionists have suggested that some form of power-sharing government would be possible.[7] Despite this increased flexibility, even the most accommodating unionist thinks that the unionist majority should count for something in any new structures of devolved government. Many unionists see the offer of power-sharing as a major concession to nationalists, rather than a basic right. It is therefore proposed as a final settlement, in exchange for which nationalists should accept the legitimacy of the state and 'forfeit the role of the Government of the Irish Republic as custodians of the nationalist interest'.[8]

Unionists think that security policy should be strengthened so that the I.R.A. can be militarily defeated. The security forces have their full backing because they are seen as the legitimate forces of the state; attack on them is attack on the state and all its citizens. For similar reasons they believe that exceptional legal measures, including internment, should be introduced in the battle against the I.R.A., and that paramilitary prisoners should be treated as simple criminals.[9]

The unionist view of the Irish dimension follows from their view of the legitimacy of the state. Just as in the early years of the state James Craig was willing to have friendly relations with the South if, and only if, each government recognised the legitimacy of the other, so today North/South relations are acceptable to unionists only when they are based on such mutual recognition.[10] Any intervention by the Republic in internal Northern Ireland affairs is seen as illegitimate.

Unionists do not accept that nationalists have a right to cultural equality. Since they believe that they have a right to a British state, they believe that British symbols should have public prominence.

The unionist position on fair-employment legislation is less closely linked with their constitutional views than with their concern with the immediate economic interests of their constituents. There may, however, be a connection between their general attitudes to reform and their resistance to strong fair-employment legislation. In both cases, formal equality of opportunity is offered while substantive equality of the traditions is resisted.

Unionists tend to offer concessions to nationalists only when they are pushed. For example, the present series of power-sharing proposals is a response to the pressure of the Anglo-Irish agreement. In 1984, only administrative power-sharing was acceptable to them. Now, as Harold McCusker reportedly put it, many realise that they would prefer to be ruled by Northern Ireland catholics than by Dublin.[11] Because the concessions have come in this context, unionists appear to give them grudgingly and nationalists do not appreciate them. But if there were no such pressure, unionists genuinely would not see the need for further reform.

Only very recently, when unionists believe they are under intense pressure from nationalists, have a few more radical noises emerged from the Official Unionist camp, which may show that some unionists would be willing to construct a new state in Northern Ireland rather than reform the old one.[12] If this were the case, it would mark a break from the view that the Northern Ireland state was and is legitimate; it might allow unionists to offer constitutional nationalists a deal which they would find difficult to refuse. Up to the present, however, there is little sign that the mainstream unionist parties have been willing to offer such a settlement.

II. The nationalist position

Nationalists' demands for institutional reform are influenced by their constitutional views. Republicans argue that partition has created a set of power relations which make the Northern state irreformable; no institutional settlement will bring full equality for nationalists and it is a waste of time to look for one. This paper considers only constitutional nationalists, who see some possibility of an institutional settlement within Northern Ireland. Such a settlement, in their view, cannot be separated from constitutional changes: their institutional demands derive from an analysis which sees the institutional conflict as a symptom of the deeper problem of relations within and between these islands.[13]

There are very different perceptions of the constitutional nationalist position. The Social Democratic and Labour Party presents itself as rational, realistic, pragmatic and moderate. Individuals in the Unionist and Alliance parties are angered by its ability to wrongfoot them and appear moderate even while refusing their offers of compromise. The Workers Party accuses it of intransigent nationalism, while Sinn Fein thinks it has given up on the aim of unity. Observers suggest that it might gain more if it held off on its nationalist demands.[14] These differences reflect different conceptions of what constitutes a reasonable compromise. The S.D.L.P.'s view of an acceptable compromise is intrinsically linked to its view on the legitimacy of the state: ambiguities in its demands reflect the ambiguities of its constitutional stance.[15]

The S.D.L.P. does not see Irish unity as the only or the priority goal. It recognizes that unionists have as much right to be British as nationalists have to be Irish. These positions mark a major change from traditional nationalism. Yet contemporary constitutional nationalists still share some traditional nationalist assumptions: that the Irish people have a right to self-determination; that the Northern state was deeply sectarian in the methods by which it was founded, in its boundaries and in its institutions.[16] The S.D.L.P. neither affirms nor denies that unionists have a right to self-determination and partition;[17] thus it leaves open the possibility of an institutional settlement without closing the possibility of Irish unity, and allows the coexistence of very different perspectives within the party. Even the most accommodating nationalist, however, only accepts unionists' right to self-determination if nationalists' aims and projects are treated as equally valid. From the nationalist perspective, the minimal necessary reforms are a total change in state structures so that both unionists and nationalists can start anew in a state equally grounded in each tradition. They cannot be satisfied with what they see as piecemeal reform of a fundamentally flawed political system. Their minimum demand is for full equality of the traditions within Northern Ireland and an open agenda on the constitutional issue.[18]

In a Northern Ireland context the nationalist position is radical. It means that unionists can no longer use their majority status in Northern Ireland to justify inequality of power. Even when nationalists accept the boundary of Northern Ireland in the middle term, they do not accept unionist power within it. Whatever the detailed structure of a power-sharing executive, it is not acceptable that unionists have the last say or, as it is usually put, a veto on reform. Thus the S.D.L.P. is committed to the Anglo-Irish agreement as a framework which makes it impossible for unionists to dominate nationalists simply by virtue of demography. Partition may be accepted as an unavoidable fact, but it is not accepted that it gives the unionist majority rights over the nationalist minority.[19]

Nationalists demand full cultural equality with unionists. This means that British symbols should not have public pre-eminence over Irish in any respect: the 'British' character of the state should not confer any priority on British state symbols. It also means that the nationalist view of the illegitimacy of Stormont, its perspective on the history of the state and its aim of a united Ireland be accepted as legitimate and should have as much and as free public expression as the official British and unionist views.

The nationalist view that a legitimate state has still to be constructed also affects its view of security policy. From the constitutional nationalist perspective, the defeat of the I.R.A. is possible only by political means. Security policy cannot be considered in isolation from reform of legal structures and of the political system. It cannot be pursued as if there were already consensus about the legitimacy of the state.[20]

The constitutional nationalist view on economic and fair employment issues does not appear to be a product of their views on the legitimacy of the state. On these issues, compromise with unionists is prevented by the direct economic interests of the different parties, rather than by their different stances on the constitutional issue.

Finally, nationalists demand an open agenda on the constitutional issue; there can be no 'final settlement'. They emphasize that their constitutional aspirations are just as valid as the unionists'.[21] Many feel that only when this is recognized will unionists accord full equality to nationalists within Northern Ireland. They believe that the national question must be left open if unionists are not to take the legitimacy of the Northern Ireland state for granted and revert to their old habits of majority rule.

Radical as these demands appear to unionists, nationalists think they have already made major changes in their own perspective and major concessions to unionists even before serious negotiations on an institutional settlement have begun.

III. Conclusion

At the root of the institutional conflict lie very different views on the legitimacy of the state. In consequence, each side has very different ideas about what counts as a compromise: what one thinks a major concession, the other does not recognize as such; what one thinks a generous compromise, the other sees as 'too little too late'. The constitutional issue, in this sense, is internal to the institutional conflict and prevents an agreed institutional settlement. Even if devolved government with power-sharing were to come about, serious conflicts over power, security and the speed and urgency of change would remain while the conflict over legitimacy is unresolved.

This problem is unlikely to go away. Both unionists and nationalists have a political interest in retaining their respective views on the legitimacy of the state. It may, of course, be in the best long-term interests of either or both groups to change their views. This is not now evident to them.

Unionists, for example, have an interest in believing that their original project of setting up their own British state in Ireland was legitimate. Otherwise they would lose their strongest argument for the union with Britain. They would have to admit that the protestant unionist people do not have an unconditional right to self-determination. They would be obliged to retreat to more pragmatic arguments about the economic or other benefits of the union.

Equally, nationalists have no reason to give up their aim of Irish unity or whole-heartedly to accept the legitimacy of the Northern Ireland state. If they were to do so, they would lose any chance of achieving Irish unity. Further, their argument for full equality of the traditions within Northern Ireland would be undermined. This argument depends on the view that the boundaries of the state give no special rights to the majority within it: in effect, it accepts the factual existence of the boundaries but denies their legitimacy.

It appears, therefore, that the Northern Ireland conflict is deeply rooted at the constitutional level. Calls for compromise on institutional structures are shallow unless they recognize that the conflict is in large part about what counts as a compromise. Unionists and nationalists sincerely believe that they have already made generous concessions and, from their respective standpoints, they have. To force either side to concede what it sees as its basic rights is unlikely to bring lasting peace. Until a way is found to bring all the issues in dispute – constitutional as well as institutional – on to the agenda for discussion, it is not clear how the conflicting interests and demands can be accommodated.

CHAPTER 2

Some comparative aspects of Irish and English nationalism in the late nineteenth century
by
James Loughlin

Our view of Anglo-Irish relations in the late nineteenth century is one that identifies nationalism almost solely with Ireland. That the opposition to Irish nationalism in England might itself be described as nationalist has not usually been acknowledged. This can be attributed partly to the fact that English scholarship has tended to regard England's historical development as unique and unaffected by the nationalist traumas affecting other peoples, while the burden of scholarly work in general has concentrated on 'new' nations in pursuit of national independence rather than 'old' national entities long in possession of it.[1] This paper will attempt to outline and compare some of the central features of Irish and English nationalism in this period and suggest that to see Anglo-Irish conflict in terms of opposing nationalisms enhances our understanding of the issues involved, in particular the rejection of Irish home rule.

Carlton Hayes has described nationalism as the fusion of patriotism with the consciousness of nationality, when love of country – an emotion involving fondness, sympathy, fidelity and loyalty – is channelled through the perspective of the history, population, territoriality, political institutions, cultural interests and ambitions of the nation.[2] Of these elements, history is undoubtedly one of the most important. History, or more exactly, a nationalist myth which unfolds the story of the nation, performs important functions. For example, it shapes perceptions of national identity and characteristics, gives meaning to 'national prestige' and generally contextualises the nation's place in the world. The myth, however, is not disinterested or devoid of political motive in the way that it deals with the national past. Its perspective is present-centred, its purpose instrumental. Its chief function is to provide a stimulus to political change, towards the realisation of nationalist objectives. To this end the nationalist myth organises the past as a morality tale. The desired political objectives and conditions are presented as having existed or having been paralleled sometime in the distant past; this ideal state of affairs – which points up the contrast between the dissatisfactions and indignities of the present and the glories that once were – is seen to have been destroyed by both domestic and external enemies with consequent oppression for God's own people. The path of glory, however, will soon be re-established by the exertions of the nation and its leaders. For those engaged in nationalist struggle, history does more than hold up a national objective; in detailing the indignities and humiliations visited upon the nation it provides a means of heightening nationalist consciousness by focusing the animosity engendered by the memory of those experiences on to the present-day successors of the original persecutors. Thus nationalist myth uses history both to identify a goal for the future and as an immediate context to explain the meaning of present political events. This kind of myth is essential to most nationalist movements and is present in both the Irish and English versions.

Irish nationalist ideology in the late nineteenth century was a complex web of images shifting between revolution and rebellion on the one side and constitution-alism on the other, and reflecting centuries of historical experience – the wars of the seventeenth century, Grattan's Parliament, the 1798 rebellion, O'Connell's repeal campaign, Fenianism and others. Within this spectrum were the central features of the national myth outlined above. The form of its expression though was condi-tioned by the nature of the audience addressed, and the need to take account of the several constituencies that made up the nationalist movement. The movement combined a number of viewpoints reflecting the varied nature of nationalist ideology itself. Parnell had, in the later 1870s and early 1880s, united agrarian agitators, Fenians, militant Irish-Americans and his parliamentary party under one broad nationalist banner.[3] To meet the needs of this heterogeneous grouping the national myth had at one and the same time to draw on its revolutionary and constitutional imagery. In fact, the myth included two distinct perspectives on the nation's fall from glory, reflecting these viewpoints. One, focusing on the glories of pre-invasion Ireland, concentrated on the persecution inflicted on the 'native' Irish and emphasised Celtic ethnicity and catholicity as essential ingredients of nationalism. The other, more recent in time, took a more comprehensive view of the Irish nation and received a major boost when Gladstone took up home rule in 1886. In this perspective, Grattan's Parliament of 1782 was associated with a golden age of economic prosperity, religious tolerance and strong nationalist sentiment on the part of Irish protestants. Betrayed by English corruption and followed by repression, it also provided an indication of the benefits that follow self-government. Distinct though these perspectives were, in practice they were often integrated, with the emphasis depending on who was being addressed and where. The flexibility of the nationalist myth was undoubtedly a major source of strength to the Parnellite movement, as indeed was Parnell's facility at exploiting it through his ability to pose as both a revolutionary and a moderate, as and when the occasion demanded.[4] It was also important that the objective of the movement could be described in 'value-free' terms: 'legislative independence', 'national emancipation' and 'home rule' could be interpreted in ways to suit either the most resolute republican or the mildest constitutionalist. As one commentator said of 'Home Rule', there was a 'transfig-uring vagueness' about the phrase:

> To moderate men 'Home Rule' meant nothing more than an Irish parliament for
> the management of Irish affairs in subordination to England. Fenians saw in home
> rule the beginnings of a movement which might possibly end in the establishment
> of an Irish republic.[5]

If the outline of Irish nationalism seems relatively straightforward, that of English nationalism – a subject that has only recently begun to be extensively studied[6] – is much more complex. The term 'English' is used here rather than 'British' because the concept of the nation that came to prevail by the early 1880s was one based on England – especially southern England – and took little acccount of Scottish and Welsh national characteristics. This concept was a conservative one and can be seen as the culmination of one hundred years of conflict with oppositional forms of patriotism.[7] English nationalism itself, however, was a much earlier growth. Indeed England has been described as the seat of modern nationalism. By the early seventeenth century there was a national language spoken throughout England and the Scottish lowlands, a national monarchy following defeat in the French wars and a national church following the break with Rome. During the English civil war both Royalists and Cromwellians shared a belief in the English as a 'chosen people' and venerated the 'ancient' British constitution.[8]

The evolution of the constitution was at the centre of the English national myth. Writers as diverse as Viscount Bolingbroke, David Hume and Edward Gibbon located the origin of English liberties in the Germanic peoples who had migrated to England from the continent and in the ancient, pre-Norman, Saxon form of government, the Witenagemot. In fact, by the later eighteenth century, one of the chief ideological weapons used by radicals complaining of the corruption in government and the French manners practised by the Whig oligarchy, was the theory of the 'Norman Yoke' – the belief that the Norman invasion had destroyed the constitutional freedoms which Saxon Englishmen enjoyed, and imposed instead a lasting tyranny on the people, a tyranny represented by the existing ruling class of crown, church and landlords, and a tyranny which it was their duty to overthrow.[9] The advent of the French Revolution and the wars that followed, however, enabled the Whigs to seize the patriotic initiative. Edmund Burke's, *Reflections on the Revolution in France*, portrayed the English constitution as the reflection of divine law and he celebrated the excellence of the English political system as it developed through the ages, reaching its culmination in the 'Glorious Revolution' of 1688. Burke presented the archaic oligarchical system of his own day as the essence of political wisdom, and it would be difficult to overestimate the influence of his *Reflections* as propaganda. It established some of the central themes of Tory national patriotism throughout the nineteenth century: organic unity versus social disintegration, common sense versus abstract theorising. These themes were used, not just against French and 'continental' theorising but against domestic enemies, such as utilitarianism, liberalism, popular democracy and socialism.[10]

Radical forms of patriotism continued to exist and, by the 1870s, were incorporated within liberalism; however by the end of this decade the liberal concept of patriotism was being decisively displaced by its conservative opposite. Liberal patriotism, in large part, was earnest and lacking in emotional dynamics. The thrust of its foreign policy – an area astutely used by Tories to heighten national consciousness and aggression – was the pursuit of peace and international conciliation, subjects about which it was difficult to arouse public excitement. Moreover a series of imperial disasters under Gladstone's second ministry of 1880-85, appeared to demonstrate that it also failed the test of practical politics.[11] Tory patriotism, on the other hand, was a more heady mix.

Claiming self-consciously to be the 'National' party, defender of the constitution, monarch, church and estates of the realm, Tory patriotism drew on a potent and integrated mix of popular protestantism, racial and class prejudice – most noticeable in relation to Ireland – xenophobia and jingoism. Indeed, the close relationship between religious and political conflict in the history of the nation led to protestantism being considered not only as a body of religious beliefs but as an aspect of English national character. Lord Salisbury, for example, expressing disapproval of the catholic practice of confession, had no hesitation in describing it as foreign to the English national character, as 'injurious to the moral independence and virility of the nation ... this practice is deeply opposed to the peculiarities and idiosyncracies of the English people ever since they became a free people'.[12] Religious and racial prejudice could, moreover, combine to reinforce each other. The constitutional lawyer, A.V. Dicey – no rabid racist – regarded England and Ireland as being at 'divergent stages of civilisation', with an injurious effect on Anglo-Irish relations: 'That the people of England should have been ripe for protestantism at a time when the people of Ireland had hardly risen to the level of Roman Catholicism was to each country a grievous misfortune.'[13] Perceived threats to the 'constitution' and the empire gave focus to these prejudices in the late nineteenth century. Concerned to limit the damage to the constitution posed by increased democratisation and the threat of 'socialism' – of which Irish nationalism was perceived as an aspect – Disraeli had consciously used an aggressive foreign and imperial policy to heighten national consciousness – to concentrate the minds of the people on those things which they could claim to have in common, thereby thwarting the development of a class-based politics. The 'Russophobia' engendered by the Tories during the Russian-Turkish war of 1878, and a series of military defeats during Gladstone's second ministry, favoured and seemed to vindicate a policy of aggressive imperialism at a time when other European powers were similarly engaged.

What told decisively in favour of Tory national patriotism was the home rule crisis of 1886. One way of seeing this crisis is as a barometer of nationalist and patriotic feeling. For many – Joseph Chamberlain is the most prominent example – the crisis worked to place nationalism and patriotism at the centre of their political interests. It intensified the ideological coherence of the Tory party itself by destroying the tradition of cross-party voting; in 1883, to take one year, the leadership of both parties had voted together in 46 per cent of 'whipped' divisions. After 1886, party leaders became more dependent on their own back benches, which in the Tory case meant an increased emphasis on the defence of established institutions.[14] More generally, the home rule crisis led to a substantial increase in support for Tory patriotism. Membership of the Tory propaganda movement, the Primrose League, rose from 200,000 in March 1886 to 500,000 in March 1887.[15]

Tory patriotism was instrumental in the defeat of the Irish nationalist campaign for home rule in 1886, and it is an interesting historical parallel that the period from the late 1870s to the early 1880s, a time when the forces of Irish nationalism were developing that would persuade Gladstone to introduce a home rule scheme in 1886, was also the period when the nationalist forces in England that would ensure its defeat were also coming to the fore. But these two forms of nationalism have more in common. Both were the products of the same religious/political conflicts and the close identification of religious and national characteristics. Popular protestantism exerted a significant influence on Tory perceptions of the dangers to England represented by a 'priest-dominated' Irish parliament. The Irish preoccupation with episodes long past was much commented on, but it had a parallel in the obsession of English popular protestantism with an historically-determined view of papal tyranny, whose chances of being established in the late nineteenth century were remote.

Interesting comparisons can also be made about the role of the nationalist myth in both Tory national patriotism and Irish nationalism. By the mid 1880s, the Tory patriotic myth of an ideal constitution was being contextualised within an appropriate ideological landscape. In this period the national perception of England as an 'imagined community', to use Benedict Anderson's phrase,[16] underwent a radical change. The desire of new economic elites to adapt themselves to aristocratic values and a widespread reaction against urbanisation and industrialisation, led to the redefinition of England in terms of an arcadian paradise based on the south of England.

This mythologising of England in terms of a rural, timeless and unchanging environment, the repository of authentic English values, was not simply the preserve of Tories; radicals and socialists had their own versions, but the Tory version was the most emotive.[17] Propagated by prominent Conservatives such as Lord Tennyson and the Poet Laureate, Alfred Austin, it sketched out a mythic ideological landscape within which the Conservative myth of the constitution, idealising the hierarchical, rural social structure, was contextualised. This idealised rural landscape was the necessary environment for a political concept of the nation centred on the stability of the constitution – church, crown, lords and commons.

Comparison of the Tory arcadian myth with that of Irish nationalism is instructive. The 'Gaelic garden of Eden' could inspire Irish nationalists in much the same way rural England inspired Conservatives. Both were critiques of current political realities. In Ireland's case it was an 'alien' landlord domination; in England, cosmopolitanism, industrialisation, and the perceived threat posed by democracy and socialism to the established order. Both were inspirational visions, in that the social and political realities which they described were politically non-contentious. In England the countryside had long been integrated into national life. There was no rural society distinct from the 'national' society based in the cities.[18]

In Ireland the same was true, though in reverse order. There was no contradiction or substantive difference between town and country society because the towns themselves were overwhelmingly rural.[19] With no substantial industrialisation there was no opposition to industrialisation; in fact, it was a standard complaint of nationalists that England killed Irish manufactures at birth. And though Irish society was rural, the arcadian Gaelic myth employed by nationalists was so remote from current realities that it could be invoked without political cost. Certainly the land legislation promoted by national politicians hardly tended towards the recreation of a Gaelic social order. The essential difference between the Tory national myth and that of Irish nationalists was that the former was directed towards thwarting social and political change; the latter sought to hasten it. To put it another way, their differences lay in the fact that one was the myth of a 'possessive' nationalism, whose independence had long been gained, the other was that of an 'aspirant' nationalism, anxious to secure it.

The territorial unity of these national myths may also be compared. The myths of Irish and English nationalism were conceived in what might be called 'heartland' terms. For Tory patriots, the heartland was southern England, particularly the home counties; for Irish nationalists no specific locality was defined as ideally Irish, rather the heartland was conceived in terms of the island as a whole. In both cases, important regional differences were ignored. Wales and Scotland, not to mention Ireland, hardly conformed to the south of England model and the national myth was hardly a reliable guide for dealing with the problems of these regions. For example, a Conservative writer in the *National Review* writing in 1913 on 'The problem of Wales', with reference specifically to nationality, landlordism and the question of Welsh disestablishment, failed to find any merit in Welsh grievances on these subjects: Wales was 'priest ridden'; the driving force of Welsh radicalism was 'greed and bitterness' especially greed; no freedom of conscience was allowed to those who differed from the majority; 'boycotting, social ostracism and unemployment' were frequently applied; the country in general was obsessed with ancient grudges while Welsh nationalism, such as it was, was 'only an artificially stimulated electioneering dodge'.[20] The stock range of Conservative reactions to Irish problems in the 1880s is immediately recognisable here. For Tory patriots, the essential homogeneity of British national life had to be insisted on, whether in Ireland or in Wales, and anything that appeared to conflict with, or disrupt it, could not be accepted as valid.

This reaction to dissident views on the part of Tory patriots had a parallel in Irish nationalist myth. The Gaelic vision of the myth ignored such an unpleasant reality as the existence of protestant north-east Ulster, while the version based on Grattan's Parliament failed completely to take account of the great changes that occurred in the political views of Ulster protestants after the 1780s. For both Irish and English patriotism, mental maps of the national territory existed, sanctioned by either nature or God, and against which no objection could be accepted. The evidence of both Tory and Irish nationalist reactions to unpalatable realities suggests how important stereotyping was to the internal consistency of their national myths. The consistency of Tory rhetoric used to condemn 'invalid' political movements and forces, indicates not only its importance but also the narrow rigidity of the framework within which these issues were viewed. On the Irish side, these characteristics are most clearly in evidence in the nationalist response to the emergence of Ulster unionism in the 1880s.

The growth of Orange opposition to nationalism in the Ulster countryside of the early 1880s was seen as unrepresentative of any section of rural protestant opinion. It was regarded as an urban phenomenon, imported into the countryside by landlords wishing to hold on to powers that were under threat from the nationalist movement. This attitude was maintained despite the continued growth of Ulster unionism, while during the home rule crisis of 1886, when unionism in the north organised itself across the province as a movement representative of the protestant community, nationalists continued to claim that the only real unionists were a reprehensible and unrepresentative clique of Orangemen and landlords, that the main body of Ulster protestants was open to persuasion on the home rule question, and in any case they would never consider armed rebellion.[21] This attitude, moreover, survived considerable evidence to the contrary, such as riots in Belfast and a multiplicity of demonstrations against home rule; indeed it survived almost intact until quite recently and its persistence provides striking evidence of the power of political myth to structure reality in accordance with the needs of those who subscribe to it.

That English nationalism of the Tory variety had many similarities with its Irish counterpart would not have been accepted by Tories. From their point of view, Irish nationalism and the land struggles associated with it formed part of the democratic and socialist threat to established constitutional order. Yet this was far from being the case. The revolutionary rhetoric of Parnellite nationalism served to disguise what was an essentially conservative movement. By the mid 1880s the radical elements of the parliamentary party were only a fraction of the membership. Parnell was no enthusiastic supporter of democracy and certainly had no time for such socialistic innovations as trades unions. Many of his M.P.s lived in England, were respectable members of their communities, while some even supported British imperialism.[22] Gladstone, by the time he decided to introduce his first home rule bill, appears to have recognised the real nature of Parnell's party, though the hopes he had for the political restoration of the Irish landlords when home rule was established were clearly misplaced.[23] It is indicative of the party's social conservatism, for example, that it had no specific programme to deal with Ireland's social and economic ills. As one close and sympathetic observer of the home rule movement noted:

None of the very able men enlisted in its cause hardly ever attempted construc-
tively to show how home rule, which was to consist of political machinery of the
English type (and) worked according to old established principles, by legislators
and officials of the same social class, and fundamentally of the same types of
mind and ideas, however they might differ in race, was to set to rights the
economic disorders of Ireland, merely because the same kinds of strings,
legislative and administrative, were to be pulled in Dublin instead of at Westminster. ... Vague and indefinite hopes prevailed to some extent that a good time
would follow – that the worker would have more regular employment and better
wages; that the farmer would get higher prices for his produce, that the shop-
keeper would have quicker sales and larger profits and so on.[24]

The reality of what nationalist rule in Ireland would entail was obscured from
Conservatives by the perspective within which Irish nationalism was viewed. It was
left to such unorthodox Tories as Wilfrid Scawen Blunt, who was that rare bird, a
Tory home ruler, to see the similarities between Conservatism and Parnellite
nationalism. Having examined the nationalist movement during tours of Ireland in
1886 and 1887, and noted how non-revolutionary and socially conservative were
the views of leading figures such as John Dillon and Michael Davitt, Blunt recorded
that the Tory view of home rulers as 'Jacobins' was absurd: 'There is nothing more
absurd than to talk of home rule as Jacobinism. Ireland under her own parliament
would infallibly be retrograde, at least for several years'.[25]

However, Blunt's complaint that the Tory concept of Irish nationalism was
inaccurate was rather beside the point; the purpose of that concept was not
dispassionate analysis but the arousing of patriotic emotions through the identification of national enemies against whom all could combine. It was no less true on the
Irish side. William O'Brien, editor of *United Ireland* and the leading propagandist
of the Parnellite movement could, on occasion, explain Anglo-Irish relations in
terms of simple national hatred: 'They hate us and we hate them in return'.[26] In both
cases, black and white stereotyping left little room for political accommodation.

In this context it was hardly surprising that Gladstone's home rule scheme,
premised on the idea that Irish and English patriotisms were compatible rather than
fundamentally antagonistic, failed as a solution to the Irish question.

CHAPTER 3

Revolution and radicalism in county Dublin, 1913-21
by
Cormac Murphy

There were two struggles fought in the period 1913-21: the national revolution for self-determination, a conservatively-led revolution which was an extension of the bourgeois nationalism of the late nineteenth century, and the social struggle, largely led by the Irish Transport and General Workers Union (I.T.G.W.U.), to improve the living and working conditions of the Irish working class. The manner of their interaction is complex and Irish historiography has tended to see one in terms of the other: most typically, the social struggle has been fitted into the broader national struggle. This, however, has tended to obscure the parallel, but separate, development of revolution and radicalism. A case study of county Dublin for the period can help illustrate the relationship between the two.

County Dublin was predominantly agricultural in the early part of the century. Farming was labour intensive and the largest employer; the main types of farming were market gardening, grazing and fattening. Fishing was relatively small-scale. The only industry of note was in the west and north. There were wool, paper, flour and other mills in the west, and a number of factories around Balbriggan in the north.[1] The area of study excludes Dublin city itself but its proximity to the city is an important factor. The county was economically tied to the city and Dublin was the centre of all the major political forces in Ireland; the military and civil establishments, all shades of nationalism, organized labour, and unionism. Dublin was the centre for the arbiters of both the 'national' and the 'social' questions. Political events in the city therefore had a direct bearing on the county.

County Dublin was predominantly a constitutional nationalist stronghold by 1913. The Irish Parliamentary Party (I.P.P.) enjoyed the majority support of the electorate with the Unionists their close rivals in the south.[2] There was little activity among the I.P.P. and kindred organizations like the United Irish League (U.I.L.) and the Ancient Order of Hibernians, between the introduction of the Home Rule Bill and the summer of 1914 as people confidently awaited its passing. However, the appearance of four branches of the Irish Volunteers by May 1914 indicates that a small group in the county were perhaps not so confident. These branches – three in the north and one in the west – were set up in those areas which had been centres for the recently defeated strike. The potential for all the forces of nationalism to come together despite their differences was demonstrated in June 1914, with John Redmond's takeover of the Volunteers; the number of Volunteer branches shot up from three to thirty-three by September with membership reaching over 4,000.[3]

The split in the Volunteer movement over the war issue in September signalled the end of the National Volunteers in county Dublin. Several branches in the north

17

broke away from the Redmondite umbrella and others throughout the county split into two factions. Their numbers never exceeded 300. In addition, many who opposed Redmond left the Volunteer movement for good. A core of about 100, mostly in the north, were advocates of physical force – two branches had split by August 1914 on these grounds. Many of these had been involved in the bitter strikes in the county. They were frequently described as 'persons of no influence', shopkeepers assistants, small farmers' sons and labourers, a group definitely not part of the establishment.

For a time both groups carried on their activities side by side. There were never any clashes but there was plenty of cat-calling – shouts of 'Up the Kaiser!' were met with 'Up Redmond!' Irish Volunteer parades were occasions for anti-British sentiment. The vast majority of nationalists, however, were supportive of Britain in its war effort. A number of the county's Volunteers followed Redmond's advice and enlisted in the British army.[4]

Neither of the Volunteer bodies carried out its activities in isolation. They maintained regular contact with city companies who would come out to the county area to drill where they would be joined by the locals. This regular contact was important – it is doubtful if the relatively scattered county population could have maintained an organization by themselves. The long working day and, frequently, the long distances to be travelled were additional factors that were not conducive to organization.

In fact, local considerations were important for all groups in the county. As well as the proximity of Dublin and the regular contact with city groups, all eleven members of the Irish Volunteer executive lived in Dublin city and county. Their influence at the local level was strong: Padraig Pearse built up a very active branch of the Irish Volunteers in Rathfarnham. Similarly, local persons of note, socially and economically, could dictate the allegiance of Volunteer branches after the organization split: Thomas Francis Healy was a prominent publican in Clondalkin and also a staunch Redmondite. He managed to maintain a National Volunteer organization around Clondalkin long after it had fallen apart elsewhere in the county.[5] This sort of situation does not allow for the small number of individuals in such an area who were undoubtedly inclined towards the Irish Volunteers. There were certainly many members of Redmondite-controlled branches who sympathised with the Irish Volunteers and who, had the circumstances been favourable, might have joined or formed branches of their own.

The National Volunteers and the U.I.L., despite reorganization efforts in 1915 which varied from locality to locality, lost ground to revolutionary nationalism. On the eve of the rising both organizations were merely nominal. The U.I.L. was redundant except for electioneering since most tenants were now owners of their land and the National Volunteers had been depleted by those who had enlisted, the suspensions of home rule for the duration of the war and the mounting casualties. They also lacked consistency and real conviction in their local reorganization efforts. The threat of conscription, although partly removed in March 1916 with the exclusion of Ireland from the Military Service Bill, ensured continued support for the Irish Volunteers but far more important were their superior organization and enthusiasm which they maintained right up to the rising. Their influence, if not their numbers, increased substantially. They stirred up latent prejudice against Britain. Irish Volunteer numbers in the county were small but they remained consistently active. This in turn led to speculation that they were about to start a rising as early as July 1915.[6]

A substantial proportion of these county Volunteers took part in the actual rising. Public reaction reflected that around the country in general; immediate shock and anger was quickly followed by revulsion and then sympathy after the executions, first among the poorer sections and then amongst a broad spectrum of nationalist opinion. Organizations like the Gaelic Athletic Association which had been inactive before the rising enjoyed a boom period following the summer release of internees. Many middle-class I.P.P. supporters turned to the 'new' nationalism. A period of militant rhetoric ensued in which the new 'buzz word' 'Republic' replaced the old cry of 'Home Rule'. Rhetorical bravado and flag waving was compounded by the activities of the returned, unrepentant, heroes. It had its effect, especially in the north of the county. But although the national issue had again united all classes of nationalists, the politics were ephemeral and belied the underlying realities. The new nationalism was divided in its goals and methods between moderates and extremists. The same small core who took part in the rising were the ones who continued the struggle. By July 1917 the R.I.C. County Inspector, believed: 'There is no doubt but that Sinn Féin has for the present absorbed all that is active and extreme in nationalist politics and that there is no real vitality in anything political but Sinn Féin'.[7]

Sinn Féin and the Volunteers successfully consolidated their position by reorganizing in the county. Their organizers there were usually 'veterans' of the rising. The first Sinn Féin clubs in the county were set up around men like Frank Lawless in the north and Desmond Fitzgerald in the south. Reorganization efforts were given added impetus following the death of Thomas Ashe from Lusk, north county Dublin, in September 1917. Former supporters of Redmond also used their local influence to establish branches of Sinn Féin and many former National Volunteers joined these new branches and clubs.

The county entered a very disturbed period with the increasing use of repressive measures to keep the peace. Police reports describe a 'rebellious atmosphere' particularly after Ashe's death. Speeches by Eamonn de Valera and others in the north compounded their fears. At Balbriggan, de Valera called for all Volunteers in the county to be well organized and 'to be in a position to make government by England impossible'.[8] Speakers and organizers harnessed the growing dissatisfaction with the I.P.P. and the renewed threat of conscription to swell the ranks. As yet the majority of the Roman Catholic clergy were not supportive of these sentiments but a few younger priests were active in the organization. One young curate was president of the Sinn Féin club in Clondalkin in the west.[9]

The growing discontent was enough to lead the Chief Secretary to implement precautionary measures to protect government officials and to secure police barracks in county Dublin in January 1918. Isolated barracks were closed from early 1918 – probably sparked off by an arms raid on the site of a new aerodrome at Gormanstown in January. There was alarm among the authorities about the potential for further such raids since large numbers of Dublin labourers were employed in aerodrome construction at Collinstown and Gormanstown in the north and Baldonnell and Tallaght in the west. Since the vast majority of them were probably either members of Sinn Féin clubs or in sympathy with Sinn Féin, it was questionable whether these men could be trusted to work on these sites. Private houses on the outskirts of the city, mainly those of retired policemen and demobilised soldiers, were also raided for arms. Military units were moved into the towns of Swords and Balbriggan in the north around the aerodromes in order to prevent arms raids and drilling both here and on the outskirts of the city.

There was immense anger and opposition to the Military Service Bill. The Roman Catholic clergy were prominent in voicing their dissent in county Dublin. When the R.I.C. started to report on parish sermons in June 1918 they were further alienated from the nationalist population. This had a lasting impact at parish level. The depth of feeling was such that the arrests following the revelation of a 'German plot', the proscription of Sinn Féin and the introduction of a permit system for all meetings simply drove Sinn Féin and the Volunteers underground, making them more dangerous and causing resentment among I.P.P. supporters. The Volunteers operated with greater secrecy. There was a lot of activity in the county, mostly by city Volunteers. They set up schools of instruction in explosives in the Dublin mountains and tightened up their organization. It was at this stage in the autumn of 1918, that the authorities began to guess at Volunteer strength and to lose the intelligence battle. In their efforts to control the situation, the police alienated themselves from those who had formerly supported them. The 'German plot' arrests, the frequent raids on prominent nationalists' homes, the dubious arrests for 'sedition' and 'unsatisfactory answers' plus the conscription debacle did not improve the situation. By the time of the armistice even a section of the clergy was tired of the government and the I.P.P. due to the failure of Home Rule Bills.

The outcome of the 1918 general election campaign in the county was predictable. The I.P.P. only carried out a half-hearted campaign in the north where they got the support of the older clergy. The rest of the clergy remained quiet during the elections save a few who canvassed for Sinn Féin. The election campaign saw a return to the militant rhetoric of post-1916. Speeches varied in their content, some being very republican. There was some heckling at I.P.P. meetings, but no violence. Sinn Féin won three of the four county seats, losing out in Rathmines to a Unionist candidate. The Unionists were their closest rivals at the polls, indicating that they had held their own support while the I.P.P. had been swamped by Sinn Féin.

The election victories were followed by constitutional efforts to obtain independence. There were a number of meetings in Dublin concerning the Peace Conference; Dublin Corporation talked about bestowing the freedom of the city on Woodrow Wilson.[10] Political activity of this kind, however, was grinding to a halt and being replaced by military action. Increased military presence in the north restrained local activities but could not control the better organized city groups who operated around the city, helped by local Volunteers and sympathisers. The first attack on policemen took place in the Dublin mountains in January 1919.[11]

The Irish Republican Army (I.R.A.) raids became more daring. At Collinstown in March 1919 they managed to hold soldiers hostage for over two hours and got away with 75 rifles and a large quantity of ammunition. The number of raids increased dramatically although on a smaller scale. City units were almost entirely responsible for these operations. County units did not have the advanced organization or numbers to plan or carry out such raids. In fact, county Volunteers played a relatively minor role in the ensuing guerrilla campaign.

The campaign of violence increased between February 1919 and the truce of July 1921. County Dublin remained in a state of upheaval and economic dislocation. This can largely be attributed to the activities of the revolutionary leadership, many of whom lived in the county, and the work of the city active service units. The theft of mail, attacks on military convoys, the burning of vacated police barracks, raids for arms and the destruction of government property became regular occurrences during the spring and summer of 1920. Government reprisals, such as that at

Balbriggan in September 1920, were followed by counter-reprisals. Police officers, spies and informers were frequent targets of assassination. The murders continued at a rate of about three a month. The police found it increasingly difficult to assess what was happening, especially in the more isolated areas of the county. I.R.A. resources were being drained by these efforts although it is not clear if there was any lessening of their resolve. The level of support for the truce suggests that it came as a relief to all.[12]

Farm labourers had fared badly from social welfare and other legislation. They were excluded from many of the Bills brought in before the war. Their working conditions varied but were never comfortable. Wages were poor and varied from farm to farm. When Jim Larkin began organizing around the county in the summer of 1913 he felt that 'the harshness and misery of the agricultural labourer's lot rivalled in intensity the worst experiences of his inner-city colleague'.[13]

Larkin's organizing efforts brought results. After a series of meetings throughout the county a small number joined the I.T.G.W.U., struck for higher wages and were largely successful. They held out for 17 shillings a week (a 20 per cent increase) and a set working day of nine hours in winter and ten in summer.[14] Most farmers agreed to the terms since the harvest was approaching. Those who did not received police protection. The strike spread quickly, particularly in the north and west, and soon included mill workers. Some farmers held out and refused to deal with the union. The County Dublin Farmers' Association, prompted by William Martin Murphy, pledged in September not to employ any member of the I.T.G.W.U. A large number of labourers in many parts of the county were either out on strike by order of the union, in sympathy, or were locked out by their employers – by the end of September over 25,000 were out in both city and county.

In the rapidly deteriorating situation, a large number of police reinforcements were drafted into the county to protect farmers and their employees who continued to work. Similar protection was offered to the mill owners and their employees. In addition, many labourers were evicted from their cottages as a result of the strike. By October, batches of 'free' labourers were being imported from counties Cavan and Wicklow. The use of non-union labour weakened the strikers' bargaining position and put the onus on the labourers to solve the problem. These factors, coupled with the growing distress and hardship, found an outlet in 'traditional' methods of protest. There was large-scale petty intimidation, several riots, maiming and killing of livestock, the burning of crops and the destruction of farm machinery.

The huge police presence protecting the 'rights of the employers' and the labourers' own lack of bargaining power brought the strike to an end in Dublin city and outlying parts of the county early in 1914. It lingered on, with increasing bitterness, in those parts of the county within a six or seven mile radius of the city, but by March 1914 the last strongholds, Swords in the north and Lucan/Clondalkin in the west, were forced to give in.

The strike had been long and general in county Dublin for a number of reasons. The proximity of the county to Liberty Hall was an important factor. Leading figures in the Transport Union like Larkin, James Connolly, William Partridge, Countess Markievicz and many others made frequent trips to the county area, addressing large gatherings of labourers to encourage them not to return to work without a settlement. In addition, local conditions were ripe for organization. There was a higher ratio of labourers to farmers in county Dublin in comparison with other counties. Farm labourers made up about 33 per cent of the workforce. Very few labourers lived in with their farmer-employer, a factor that might have discouraged many from striking for fear of eviction or maltreatment. This discontent was then harnessed by the enthusiasm and ability of city-based union organizers.

The outcome of the strike left the labourers disillusioned. The union, it appeared, had failed to deliver them from their predicament, so they sought an alternative in militant nationalism. Within a few weeks of the strike ending, the first county branches of the Irish Citizen Army and the Irish Volunteers were formed in those areas which had been the strike centres, Swords and Clondalkin. The union lost its influence in the county – Dublin number one branch, the largest branch in the country, had only 63 agricultural labourers by the end of 1915.[14]

The legacy of the strike opened the eyes of the strikers to other possibilities and raised their expectations. The more prominent local strikers found it very difficult to get employment even as casual labour. These wounds only began to heal by late 1916. The R.I.C. County Inspector, described employee relations in May 1916 as satisfactory '... though the relics of the Larkinite strike still lurk'.[15]

The outbreak of the war and the resulting increase in production, both agricultural and industrial, brought plenty of employment opportunities, but war also brought the added burden of spiralling prices. Basic commodities like bread reached exorbitant prices and it became increasingly difficult to feed a family. Many were attracted by army pay and the dependents' allowance. Wages rose accordingly but lagged way behind the inflated prices. The price of meat, which was already beyond most labourers' wages, rocketed further: sheep, cattle and fowl were frequently stolen and butchered from early 1916. Labourers' frustrations and distress were compounded by the fact that their employers and their shopkeepers were making enormous profits out of the war which did not find their way into labourers' pockets to ease the increasing burden.

This situation produced conditions that were again ripe for the organization of labourers. The I.T.G.W.U., which began reorganizing in the labour centres of the county at the beginning of 1917, stepped up its efforts in the early part of the summer. This was always the best time to organize since the threat to the harvest would put the labourers in a better bargaining position. Branches were formed in those same areas which had been centres of the lock-out. The union enjoyed its period of greatest influence from this stage to 1922. Success was almost immediate. The number of strikes and threatened strikes increased dramatically both on the farms and in the mills and factories. Most employers capitulated to union demands and the outcome usually favoured the strikers. The construction of four new aerodromes in the county throughout 1918, employing over 1,000 labourers at good wages, compounded a situation of labour shortage. Farmers and other employers were forced to pay comparable wages. Farm labourers could demand 35 shillings a week without fear of recrimination.[16]

The Transport Union worked very closely with Sinn Féin from late 1917 in a period of growing confidence. It was believed that most of the county's union activists and a large part of the membership were in Sinn Féin. Sinn Féin organizers like Laurence Ginnell made speeches during the early part of 1918 encouraging labourers to agitate for land, to join Sinn Féin clubs, the volunteers and the Transport Union. Sinn Féin also established food stores in the northern part of the county in an effort to interfere with the food regulations.

Although the authorities interpreted these activities as the flowering of a Bolshevist revolution, this was a mistake. Labourers in the county were too scattered to agitate effectively, and the underlying realities of the situation became obvious at an early stage. The Sinn Féin-controlled food stores were a failure because they charged the same prices as the retailers for inferior quality produce and the farmers did not make a profit – their real purpose was to disobey government food regulations rather than to alleviate the hardship of the working population. It became obvious to Sinn Féin's leadership in early 1918 that the policy of agitation was alienating farmers. By March there were no Sinn Féin organizers encouraging labourers to take the land, preferring instead to attend auctions and ensure that tenants secured their property, but they had to pay good prices. March 1918 marked the point at which Sinn Féin and the Transport Union effectively went their separate ways. This situation was no doubt encouraged from Sinn Féin headquarters.

The Transport Union continued to organize and press for improved conditions, consolidating its position throughout 1918. It became an accepted arbiter in employee relations although disliked by the employers. An important factor in the success of organized labour was the ability of the Transport Union to operate legally throughout the dislocation of the troubled period. The I.T.G.W.U. was an open, agressive force, independent of, and often in opposition to Sinn Féin, despite the overlap in membership. The Transport Union was not the 'socialist and labour wing of the Irish revolutionary movement'.[17] Despite the rhetoric its purpose was very different from Sinn Féin.

Local branches of the Transport Union found themselves at odds with the Sinn Féin branches, especially in the north. Many of the local farmers in Garristown, for example, had voted for Sinn Féin in the general election of 1918. When a branch of the union was set up in January the farmers resented being dictated to. Similar tensions followed the Irish Congress of Trade Unions conference that year where there was a call for a 44 hour week and a minimum wage of 50 shillings. Local farmers and shopkeepers were accused of profiteering by charging high prices long after the war was over. Prominent Sinn Féin members in Rush, north County Dublin, bought a farm which a group of local people, backed up by the Transport Union had intended to divide amongst themselves. There were other signs of less than perfect harmony. The County Inspector reported in January 1919, 'Labour appears to try to take the first place and to regard the obtaining of higher wages and better conditions of living as more urgent than anything else. It is more concerned with realities than ideals'.[19]

The inflationary prices and prohibitive cost of basic foodstuffs continued. The authorities believed that much of the disaffection and intimidation in the county was due to the hardship endured by those on low or fixed incomes – a minimum wage of 40 shillings to 50 shillings a week was needed to simply meet basic requirements. Luxuries such as alcohol became both scarce and very expensive, a fact that seemed lost on Sinn Féin who called for sobriety among their volunteers in order to protect plans. The cracks deepened between both organizations within the county, and the Transport Union asserted its independence with more vigour. It became involved in land grabbing – 'land for labourers' – at auctions during the later part of 1919. Sinn Féin was still assumed to be colluding with the unions by the local farmers and suffered in the north as a result. But such incidents were isolated. The Transport Union's position as arbiter was determined, and employee relations began to improve by the end of 1920. Although strikes continued to break out with regularity they were soon settled, almost invariably involving the I.T.G.W.U.

The Union's position of strength was slowly ground away in the period following the Treaty due to a number of factors. Conditions were never as favourable as they had been in the period 1918-21 when the economic prosperity of employers and the shortage of labour were ideal bargaining tools. Organized labour's failure to consolidate its position of strength in the years following independence was as much a testimony to its own shortcomings as to the factors working against it.

The majority of social radicals did not abandon their socialism after 1913 to become nationalists. They maintained their separate identity and organization throughout the revolution. They were prepared to throw in their lot until it became clear that their interests were diametrically opposed. The potential for common action was limited by a revolution which placed the rights of private property before the rights of labour.

The emerging differences between Sinn Féin and the Transport Union clearly demonstrate the conservatism of the revolution between 1913 and 1921. The socially-radical rhetoric of some nationalist leaders should not mask the reality. The unity of radicals and revolutionaries was more apparent than real, and divisions were demonstrated by the Civil War and the repressive legislation of the new state.

Radicalism did not end with the defeat following the lockout. It met its end with the foundation of the Free State. Social radicalism reached its peak not in 1913 but in 1921 at the height of the nationalist revolution. It was defeated by the forces of conservatism within the Free State and by organized labour's failure to consolidate its position in the 1918-21 period.

The success or failure of both the revolutionary and radical movements depended on the availability of local leadership and favourable local conditions. The initiative for action may have come from the city but little happened unless the 'parish pump' could be worked effectively. A greater number of local studies need to be done to give us a better insight into political behaviour and industrial conflict. Only through a closer examination of local diversity can we hope to come up with a more unified picture.

CHAPTER 4

'Quotas' : affirmative action, reverse discrimination
by
Maurice Goldring

It would be boring and pointless to recall the results of research that all point to the same conclusion: Roman Catholics in Northern Ireland have been discriminated against in employment, education, training, housing, etc.[1] The typical protestant male in industry is skilled. The typical Roman Catholic male is unskilled or unemployed. Roman Catholics, though they constitute one third of the economically active population, form the majority of the unemployed. The difference is even seen in gender: occupations that are strongly protestant tend to be male, whereas jobs where catholics are overrepresented tend to be predominantly female. The most striking feature is among young people. R.D. Cormac and R.D. Osborne have shown that among the 16-18 age group, there are 18 per cent unemployed catholics to 17 per cent protestants. But in the 19-24 age group, that is to say when school and youth training programmes are over, unemployment rises to 19 per cent for protestants and to 32 per cent for catholics.

Some unionists, trying to find reasons for such a situation, put the blame on catholics themselves. Gregory Campbell, a Derry Democratic Unionist Party councillor, wrote a pamphlet called *Discrimination, the Truth* in which he claimed the statistics of the Fair Employment Agency or of various academics overlook a series of factors.[2] For example, since catholics have a higher birth rate, more catholic school-leavers are seeking too few jobs. This argument was answered a few years earlier by A.C. Hepburn, who showed that the same differences in employment existed in Belfast in 1901 whereas the difference in fertility rate was negligible. He pointed out that the gap did not narrow between 1901 and 1951. In fact, the gap between catholics and protestants was bigger than that found between blacks and native whites in Birmingham in 1975.

Gregory Campbell also argues that Northern Ireland is entering a process of reverse discrimination. The future is grim. Older protestant employees are gradually being replaced by younger catholics, and it is only a question of time before the balance of the entire workforce is fundamentally altered.

The Fair Employment Agency was established in 1976 to promote equality of opportunity in employment and to eliminate discrimination. The original working party was very much against quotas and chose to stress 'affirmative action'.[3] Discrimination was to be made unlawful – but through a process of talking and negotiation. 'Criminal penalties' were assumed to be likely to provoke sectarian feelings and thus be counterproductive.

In the *Guide to Effective Practice* published by the F.E.A, extraordinary precautions are taken to avoid the label of quotas. Affirmative action is thus defined as:

those special measures that an employer can take to promote a more representative distribution of employment in the workforce in the event of the existing representation of either the protestant or Roman Catholic community being less than might reasonably be expected.

However, recruitment remains subject to the operation of the merit principle. Or again, discrimination is illegal; reverse discrimination may involve reserving a set proportion or number of jobs for particular groups or individuals. These are known as quotas and are illegal. It is also illegal to favour certain individuals or groups to help correct an historical imbalance in employment.

What is meant then in effect by good practice? First the employers should monitor their workforce, that is, record the 'perceived religious affiliation' of employees. The F.E.A. suggests the advertising of all vacancies through channels which will reach all potential candidates, and the ending of 'word of mouth' recruitment. Employers should increase the awareness of pupils of any underrepresented minority. Preferential treatment of ex-members of security forces should end. There should be no display of flags or emblems in the workplace that might give offence. The management should give firm goals and timetables for a redress of balance. This is sometimes understood as tantamount to quotas. This is wrong. Quotas are illegal. Once more, they are incompatible with the merit principle. It is not permissible to take religion into account in the recruitment process. All selection must be – and must be seen to be – on the merit principle.

The same set of advice is given to the trade unions. They must co-operate with the employers in fighting discrimination. They must not discriminate themselves by treating certain members less favourably in terms of benefits, social events, etc. Trade unions should treat as statutory offences, acts of discrimination by their members such as intimidation or unfair dismissal. Let us note here that the F.E.A. is much more direct with the unions than with employers. They ask them to dismiss any members guilty of discrimination. Their demands are much less drastic when addressing employers.

The F.E.A. guideline for effective practice, though meant to promote 'affirmative action', is mostly negative advice: 'Stop doing this, don't do that.' The result is that it gives a fairly accurate picture of the way discrimination works.

The F.E.A. has had limited success. There are very few complaints and most of them are not followed through. Discrimination is very difficult to prove in court. The main reason of course is that it simply appears as 'natural' or 'traditional' proceedings. Informal recruitment practices are a major factor. The way skilled crafts wanted to control recruitment and apprenticeship in Britain has assumed a sectarian aspect in the Northern Ireland context. This is why the F.E.A. has had greater effect in the public sector, in higher grade non-manual occupations and in larger firms in the private sector.

The relative failure of the F.E.A. has given rise to a lot of criticism. The Social Democratic and Labour Party claims that the only improvement is to be found in the public service, but mostly in lower grades and middle management. According to the S.D.L.P., the signing of the declaration of intent has been an empty gesture for most employers. The main incentive for signing has been the government's announcement that public tenders would be available only to firms having signed the declaration of intent. Only twenty-four firms had signed before the announcement in 1981. Within six months there were 497, and in 1984, 6335. Not a single employer has been removed from the register for discrimination. But the

S.D.L.P. still holds the same basic position as the F.E.A.; it is asking for 'targets' and not 'quotas'.[4]

In spite of all precautions, the F.E.A. is criticized by unionists because they claim its principles are reverse discrimination: counting heads in factories creates social disturbances because it is discriminatory. The very failure of the agency is used against it: If, between 1976 and 1979, there were only eight proven cases, it proves discrimination does not exist in Northern Ireland.

The MacBride Principles

The MacBride Principles[5] created such an uproar that one might have assumed they would have differed from the F.E.A. on the one and only controversial issue, that of quotas and of 'reverse discrimination'. Well, they do not. Their aim is to 'increase the representation of underrepresented religious groups' and to protect minority employees. This should be achieved by active recruitment of minority employees, by public advertising of all jobs. To sum up, the principles are the same, and share almost the same wording as the F.E.A. One finds even the same caution: the efforts for minority recruitment 'should not be construed to imply a diminution of opportunity for other applicants'. It is not quotas, it is not reverse discrimination. Peter Archer, Labour Party spokesperson on Northern Ireland, supporting the MacBride Principles, said he distinguished between affirmative action and the imposition of quotas. Affirmative action is possible without resorting to reverse discrimination which could increase tension and prove counterproductive. This is a familiar line of argument.

The MacBride Principles have been presented as 'reverse discrimination'. I have yet to read any convincing demonstration showing how they differ fundamentally from the F.E.A. The only strident criticism applies to a side issue: the employer must ensure that applicants are not deterred from seeking employment because of fear for personal safety.

If there is such an array of precautions, of negative clauses, in both the F.E.A. and MacBride Principles, could it simply be because these principles are what they are claimed not to be; that is to say, reverse discrimination? In times of layoffs, closures, shrinking employment, they are necessarily so. The passage from word-of-mouth recruitment to public advertising is reverse discrimination if jobs are scarce. Take this admirable principle about layoffs: those that involve seniority only can result in discrimination if the bulk of employees with greatest seniority are disproportionately from another religious group. Does it mean the management has to sack older protestant employees and keep younger catholic employees? If it does, isn't this reverse discrimination? If it does not, what does it mean? Affirmative action is made up of more pleasant words. Affirmative action means sharing a bigger cake. Sharing a smaller one is less pleasant. When the F.E.A. says it is illegal to favour groups to help correct an historical imbalance in employment, if one takes this statement literally, it would be the death warrant of the agency. Why on earth was it founded if not to help correct an historical imbalance in employment?

When there has been long-standing inequality, any concrete step of redress necessarily appears as 'reverse discrimination' to the holders of ancient privileges, however minor they may be. The very research on that inequality is seen as a threat and becomes an ideological battlefield.

Conclusion

One side issue is about the link between the question of equal opportunity and the national question in Northern Ireland. In the North, nationalists do not consider the state as legitimate, and they are considered as 'disloyal' by loyalists. Equal opportunity becomes a pressing issue for groups that are undoubtedly part of the nation-state. Blacks in the United States are obviously American citizens. In the same way, equal opportunity for women becomes a pressing issue if their presence in the workplace is not casual, residual, transitory – an interval between youth and marriage. In other words, if they become 'citizens' in the workplace.

From that point of view, it appears that the extreme arguments that are used against affirmative action are roughly the same as the ones used in France against the immigrant workforce. In other words, the nationalist community in Northern Ireland is seen as a group of 'foreigners' to whom the country owes nothing.

But this is not the central idea that has been discussed in this paper. My main point is trying to understand the difference between affirmative action in industrialised countries: the United States, France and Great Britain. The Plowden Report in Britain, as far back as 1967, and reforms in the French educational system, pointed in the same direction: the underprivileged need better schools, a larger number of teachers and smaller classes. Various urban programmes, in Great Britain, France and the United States grant resources to specified areas. In Great Britain and France they officially benefit everybody, blacks and whites, citizens or immigrants. But in effect, they benefit the black or immigrant population disproportionately. So, the discussion is, or seems to be, more about words than fact. The trend in Great Britain and France is to present such actions as mere applications of welfare, in job training, social services, housing, etc. They are not presented as consciously anti-racist and anti-discriminatory policies. How is it that the conscious use of quotas (in gender and race) is found in the country that is the least welfare-minded? Whereas in Britain, and even more in France, politicians are afraid of using the word. Are they afraid of the backlash? The backlash is there all the same. When there is a large slum-clearance in a predominantly Algerian district, the National Front is quick to point out that all the public money is spent 'on them'. We have already noticed the reaction of the D.U.P. to the F.E.A. and affirmative action. They call it reverse discrimination. The phrase is even used strangely in the political field. In a conversation about the Anglo-Irish agreement, it was presented to me as 'reverse discrimination gone mad'.

These precautions may be legitmate. But for an observer who does not have to take a political decision, it is quite clear that the difference between affirmative action and reverse discrimination lies in the result. Quotas are targets that have been reached, and reverse discrimination is affirmative action that works.

CHAPTER 5

Typical case or deviant? Nationalism in Ireland in a European Perspective*
by
John Coakley

1. Introduction

The object of this paper is to present an alternative to the view that nationalism in Ireland is a unique phenomenon, having few elements in common with nationalism elsewhere. Nationalism in Ireland, it is frequently argued, is a product of the unique set of circumstances which conditioned relations between competing groups in the nineteenth century, and it is to the distinctiveness of the Irish experience that one must look in accounting for the phenomenon of modern nationalism.[1] It is not, of course, possible to discount the significance of factors unique to Ireland as formative influences on the course taken by nationalist movements; this paper takes it for granted that certain unique factors are not susceptible to explanation in terms of general theories. This need not, however, prevent attempts to account for certain aspects of Irish nationalism which recur or have recurred elsewhere, and to use comparative analysis in doing so.

The paper begins in section 2 by pointing to certain of the more obvious parallels between nationalism in Ireland and nationalism elsewhere in Europe. This picture is qualified in section 3 by an analysis of certain of the more obvious differences that set the Irish experience apart. In section 4 the focus switches back to similarities, but this time to less obvious ones. In section 5 this set of similarities is, in turn, balanced by an examination of some less obvious contrasts between the Irish experience and that elsewhere.

In each of the four following sections reference has been made (though in varying degrees of equality of treatment) to three principal domains of analysis: political, cultural and economic. This distinction corresponds crudely with the territory/identity/economy trichotomy that forms the background to a well-known recent comparative study of political nationalism in Europe.[2] The basis for comparison needs to be made explicit. Although several references are made below to nationalist movements in Western Europe, it is assumed here that the most fruitful comparative context for the study of Irish nationalism is a Central and East European one, and that the closest parallels are with those nationalist movements which succeeded in creating new, independent states at around the same time as the Irish Free State came into existence.

* I am indebted to conference participants and especially to Joseph Ruane and John Whyte for comments on an earlier draft.

2. Nationalism in Ireland and Europe: some obvious similarities

The most obvious similarity between nationalism in Ireland and that elsewhere depends on matters of definition. If by the term is meant *separatist* nationalism (in contradistinction to the forms of nationalism found in Germany and Italy in the nineteenth century, which had national unification rather than independence as the objective), then Irish nationalism resembled nationalism elsewhere in defining an external ruling power as the enemy. As in the peripheral territories of the Habsburg and Russian empires, nationalism was initially directed towards a restructuring of the state along federalist or quasi-federalist lines, and moved to more extreme demands for national independence only during the years 1914-1918. (In Poland and in the Balkans, by contrast, full independence had already been widely articulated as a nationalist goal in the nineteenth century.)

The similarities go further. In few cases was the nationalist struggle a simple, two-way contest. Typically, at least a third party was present: a substantial, ethnically-distinct, indigenous population whose members occupied positions of relatively high economic, social and political status. In its most simple form, this minority was ethnically related to the metropolitan power and was allied to it politically. This was the case among Irish protestants, Germans on the western frontiers of Poland and on the Bohemian rim of western Czechoslovakia, and Hungarians in Slovakia and in the predominantly Romanian province of Transylvania. In a more complex form, the privileged ethnic minority was unrelated to the metropolitan ruling power but this did not necessarily impede a close alliance of convenience between the two: the German minorities in the Estonian and Latvian provinces of the Russian Empire are an obvious example. In yet another variant, as exemplified by the Swedish-speaking minority in Finland, the Polish minority in Lithuania and the Greeks in Bulgaria, the privileged minority played a more detached role, leaving open other alliance possibilities.

Second, the relationship between the movement for the revival of the Irish language and the political nationalist movement resembles the pattern to be found in the case of almost all other peripheral nationalities. The revival of a decaying culture and the linguistic standardisation and development of a rural patois were important concomitants of nationalist movements, and served to strengthen the national sense of solidarity and distinctiveness. Persons active in the linguistic revival movement, in Ireland as elsewhere, also played a major role in the political nationalist movement.[3]

Third, the Irish nationalist movement, like its counterparts elsewhere in Central and Eastern Europe, but especially in the Baltic provinces of Russia, was given added vigour by a striking coincidence between ethnic differences and social stratification – the phenomenon known as a 'cultural divison of labour'.[4] The fact that most members of the peripheral nationality were peasants (Irish catholics, Estonians, Latvians, Lithuanians) whose landlords adhered to the culture of the privileged minority (Irish Protestants, Germans in Estonia and Latvia, Poles in Lithuania) added a further dimension of class warfare to the already bitter one of cultural conflict. The struggle of the majority for democracy and political autonomy was simultaneously a struggle for an improvement of its economic position.

3. Nationalism in Ireland and Europe: some obvious contrasts

The three points made in the last section need to be qualified. In the first place, there was an important difference between Ireland and the typical European case in terms of the political balance of power. That portion of the Irish protestant minority that was concentrated in Ulster was able, with the assistance of powerful British support, to secure its exclusion from the new state that appeared after the First World War. In this it resembled the Polish minority in southern Lithuania, which succeeded in ensuring that the area around Vilnius, the historic capital of the old Lithuanian state, was detached from the new Lithuanian Republic and absorbed instead by Poland. More typically, however, the integrity of the so-called 'historic national territory' was not breached. Thus the Czechs succeeded in retaining the overwhelmingly German Sudetenland and the Finns remained masters of the almost exclusively Swedish-speaking Aaland Islands on the grounds that the drawing of frontiers along ethnic lines in these cases would violate the integrity of the 'national territory'. In other cases such as Estonia and Latvia, the fact that the minorities were not concentrated in a borderland adjacent to their 'spiritual homeland' made their exclusion unrealistic.

Second, for all the superficial similarities between the language revival movements in Ireland and elsewhere, the Irish case stands apart in terms of the cultural basis of its nationalist movement. The language revival movement in Ireland began extremely late, at a time when the language had ceased to be the domestic language of a majority of the population. Already by 1851 the monoglot Irish-speaking population had dwindled to 5 per cent, and 77 per cent of the population were able to speak English only. Given the pace of the decline, the challenge of even preserving the language was an enormous one, and the task of the revivalists was foredoomed to failure. Though it differed in this respect from the position in Central and Eastern Europe, the Irish experience bears some similarity to that of Welsh, Breton and Basque nationalists more recently, groups that have been faced with the prospect of attempting to mobilise support in the name of linguistic distinctiveness through the medium of a metropolitan language. Irish political nationalism was thus expressed formally and informally through English, and the principal marker of national distinctiveness was religion, not language. It is difficult to find parallels to this coincidence between religion and national identity within Europe (though many are to be found outside this area). Two cases may, however, be mentioned: those of the Masurians (Polish-speaking protestants in the North East of Poland) and of the Pomaks (Muslim Bulgarians), groups which found that they did not share the 'national' religion of the majority (Catholicism, Orthodoxy) and who tended to define themselves and to be defined by others as ethnically distinct. The three-way division of the Serbo-Croatian linguistic community into Orthodox Serbs, Catholic Croats and ethnic Muslims is another example.

Third, although nationalist protest has been interpreted as a function of economic peripherality and dependence, most notably by the 'internal colonialism' and related schools, it is a striking fact that most of the separatist nationalist movements whose efforts bore fruit in the early part of the twentieth century were based in territories that were more advanced in economic and social terms than the core territories from which they were seceding. Thus, by such indicators as the proportion of the population living in urban areas, involved in industry, able to read or with some post-elementary education, Finland, Estonia, Latvia and even Lithuania were more advanced than Russia proper, the Czechs were more advanced than the Austrian Germans, and the Romanians and Bulgarians were more advanced than their Turkish masters. (By West European standards, of course, most of these nationalities were not at a very advanced level of economic and social development.) By contrast, the relative under-development of Ireland vis-a-vis Great Britain was clear, though there were parallels in Europe: the position of the Norwegians in Sweden-Norway and of the Slovaks and Romanians in Hungary, for example.

4. Nationalism in Ireland and Europe: some underlying similarities

One may now consider the characteristics of Irish nationalism that have sometimes been interpreted as unique but that in reality have close parallels elsewhere. The first is the phasing of the political nationalist movement. The phenomena of Grattan's Parliament, of the United Irishmen and of 1798 may be seen either as temporary deviations from a narrower path of nationalist development or as the first stage in a broader process of mobilisation that 'went wrong' after 1800. In fact, these developments were typical of the early phases of nationalist movements. In territories that were characterised by the cultural division of labour described above, nationalism tended to go through at least two phases. In the first phase, of *territorial patriotism*, to which protestant 'nationalism' of the eighteenth century belonged, the privileged minority and its aristocratic leaders resisted the centralising efforts of the metropolitan power and invoked local patriotism as a weapon. Thus in Finland in 1788-90 the Anjala League represented the efforts of elements of the Swedish-speaking elite to secure autonomy (directed against the Swedish central state, of which Finland was a part at the time); the Baltic German nobles resisted the centralising efforts of Catherine II in the late eighteenth century; and the Bohemian German aristocracy defended their autonomy against the reforms of Joseph II in the 1780s. Such tinkering with separatism, potentially lethal to the survival of the minority, tended to stop abruptly in the second phase, that of *ethnic nationalism*: with capitalist development, social mobilisation and the growth of democratic practices the minority found its position threatened.[5] With the growth of the ethnic consciousness of the majority (Irish Catholics, Finns, Estonians, Latvians, Czechs) and their radical political demands, the minority tended to look to the metropolitan power for protection. This shift in alliance options was not necessarily to the benefit of the minority: the metropolitan power was typically prepared to make substantial concessions to the local majority (in such areas as land reform and the democratisation of local government) that ultimately undermined the economic, social and political hegemony of the minority.

Given this path of development in the political domain, it is not surprising that the role of the minority in Ireland in the early phases of the cultural revival movement forms an exact parallel to that of its counterparts elsewhere. It was the Bohemian nobility, the Swedish-speaking elite in Finland and the Baltic German pastors and gentry that initiated the first societies for the study of the local language and history. In Ireland, similarly, it was the Anglo-Irish nobility and gentry that sponsored the foundation of the Royal Irish Academy (1785), the Iberno-Celtic Society (1818), the Irish Archaeological Society (1840) and a large number of other societies devoted to the study of the Irish language, literature and history. It is to be noted that the only sustained attempt to use the Irish language as a medium of written communication in the early nineteenth century was sponsored by protestant missionary organisations such as the Baptist Society (1814) and the 'Irish Society for Promoting the Education of the Native Irish Through the Medium of Their Own Language' (1818).

The starkness of the contrasts between minority and majority that have been outlined above needs to be qualified by looking at certain of the consequences of economic development. Initially, there had been a tendency for upward mobility in the labour market to be associated with assimilation to the dominant culture (English-speaking and Protestant in Ireland, Swedish in Finland, German in the Baltic provinces and so on). With the development of a critical mass of members of the majority community in middle-class occupations, there was a tendency for this process to be halted and even reversed. There remained, however, certain intermediate groups whose economic position placed them in an ambiguous relationship with those from whose culture they had been drawn. The phenomenon of conservative catholic landowners in Ireland and 'Castle catholics' who supported the Union, finds its parallels in similar groups elsewhere: the so-called 'grey barons' in the Baltic provinces (native Estonians and Latvians who had recently become significant landowners) are an example, and similar groups, drawn from the majority population but by virtue of their economic interests detached from sympathy with the popular nationalist movement, are to be found elsewhere.

5. Nationalism in Ireland and Europe: some underlying differences

Reference has been made above to the protestant counter-nationalist movement in Ireland that successfully delayed the implementation of Home Rule and succeeded in preventing the extension to Northern Ireland of government from Dublin. This movement enjoyed a degree of political strength that greatly surpassed that of its most powerful counterparts, including even the Bohemian Germans. This may be attributed at least in part to the fact that its metropolitan ally was one of the victorious powers in the First World War, and could decide where and on what terms the Wilson principles of national self-determination were to be implemented. This meant not only that Ulster Unionists could secure autonomy for their ethnic territory but also that the boundaries of the new state of Northern Ireland were extended to include a large segment of 'catholic' ethnic territory. By contrast, the Vilnius area that was detached from Lithuania contained very few Lithuanians, though this should not be taken as implying that it was predominantly Polish: the Jewish and Belorussian groups there were of comparable size with the Poles and the Lithuanians.

A second characteristic that set the antagonistic catholic/protestant relationship in Ireland apart from similar relationships elsewhere was the weakness of its cultural base. In Central and Eastern Europe the counter-mobilisation of the minorities had a strong cultural component. A process of national self-discovery similar to that which had affected the majority population took off in the late nineteenth century, resulting in the appearance of a network of cultural, linguistic and historical societies that emphasised the distinctiveness of the minority. These were best developed, perhaps, among the Bohemian Germans and the Swedish-speaking population of Finland. Among Irish or Ulster protestants there were few signs of a comparable movement. Although certain communal rituals were given a new vigour, neither the cultural past nor the cultural present of the community was of great concern to the protestant leadership, nor was a classical historical myth illustrating the great past of the Irish protestant community created for propagation among the masses. The notion that the Protestant community dated only from the seventeenth century, however glorious its role then, was no substitute, though there were elements of a typical nationalist sense of mission in the idea that Irish protestants were the defenders of liberty in a benighted land. In general, though, the Protestant minority projected itself as an extension of the British nation, whose 'greatness' lay in the imperial present and which needed no recourse to a glorious past to reinforce its contemporary solidarity.[6]

It is true that the patterns of economic competition between the two communities bore some resemblance to those elsewhere. The leadership of the majority community was sympathetic to the idea that its resources could be built up by cultivating national economic development along the lines of the Polish 'organic work' model and intense demographic competition and conflict over the control and transfer of property between the communities took place. Although the Irish protestant minority was by no means a monolith – in addition to class divisions, there was a deep gulf between Northern and Southern protestants – it is striking that the intensity of inter-community strife overshadowed so completely potential intra-community strife. The failure of class conflict to achieve clear political articulation within each community is one of the remarkable features of Irish political development, one for which it is difficult to find parallels elsewhere. In the other cases that have been mentioned above, the nationalist movement of the majority was always divided along class lines: there were typically three parties, a middle-class nationalist one, an agrarian one and a socialist one. A similar differentiation tended to take place within the minority, though the Swedish People's Party in Finland came close to the Unionist Party in Ireland in its capacity to mobilise the minority community across class lines.

6. Conclusion

In the context of nationalist movements in Central and Eastern Europe, then, Irish nationalism may be typified as follows. First, as a political phenomenon it displayed all of the characteristics of the triangular relationships that were typical elsewhere – relationships between an external metropolitan power, a local underprivileged majority and a local ethnically-distinct minority that had exercised a near-monopoly of domestic economic, political and cultural influence. The early efforts of the minority to form an alliance with the majority against the external power could not survive the ethnic mobilisation of the majority in the nineteenth century, and the second phase of the nationalist movement saw clear-cut antagonism between majority and minority, with the latter looking increasingly but not always successfully to the external power as a guarantor of its position of privilege. The Irish experience was distinctive, however, in the great political strength of the minority (largely attributable to its close relationship with the external power, which emerged victorious from the First World War), a factor that permitted it to secede in turn from the new secessionist state. This set of relationships in Ireland was, indeed, characterised by a degree of dependence on political violence that greatly exceeded the typical level elsewhere.

Second, the cultural basis of nationalism in Ireland was unique in the context of the post-war successor states. Despite superficial similarities between the Irish language revival movement and that elsewhere, including the tendency for the movement to be sponsored in its earliest phase by members of the minority, the language boundary in Ireland was of almost no ethnic significance. The inter-communal boundary was instead defined in terms of religious denominational affiliation, reinforced on the catholic side by a powerful myth of history and consciousness of past linguistic and cultural distinctiveness. On the protestant side the movement tended to rely overwhelmingly on economic and political claims.

Third, the coincidence between ethnic conflict and conflict between peasants and their landlords gave Irish nationalism an important agrarian dimension, one which it was to share with nationalism in Central and Eastern Europe. Although it fits well with theories of internal colonialism, the Irish case was distinctive in that Ireland was much more clearly an economic periphery than were the other European cases with which it has been compared above. Most distinctive of all is, of course, the failure of class conflict to cut across ethnic conflict in anything more than a superficial way.

It scarcely needs to be emphasised, then, that the Irish case must be taken into account in any attempt to arrive at a theory of nationalism on the basis of comparative evidence. Equally, the comparative dimension sheds revealing light on certain aspects of Irish nationalism. The similarities noted above are worthy of further analysis with a view to determining how far they may imply that a common set of causal relationships is at work; but the distinctiveness of the Irish experience also constitutes a challenge to theorists of nationalism and a test-case against which only the most robust explanatory hypotheses can survive.

PART II
PERSPECTIVES ON TWENTIETH CENTURY CULTURE

'Quiet Desperation': variations on a theme in the writings of Daniel Corkery, Michael McLaverty and John McGahern

by

Sophia Hillan King

'The mass of men lead lives of quiet desperation'. Thoreau's phrase was written originially for a nineteenth-century American audience in *Walden, or Life in the Woods*, but it has a curious relevance to the writings of the three Irish authors whose work is, very briefly, considered in this paper. The oldest of them, Daniel Corkery, quoted Thoreau's phrase as an epigraph to his novel, *The Threshold of Quiet*.[1] He explained his choice of epigraph in the novel's prologue:

> Self-knowledge is not easily won; ... to know Cork is almost as difficult. Those faces I have been looking at in its streets today, how much do they know of its 'quiet desperation', in which, according to the American philosopher, most of the citizens of the world pass their lives? And if they do know something of this quiet desperation, whether it is the stillness of the hills or the busy-body chatter of the valley that gives it its local texture and colour? ... And once again the handful of wayfaring souls that are gathered into this story would pass before me, as if they would answer for all![2]

Corkery's attention to natural detail, together with his unsentimental compassion, acted as inspiration to a younger writer, Michael McLaverty, who began in the 1930s to study Corkery's work, and later, in the 1940s and 1950s, to correspond with him. In the following extract from a talk delivered to the Young Ulster Society on 27 February 1940, McLaverty gives his enthusiastic opinion of *The Threshold of Quiet*:

> Corkery's book is quiet, mellow, thoughtful and inactive – it bears all the evidence of maturity, a mind turned inwards and catching for us fragments of a life which youth passes by. There is nothing in it of the rebellious stir of youth; there is a love theme, threading through it, but it too has unobtrusiveness ... It has atmosphere, the atmosphere of autumn: firelight leaping at the windows; water hens creasing a lake; amber skies; and man himself, with his own thoughts – quiet perhaps, but with a growing note of desperation.[3]

Later, in the 1950s, when McLaverty was himself an established writer of short stories and novels, he was tentatively approached by a young schoolteacher who had

written a first novel. This was John McGahern, and an increasingly friendly
correspondence resulted from that first letter. McGahern first asked McLaverty's
advice, and then developed his own confidence in writing of the lives of the quietly
desperate, notably in *The Barracks* and *The Dark*. McGahern's first letter is dated
13 January 1959:

> I am a native of North Roscommon, and work in a National School in Dublin. I
> came across *Truth in the Night* when I was in the Training College; I read it several
> times that month. Since then I read and enjoyed most of your work. *School for
> Hope* is the novel I think greatest. *Truth in the Night* gave me much enjoyment
> – to read it was like coming into a new country. ... More than a year ago I read your
> 'The circus pony' in the *Dublin Magazine*. I hope you don't think me stupid when
> I say it is better than any of your work. I thought it captured the same strange
> wonder of K. Mansfield's 'The young girl', or 'Vision' by Corkery. It so excited
> me at the time that I read it to a class I teach, but they were too young. ... I believe
> that it is a great achievement for any man to state, even once, a measure of his
> experience truthfully. Your books have given me a better appreciation of life as
> well as their own pleasure. I want to thank you and to wish you the health to write
> many more.[4]

McLaverty's reply, ten days later, is full of encouragement and paternal helpfulness,
as he sets out, in what was to become his characteristic method when dealing with
young writers, a programme of reading for McGahern:

> I was greatly pleased to get your letter, and pleased too to hear that you admire
> Corkery's beautiful story 'Vision'. I remember reading reviews of *Earth Out of
> Earth* and not one critic gave 'Vision' as much as a line of praise. Years later I
> met Corkery and I told him I thought 'Vision' his best story and he smiled in his
> quiet fashion, glad to hear that I had loved it. You are fortunate as a teacher
> starting out on your career by reading stories of such quiet power to your pupils.
> You'll enjoy your work and your pupils will enjoy school. May I suggest that you
> also read to them Seamus O'Kelly's 'Billy the Clown' and if you can act it, as you
> read, their enjoyment will be a memorable one. Others that you may find effective
> are Mary Lavin's 'The Sand Castle', Chekhov's 'The Runaway' and 'Kash-
> tanka', Katherine Mansfield's 'The Doll's House' and 'The Voyage'. And for
> your own private enjoyment Mary Lavin's 'The Small Bequest' and Tolstoy's
> great, great story, 'The Death of Ivan Ilyich'. Of O'Connor's I'd suggest
> 'Uprooted'; he has also written one called 'The New Teacher' but it's so silly, so
> palpably unreal I often wondered why he enclosed it between the covers of a
> book.[5]

It seems from the correspondence that there was a kind of unity of theme, and
indeed, a similarity of approach in the work of these three Irish writers. Beneath the
more obvious signs of a similarity of outlook, however, there appear fundamental
differences in their interpretations of Thoreau's phrase. As the correspondence
between Corkery and McLaverty – and later, that between McLaverty and McGahern – increasingly show, these three writers differ widely in their understanding of
the phrase 'quiet desperation'.

The central figure is McLaverty, first as Corkery's disciple and later as McGahern's mentor. Guided by the spirit of Thoreau's phrase, as set out in Corkery's

gentle novel, McLaverty began to be possessed by the idea of a daily struggle with an intolerable situation, though he did not devote himself to this theme until after the publication of his early short stories of children and islands, and his two first, largely autobiographical novels. In the early 1940s, he began increasingly to investigate the lives of the lonely, and the trapped, in everyday situations. He hoped that the novel he worked on from 1941 until its eventual publication in 1945, *In This Thy Day*, would be his best. By this he meant that it would be true to life as he perceived it, and, to this end, he gave it a bitterly stark ending. Thus, his innocent heroine and well-meaning, upstanding hero, Ned, are irrevocably parted by the workings of the mean-spirited Mrs Mason, mother of the hapless young man. She considers the girl, Mary Devlin, to be the product of a worthless family and prevents the young couple's marriage by witholding her consent. She is empowered to do so by her late husband's will, leaving the land to her 'for her day'. Ned goes away to sea, and Mary, bereft, begins a lonely existence. Although his mother repents, it is too late, and her hardness of heart reasserts itself in the closing sentences of the novel, as she feeds her acrimony with bitter thoughts of Mary Devlin's ne'er-do-well brother:

> 'O God', she moaned, 'what did I do that You're so hard on me!' She lifted her beads but her mind sped from the prayers she was saying, her heart hardened to John Devlin, and bowing her head on her crooked arm on the table she wept bitterly.[6]

These are the closing sentences of the novel, and McLaverty, despite concerned requests from his publishers to give some hope for the young people, held fast. He believed in his ending, and refused to alter it. To his astonishment and chagrin, his American publishers then rejected it. So did other publishers, until, eventually, Macmillan agreed to produce the American edition. The shock of this rejection served to strengthen, rather than undermine, McLaverty's determination to produce a truly moral novel which would reflect the value, not only of endurance of the intolerable, but of a specifically Christian, and indeeed catholic, patience in adversity. He had spent the 1930s reading and studying the work of Corkery and other modern Irish writers, and set himself in the 1940s to the task of developing his own theory of the lives of those who 'lead lives of quiet desperation', refining it further in the light of the study of the works of Gerald Manley Hopkins and Francois Mauriac. So determined was he to produce the moral, truly catholic novel, that he wrote to John Pudney, in 1949, the words: 'I have turned my back on the short story'. While it was not strictly true, it was largely so, as he wrote only seven more over the next forty years.[7]

Almost at the same time that he abandoned the short story in favour of the moral novel, McLaverty began to correspond with Daniel Corkery. Much of their correspondence, between 1949 and 1954, deals with their respective attempts to have the American pubishers, Devin Adair, deal fairly with them over royalties, and McLaverty, who had already worked with Devin Adair, seems to have guided Corkery through a maze of difficult negotiation. Some of the letter, however, contain valuable literary criticism. Corkery was here the elder, and, as McLaverty was to take over the Corkery role in his later dealings with McGahern, Corkery's opinions have a special significance. The following is an extract from a letter from Corkery to McLaverty, dated 21 May 1949:

Very many thanks for your book. One or two of the stories I had read before – 'The

Game Cock' and 'Aunt Suzanne': I was glad to see them again. And to read the others. The writing is very lovely. Only for your gift of intimacy, hardly any one of them would carry itself through – they are so slight. I enjoyed 'The Wild Duck's Nest', 'Father Christmas', 'The White Mare', 'The Mother', 'The Poteen Maker', 'The Schooner' very much indeed. It is a book one can turn to again and again.[8]

Between 1949 and 1954, McLaverty was finding that the writing of his ideal novel was a more difficult task than he had imagined, although he had not expected that it would be easy. In a letter to his friend, Cecil Scott, editor of the Macmillan Company in New York, he writes of his difficulty in delivering his fifth novel, published in 1954, under the title *School of Hope*:

I had hoped to have the book ready for you before I go off on vacation at the end of the month, but it's just not to be. I just can't manage it, and my chief delayer in this respect is my own desire for perfection; perfection of phrase and consistency of mood. I could let my imagination run wild for a while and so write easily, but then it would all be false, and falsity is, I hope, what no critic will ever accuse me of. No, nothing goes out of fashion as quickly as falsity and nothing wears so well as truth.[9]

Almost a month later, on 19 June 1953, he wrote to Scott: 'At times I have misgivings that I am too restrained and the style too bare to produce the effect intended. I try to suggest, to hint, rather than make things obvious. The long apprenticeship I spent at the short story form has taught me that'.[10] By 2 November 1953, however, he was cheerfully optimistic, if still deeply conscious of the toll taken by the effort of writing the novel:

It will probably be my most successful book though I wouldn't say it's my best. No book ever gave me so much trouble. I cut out thousands of words in an effort to preserve unity of scene and to use nothing that did not give point and piquancy to the main theme. If the reviewers read me slowly and with full attention they will see that each chapter is created with the same meticulous integrity that I'd expend on a short story. I hate contrivance. I love the natural gesture and the natural event – but these can only be achieved, it seems to me, by long and reverential contemplation. When one has learned the 'tricks of the trade', it's easy to write a novel, but a novel of that kind would not be worth writing or reading.[11]

This novel was not the first since his decision to devote himself to the writing of the moral novel, but was very important to him, despite his misery in writing it. He had received from Corkery qualified, but reasonably encouraging praise of *Truth in the Night*, the interim novel, published in 1951. In January 1954, Corkery wrote to McLaverty:

I am glad to hear you are having another novel coming out. ... I thought it was not as unified a book as *The Three Brothers* – but then that was one of those things about which one says: 'That certainly has come off'. Still I thought that certain chapters towards the end of *Truth in the Night* were well done – swift and firm and true. I thought that perhaps you had too many characters in it and that what becomes the heart of the whole thing had not had sufficient space given to it. One could certainly read it again and again.[12]

McLaverty sent Corkery his copy of the 'new book', *School for Hope*, and received the following, shattering reply:

> You must be surprised at my delay in thanking you for your book. I have been having some visitors – in spite of the horrible weather. But I also wanted to get away from the book, for I had an uneasy feeling of thinness as a characteristic of it whilst reading it. And to out with an unpleasant impression, distance does not dissipate that feeling. If you don't mind me saying so, I think you should make up your mind that the next will be of a quite different size! ... I thought the surroundings in *Truth in the Night* were very real – and though I thought you had some characters in it who stood away from the action, and yet were liberally dwelt upon, the tragedy in it did not seem contrived. It was a real novel; but your latest looked like a long short story. ... I suppose Conrad is going out of fashion, but he has throughout – and especially in his long short stories, which I think the best of him – an element continuously suggestive – shade within shade – colour within colour – which gradually not alone enriches but solidifies the whole action. And I find this richly wrought background in what remains of those stories in my mind – not the particulars of it but the brooding feeling in it. I should like you to aim at something like that in your next – to try for something that seemingly delays the action and yet is always enriching it. I fear you will never forgive me for all this ...[13]

This letter, kind but certain of the failure of the novel which had been so difficult to write, must have been a blow for McLaverty, and his reply indicates his almost despairing resignation at the rejection of his work by his mentor:

> I read your kindly letter (and how well-wishing it is) – not once but many times, and when *you* say my book is thin, that is sufficient for me and I strike it off as a failure. ... The book in its original form was about twice its published length but I slashed at it in revising it, hoping to make it taut, actionless, but realise now I must have choked the life in it. I always strive after the normal, the ordinary – believing that the best fiction displays these qualities abundantly. ... I had hoped in writing that novel to suggest by hints and nudges, far more than was on the page, but I see now that it hasn't come off ... I don't know what to tackle next. I may try my hand at a play or some short stories. I'll read Conrad's stories this autumn. I have only read two of his books: *The Shadow Line* and *The Secret Agent*, one I like for its absence of women and the other for its sinister atmosphere in the old gaslit London streets. Mauriac, whom you also mention, I have read but do not like.[14]

Though no more correspondence between the two writers has survived in McLaverty's files, he did continue to write novels, and in 1958, published *The Choice*, receiving a better critical reception for it than for the previous two novels.[15] In this strong and moving story, he traces the story of a man who, after the death of his wife, returns to the town of his birth, against the advice of family and friends. He finds it is no longer home, and that the inhabitants are at first suspicious and, ultimately, hostile towards him. He dies, lonely and disappointed. So brief a synopsis cannot convey what is the real power of the book – its condemnation of blind prejudice and xenophobia, powerfully conveyed in symbol and metaphor. In *The Choice*, perhaps, McLaverty achieves his ambition to produce the moral novel.

In a sense, this achievement came ten years too late. McLaverty had begun, in the 1950s, to see himself more as a guide to the young than as a driving force in the world of letters, and the continuing failure of the public to acknowledge what he was trying to do seemed to reinforce that opinion. It is interesting to note that 1958, the year of the publication of *The Choice*, was also the time that he began to act as mentor towards the young John McGahern, advising, encouraging, and ultimately disapproving of one of McGahern's works. He was to McGahern as Corkery had been to himself.

McLaverty and McGahern met briefly, in the early 1960s, and transformed their written friendship into a personal one. They found themselves very much in sympathy, McLaverty less and less recommending reading to McGahern and more often comparing criticisms with him on an equal footing. McLaverty began to take great pleasure in McGahern's developing craft:

> Your work afforded me the same rush of delight that used to come over me when I saw my algebra teacher write on the board, Simplify. To read your work and Chekov's and Tolstoy's is to convince me that simplicity is the finest ornament of any style: the few words, the right words, chosen for point and propinquity.[16]

McGahern later acknowledged McLaverty as one of his models, and explained his reasons in a letter dated 25 March 1961: 'What attracted me years ago to your work, ... was ... what seemed to me a faithful search among the images of existence for some meaning that doesn't obviously show itself there'.[17]

When McGahern published the novel he had asked McLaverty to look at, *The Barracks*, McLaverty was warm in his praise of it, although the tone of his criticism is oddly like that of Corkery to himself in the late 1940s and early 1950s.

> There were one or two places where my Northern eye or ear stumbled, found the rhythm upset, or the object blurred. I tripped on 'blinded windows', and would have preferred 'that beat on the slates and on the windows'. And in the dialogue found that the addition of 'on us' knocked off balance the line 'rich Americans didn't run off with a girl like you'. And a point that seemed to me to lack *general* truth was Regan's use of 'bejasus' in front of his children. The rest was a thing of real beauty: the intimate atmosphere, the children, and above all the quiet power of Elizabeth who says so little and yet floods the whole scene with her presence. 'Feeling the shirt for dampness' is a delightful stroke. More power to you.[18]

McGahern's reply pays warm tribute to McLaverty: 'All my masters wrote with care: and you were one'.[19]

When McLaverty's health troubled him and he took early retirement in 1963, McGahern was concerned and supportive, and McLaverty extended the hand of friendship to the younger man in all the various troubles of his own life in the early 1960s. For both, this was a time of cautious optimism. McGahern was writing his second novel, and McLaverty was nearing completion of his eighth, published in 1965 as *The Brightening Day*. In the same year, McGahern's novel, *The Dark*, was published, and while McLaverty praised it, he also, in his own words, 'recoiled' from some of it:

> I have read your new novel and was greatly impressed by its painful sincerity and its pared-to-the-bone style, a style that has caught the essential and has left the

verbal flotsam and jetsam to the best-selling novelists. In spite of the pressure upon me of the fine reviews it has received, *The Barracks*, because of its wider scope of characterisation, seems to me the better book. Still, *The Dark* could be read as a continuation of *The Barracks* with Regan and Mahoney one and the same person. I haven't the book beside me as I write, but when I recall it there stands out: the fishing on the river, the throwing of water round the screeching tholepins, studying for exams, thoughts engendered by two old boots on a hearthstone, and the rain-damp atmosphere of an old garden. It would be difficult to analyse how you achieved this and to attempt to do so would be to kill it – it's your own natural gift as a writer and if you were fully conscious of it, it would blemish the ease and inevitablity of your style. The book rings with truth at every turn and it must have been a heart-breaking and exhausting book to write. I recoiled from one or two pages (a priest's thoughts) and wished they hadn't been there, though I realise that not a line of it was written out of a weakness to shock or degrade. The final chapters, which I found compassionately moving, do justice to Mahoney as a father and as a man and demonstrate that you have the maturity and fair-mindedness of a true novelist.[20]

This represents the end of the master-pupil relationship between the two writers, just as Corkery's withdrawal of support after *School for Hope* marked the end of a similar relationship between the two older men. On no side was there a falling out, but the correspondence that follows the publication of *The Dark* is no longer concerned with mutual, constructive criticism: something bright and enthusiastic seems to disappear. In the case of McLaverty and Corkery, no further letters exist in McLaverty's collection. McGahern and McLaverty continued to correspond, sporadically, as McGahern travelled further afield, both literally and metaphorically. It is true to say, however, that they maintain to the present day a warm regard and profound respect for one another. As for McLaverty's eighth, and as it happened, his last novel, *The Brightening Day*, it received a less than satisfactory response from the critics, and, sadly, McLaverty wrote no more.

Daniel Corkery died in 1964. Of the three writers, Corkery, McLaverty and McGahern, there was, after 1965, only McGahern left to continue exploring the theme of 'quiet desperation'. It is virtually certain that, despite the fact that both men had great admiration for skill and fine writing, neither McLaverty nor Corkery would have accepted the McGahern of, for example, *The Pornographer*.[21] The 'quiet desperation' of the characters of whom they wrote seems, in retrospect, to have a poignant relevance to the plight of such men, grown suddenly old in a world increasingly foreign to them. McGahern was the inheritor of that world, and the only one of the three able to contemplate writing in it. As for Corkery and McLaverty, perhaps the final judgement on these two careful delineators of good and careworn people, can best be found in Corkery's own words, written, in valediction, at the end of *The Threshold of Quiet*:

The room was filled with quietness; not with the quietness of peace that leaves men's souls gentle and deep and rich, even if just a little, a very little, pensive, not to say bitter. Bitter! but when such souls quit our company it is the sweetness of their quiet spirits that remains like a fragrance in the air.[22]

CHAPTER 7

Irish landscape painting in a political setting 1922-48*
by
Brian Kennedy

Paintings of the Irish landscape by artists such as Paul Henry, Charles Lamb, James Humbert Craig, Frank McKelvey, Sean Keating, Maurice MacGonigal and many others of their generation, working during the inter-war years and immediately after, often appear to be quite innocuous, merely sentimental depictions of a landscape otherwise much dramatized in the printed word and in folk memory. If the subject-matter of these artists more often than not was the west of Ireland, then it is assumed that that is because there lies the finest, the most barren and beguiling of Irish scenery. But artists, like everyone else, are influenced by every-day events around them and so, despite the appearance of their works, Henry Lamb and company were products of their times and shared the common hopes and aspirations of those times.

Much has been written of the social and political developments of Ireland in the years following independence. Broadly speaking, during the 1920s and to a greater extent in the 1930s, a form of stasis evolved as successive Dublin governments encouraged a way of life quite different to that which was already led by the great majority of the population. Official policy increasingly dwelt on a romantic view of the west where the old Gaelic or 'Irish' Ireland best survived, unsullied by the centuries of English rule which had influenced so much of the rest of the country. These views were especially characteristic of Eamon de Valera's governments between 1932 and 1948, the longest period of unbroken government in the history of the state. Consequently, the 1920s and 1930s in Ireland brought considerable isolation, which at times verged on xenophobia. As far as the arts were concerned, an emphasis on rural themes, and of the west in particular, pervaded everything.

In painting, the clarion call of the period was that artists should create a genuinely Irish school of painting, although no one knew quite what this should consist of. Indeed, from the closing years of the nineteenth century, George Russell (AE), Sarah Purser, Hugh Lane and others, had worked towards a similar aim but apparently with little success. Now, in the new Ireland, previously held ideas of what might constitute an Irish school were anathema, for they represented the efforts of the old protestant Anglo-Irish ascendancy. Exact parallels in literary attitudes can be found, for example, in Liam O'Flaherty, who criticized Russell's management of the *Irish Statesman* newspaper. Russell saw room for both the Anglo-Irish and the Gaelic traditions in the new Ireland and frequently expressed his views in his editorial in the paper. O'Flaherty was vehement in his opposition to Russell's

* All pictures referred to in this paper are in private collections unless otherwise stated.

stance. 'I don't for a moment claim that your paper is not doing good work', he wrote
to Russell in 1925, 'But I do claim that it is not Irish, that it is not national, and that
it is not representative in any respect of the cultural forces, in all spheres, that are
trying to find room for birth in this country at present'.[1] What O'Flaherty and others
wanted from art in the period was a form of symbolism. In the words of Cyril Barrett,
works should not only arouse national and patriotic sentiment, but should also
define it; they should give some glimpse of what the people were striving for and
of the kind of life they intended to bring into being.[2]

The artists who, during the 1920s and 1930s, best satisfied these aspirations were
Paul Henry, Charles Lamb and James Humbert Craig, all, paradoxically, northern-
ers, and Sean Keating and Maurice MacGonigal from the South. Henry was the most
innovative in terms of his treatment of subject-matter and, certainly early in his
career, he had a more intellectual approach to his art. 'A Connemara village',
painted c.1923-30, typifies the best of Henry's work at the time, in which he
captured the whole sentiment of the landscape. In the humble dwellings depicted
with their gathered stacks of turf for fuel and the general suggestion of a basic but
satisfying way of life, unsullied by technological advancement and other trappings
of 'civilisation', was a view which fitted perfectly with the temper of the times.
Around 1925, another of Henry's paintings, 'Connemara', was made into a poster
by the London Midland & Scottish Railway Company and distributed to tourist
bureaux throughout Europe and the U.S.A. Such images helped to create what
became the archetypal view of the Irish landscape. And if these 'quiet' scenes did
not convince one of the values of such a life-style, then Henry's 'Old people
watching a dance', c.1910-11, or 'Potato diggers', 1912 (National Gallery of
Ireland), and similar works showing humble peasants at ease or earnestly tilling the
land would certainly do the trick. It is easy, yet misleading, to think that Henry's was
the 'natural' way to paint the landscape of the west of Ireland, but that is only
because he and many others have accustomed us to view it in that way.

If we look at how other artists have reacted to the area, for example Dermond
O'Brien's treatment of his native county Limerick, we see a different, yet equally
persuasive, way of painting a similar subject. O'Brien was president of the Royal
Hibernian Academy (R.H.A.) for most of the period under discussion and his was
the kind of painting under attack in the Ireland of the time. Charles Lamb's 'Hearing
the news', painted in the early 1920s, similarly put forward a largely romantic view
of what was in reality a very harsh life. Like Henry's early work, 'Hearing the news'
is in the tradition of late nineteenth-century French Realist painting and in it Lamb
has set down a statement of character, symbolizing the locality. In the mid 1920s,
Lamb spent some time in Brittany and his 'Breton peasants at prayer', 1926-27
(Waterford), could equally have been set in the west of Ireland. But unfortunately,
as was the case with Henry, Lamb's later works, such as 'Taking in the lobster pots'
(Armagh) of the mid 1940s, often degenerated into cliché. Humbert Craig was a less
original painter than either Paul Henry or Charles Lamb, but he worked consistently
both in the west and in county Donegal. Through frequent exhibitions he helped,
perhaps more than anyone else, to perpetuate the landscape tradition which had
begun with Henry. There is invariably a luscious quality in Craig's work and he
brilliantly managed to convey the dankness of bog landscape. Craig worked quickly
in a loose, semi-Impressionist manner which was characterized, as John Hewitt
observed, by 'the swift notation of the insistent effect, the momentary flicker, the
flash of light, the passing shadow',[3] qualities which are evident in his 'Glendun,
Cushendun' (Bangor).

Frank McKelvey, another Belfast painter, was prominent as a landscapist in the 1920s and 1930s and exhibited regularly at the Royal Hibernian Academy, but his work is more in the style of Dermod O'Brien. It is notable that this school of landscape painting, which descended from Paul Henry through Lamb, Craig, McKelvey and numerous others, and which was an almost entirely northern-inspired affair is, perhaps, the nearest thing to a distinctly Irish school which has emerged this century. In passing we should note that not all the critics longed to see endless views of the west. Stephen Rynne, for example, reviewing the R.H.A. exhibition as late as 1945, lamented the dominance of subjects relating to the west. 'The Academy', he said, was 'threatened by peasant habitations' which seemed to be ousting all others. Could the authors of such works, he pleaded, 'not ease off a little? Say, for this year only, eschew Connemara, cancel reservations in Aran and have a think about the whole matter.'[4]

It would be wrong in passing such comments about these artists to suggest that they deliberately made pictures for propaganda purposes, although their works were so used, as a glance at the illustrations in some contemporary publications – such as the *Book of Dublin* (1929) or the *Irish Free State Official Handbook* (1932) – show. With some of their contemporaries, in particular Sean Keating, what one might call 'soft' propaganda was certainly part of their intention.

Sean Keating had first gone to the Aran Islands around 1913 or 1914 and, like John Synge before him, at once fell captive to their spell. In Aran, he wrote many years later,

> The contrast between the petty bourgeoisie life of my home town, the decayed grandeur and second rate provincialism of Dublin; the riches, wastefulness and utter conventionality of upperclass London life repelled me. By contrast Aran, wrenching an existence from the sea against a background of endless labour, danger, poverty, ignorance, patience and religious belief; charming gentle manners, the sonorous musical cadences of spoken Irish, the individual racial types waking old race memories; all these things decided me that here was where I wished to live and work'.[5]

In these comments we have a veritable catalogue of the social aspirations that pervaded both the times and many of Keating's paintings. In many respects Keating was the personification of the times: here was the rugged Gael seizing the mettle to mould the future as he dreamt it could be. Keating was strongly nationalist. He had made his name with his 'Men of the west', 1916 (Lane Gallery, Dublin), a splendid picture which extols the fibre of the people in their struggle for independence. In 1922 it was followed by a companion work, 'Men of the south' (Cork), but the latter does not have the concise rigour, either of concept or execution, of the earlier picture.

In the mid 1920s, Keating was commissioned by the Electricty Supply Board to paint a series of pictures chronicling the construction of the hydro-electric scheme on the river Shannon at Ardnacrusha in county Limerick. In all, more than twenty paintings were made of the scheme. Most of these are rather dull, unimaginative landscapes but in 'Night's candles are burnt out', 1928-29 (Oldham), he produced what is possibly the most allegorical picture made in Ireland this century. The picture is an allegory of Keating's hopes for the emergent new Ireland. We see the advancing power of electricity about to oust the candle, which is placed beside a priest at the bottom right-hand corner, and the oil lamp, held by a workman to the left of centre. This change is epitomized in the figures of a mother and father with their children in the top right, the latter representing the new generation. The hanging skeleton at the left-hand side of the composition represents the death of the old era, while the workmen to the left of centre and the contractor in the foreground, represent latent entreprenurial skills. The contractor's contemptuous stare at the gunman to his left is an historical reference to the recently ended civil war of 1922-23 and also symbolizes the birth of the new era and confidence in the future. The immensity of the whole Shannon project and the determination with which it was carried through are vividly illustrated in 'The key men', c.1928-29 (Institution of Engineers of Ireland), another work in the series, and one which is strongly rhetorical.

Other Keating compositions of these years, which extol the virtues of life in the west are 'Half flood' and 'Goodbye, Father', 1935 (Ulster Museum), the latter showing the departure of a priest from Inishere, Aran, to the mainland. These, along with 'The race of the Gael' (IBM, New York), in which Keating eulogized the rugged fibre of the Gaelic temperament, are excellent examples of what was thought at the time should comprise a 'national' art. 'The race of the Gael' was awarded first prize in a world-wide competition of contemporary painting organized by the American IBM Company in 1939. In the words of Anne Crookshank and the Knight of Glin: 'It is Keating who sums up the "discovery" of the west of Ireland as a source for patriotic, heroic, almost propagandist subject matter which seems to have been adopted by the independence movement to straight-jacket Irish art into nationalist terms'.[6]

To some extent Maurice MacGonigal shared Keating's ideals, but he was more broad-minded. In paintings like 'By the sea', of the late 1930s, he caught a similar mood to Keating's 'Half flood', but it is in landscapes such as 'Inishmor', c. 1930-35, that we see him at his best. The work is full of fresh air and vigour typically effected with a cool palette, dominated by blues and greys, to give a pristine, almost luminous quality to the paint. In the 1940s, MacGonigal, like Keating before him, did some paintings for the Electricity Supply Board – 'Errigal, Co. Donegal' and 'Co. Donegal Scheme' are good examples – but they are more freely handled than Keating's works and have less of a harsh didactic realism about them.

The most important of all the painters working in Ireland during these years was Jack B. Yeats, but he was a loner in every respect. His subject-matter has led to him being called the painter of Nationalist Ireland. One of his best-known images is 'The man from Aranmore' (National Gallery of Ireland), a watercolour done in 1905 when he toured the west with John Synge and which is the quintessence of the rugged life there. From 1915 until the mid 1920s, in pictures such as 'In memory', 'A westerly wind', 'The Liffey swim' (National Gallery of Ireland) and 'Communicating with prisoners' (Sligo) he recorded the revolutionary events of the times and documented life as it was. In his early years Yeats was regarded as an enigma: his celebrity dates from the mid 1940s. Thomas MacGreevy was the first writer to cast Yeats as the champion of Irish nationalism in the visual arts, a view which has been sustained by most subsequent writers. MacGreevy's religious and nationalist feelings prejudiced his discussion and he did not discuss his interpretation of the works with the artist.[7] To cast Yeats in this mould is to categorize him falsely and because his paintings of the 1920s and 1930s have a universality about them and evoke our sympathy that is not to say that they are instructive statements of a political view. Yeats was a recorder of events – he worked from what he called a 'pool of memories' distilled from his sketchbooks – and there was nothing intentionally didactic in his work. While he sympathized with various factions, political and otherwise, none of their causes was ever the subject-matter of his art in any real sense. In 1929, in words which might well represent his views on any attempt to cast him as a propagandist, he said that painting had 'suffered ... terribly from the admiration of the half educated, from people who ... cannot accept [it] on its own valuation, but always wish to see it as a vehicle for expressing something else'. He continued: 'Now the truth is a painting is not a vehicle for anything except itself. It is the memory of a moment.'[8]

The kind of imagery represented by Henry, Lamb, Craig and, more especially, by Keating, MacGonigal and the early Yeats was seen during the 1920s as going part of the way towards the creation of an Irish school of painting; but by the late 1920s cries were heard for a more overtly 'nationalist' art. In 1929, for example, George Noble, Count Plunkett, sometime director of the National Museum of Ireland and minister of Fine Art in the first Dail, founded the Academy of Christian Art, membership of which was exclusive to Roman Catholics. The Academy was founded to promote what Plunkett termed 'the intellectual commonplaces of catholic life'[9] in the visual and the literary arts. Through organizations such as this, the Catholic Action associations, the Catholic Truth Society and the Censorship Board, which freely repressed writings which might have disturbed conventional moral sensitivities, life and art in the new state were given a catholic complexion in all their aspects. During the 1930s this chauvinism increased. Even the more liberal *Irish Times*, reviewing the annual exhibition of the Royal Hibernian Academy in 1932, encouraged artists to emphasize aspects of life in the west so as to create a 'nationalist' art which, it said, was the only art that really mattered in Ireland at that time.[10] In 1934 the Academy of Irish Art was established to challenge the R.H.A. – a body considered by many to be an anachronism – specifically to encourage the development of a national art. The leading force behing the new Academy was Ben O'Hickey, a close friend of Sean Keating, and its members were mainly artists whose works had been rejected by the selection committee of the R.H.A. The new academy ceased to exist in about 1939; it contributed little to the development of Irish art, its title was pretentious, and it remained, in a pejorative sense, a 'salon des refusés'.

The heyday of societies and groups such as these came in the late 1930s and was epitomized by Dr Ethna Byrne's attitude in concluding her review of the 1938 R.H.A. exhibition for the *Leader* newspaper:

Not long ago Mr L.S. Gogan[11] addressing the Academy of Christian Art ... gave good advice to Irish artists in general; he recommended them to steep themselves in Gaelicism, to go back to traditions to the great Gaelic past for their inspiration ...

It is a pity that such excellent advice is not followed. Mediaeval Ireland produced works of art so beautiful that they are among the most precious treasures of subsequent civilization and models of the highest artistic ability. Modern Ireland can do the same – if she will consent to *be* Irish, if her artists will work for an *Irish* art.

She concluded, using a paradox common to the Irish mind at the time: 'We can only go forward to great achievement by looking back'[12] Much of the work of the best of those artists who did follow such advice was of a kind of 'Social realism' – Keating's 'Economic pressure', c.1920s (Cork), a picture representing forced emigration from the west, is a good example – and to that extent it paralleled developments in the work of Sean O'Casey, Frank O'Connor, Liam O'Flaherty and other young writers of the time in Irish literature.

With such an introverted view of life it is not surprising that those artists in the 1920s and 1930s, who did concern themselves with more cosmopolitan themes, met with little success. Mainie Jellett, Evie Hone and Cecil Salkeld, perhaps, were the most adventurous of them. In 1920, along with Hone, Jellett went to Paris, where she studied under André Lhote and Albert Gleizes. The latter greatly influenced her work and with him she began to make Cubist paintings, often with a landscape theme, two of which – including, in all probability, her 'Abstract', 1922 (Ulster Museum) – she first exhibited at the Dublin Painters' Gallery in 1923. The critics greeted them with derision. Even George Russell, who some years earlier had argued that the best way to establish a genuinely Irish school of painting was to make native artists aware of what their contemporaries elsewhere were doing, commented in the Irish *Statesman* : '... what Miss Jellett says in one of her decorations she says in the other, and that is nothing'. Cubism, he continued, was a mere 'sub-section' of the contemporary 'artistic malaria'.[13] Jellett and Hone continued to exhibit Cubist paintings in Dublin throughout the 1920s and 1930s, but rarely met with approval.

Cecil Salkeld was the only Irish artist of his generation to study in Germany where he was inspired by the 'Neue Sachlichkeit' movement which greatly influenced European art in the inter-war years. He exhibited works such as 'Composition' and 'Railway' at the Dublin Painters' Gallery, the New Irish Salon and other Dublin venues in the mid 1920s but, like Jellett, met with little acclaim. Reviewing the New Irish Salon in 1924, George Russell again illustrates the critical mood of the time. Likening Pointillism, Cubism, Fauvism and other trends to 'aesthetic bacteria' he said:

> We went into the New Irish Salon and saw the aesthetic bacteria at work, and the inflamations, ulcers and blotches they produced ... One speculated about the Gleizes, the Lhotes, the Salkelds and the Jelletts, wondering whether their decorations were reflections of thought forms or imitations of other Cubists ... The only excuse for these is a colour sense, and we regret to say that some of them had no more beauty of colour than is usual in a pattern on oilcloth.[14]

Apart from Jellett, Hone and Salkeld a few other Irish artists – mostly the members of the Society of Dublin painters, a group formed by Paul Henry in 1920 to fight the reactionary stance of the Dublin art establishment at that time – exhibited mildly Modernist paintings throughout these years. Significantly, no trace of Surrealism, which was so prominent as an intellectual force in Europe in the inter-war years, appears in Irish art before Colin Middleton, another Belfast painter, made just one or two Surrealist works in 1938-39. Modernism in all its aspects was regarded as an ogre in the Ireland of the 1920s and 1930s, and by rejecting it and all that it stood for, its critics were able to settle for the dubious comfort of veneration for the Irish past. John Dowling, writing about Surrealism in 1937, typified much of contemporary journalism. Describing Surrealism as a 'stealthily spreading philosophy' he concluded: 'It is ... a comforting thought that the steady stream of tradition still moves on, indifferent to these squalls, and it is heartening to remember that the gates of Hell shall not prevail against it'.[15]

Yet by the late 1930s attitudes were changing in Ireland; there was a growing realization that the country was not immune to external influences. Moreover, in 1939 the declaration of Irish neutrality, the outbreak of war in Europe and the beginning of the 'Emergency' in Ireland, compelled the adoption of a truly independent foreign policy for the first time, which ultimately led to a more confident national identity. In the arts there was a broadening of attitudes. Numerous foreigners, including a number of artists who spent the war years in Dublin, brought influences – in particular first-hand experience of European Modernism – which could no longer be ignored. Two artists who made a significant contribution to the changing climate of the times were Basil Rakoczi and Kenneth Hall. They both spent some time in the west and Rakoczi's 'Aran islander', c.1939-40 and Hall's 'Dooagh', 1939-40, show a less sentimental view of the people and the landscape than most of the native painters. The most important development in Irish painting was brought about by a number of Irish artists who had spent the 1930s in Europe and elsewhere before being forced home by the outbreak of war. The best known of these painters are Louis Le Brocquy and Norah McGuinness. In 1943, along with Mainie Jellett and some others exasperated by the intransigence of the R.H.A. towards any form of Modernism, they formed the Irish Exhibition of Living Art. This was a belated assertion of secessionism, similar to those movements which had earlier manifested themselves in other European countries.

In these years the R.H.A. was abhorred by those who craved a 'national' art and by the more avant-garde painters who espoused international trends. Mainie Jellett, writing in the journal *Commentary*, clearly stated the predicament of the times and encapsulated a number of themes – academic art, national art, avant-garde art – which dominated the era:

> Every year I go to the R.H.A. exhibition in a spirit of hopefulness, expecting there may be some change ... [from the usual] miasma of vulgarity and self-satisfaction ... [But with] the exception of Jack B. Yeats and an odd work here and there, bad craftsmanship, vulgarity, and faulty weak draughtsmanship [are] its main characteristics ...

> Then one looks for some sign of nationality, something that would tell the onlooker that these pictures were by Irish men and women ... This quality of nationality is something lacking in Irish art as a whole.

Bringing some common sense to the whole discussion about nationality in art she continued:

> It is a quality that cannot be studied and self-consciously looked for; it will show only if we artists are working creatively with our whole capacity of body and soul, and not if we continue to paint complacent coloured photographs of cottages and Irish scenery, without delving deeper into the inner consciousness of our country and its natural rhythm of life.[16]

It was in this climate that Le Brocquy, McGuinness and Jellett inaugurated the Living Art exhibition which became an annual event and which is still held each year.

The Living Art exhibitions were an immediate success. They were well received by the press and were supported by the public both in attendances and in purchases of pictures. The exhibitions were a catalyst for all that was progressive in Irish art, and in the late 1940s they brought forth a number of young painters, principally from Belfast, who dominated the development of Irish painting for the next two decades. Of the founders of the exhibitions, Jellett died young in 1944, Le Brocquy was mainly a figure painter and therefore outside the scope of this paper, and Norah McGuinness regularly exhibited pictures like 'Bachelor's Walk', c.1949, which were much influenced by French Fauvist painting. McGuinness's friend, Nano Reid, was another frequent exhibitor at the early Living Art exhibitions and it was largely through these that she came to prominence. By the 1940s she had evolved a lyrical style of landscape painting, evident in 'The hanging gate' of c.1945, although she could also be boldly Expressionist as in 'West Cork mountains' of the same period.

Of the northern painters who came to the fore at this time, Colin Middleton, Nevill Johnson, George Campbell, Dan O'Neill and Gerard Dillon were the most influential. They all produced work which was refreshingly different from that which had typified the preious two decades. Both Middleton and Johnson had a strong social conscience and were much influenced by contemporary events in the wider world. Middleton's 'Our lady of Bikini', 1946, was stimulated by the horror of recent British atomic tests on the Bikini attol in the Pacific, and the desolate wasteland of Johnson's 'Landscape, rock pool', c.1950 (Lane Gallery, Dublin), was also a reaction to the changing post-war world. Johnson exhibited works like this at the Waddington Galleries, Dublin, in 1947 and the *Irish Tatler & Sketch* saw them as macabre symbols of the new atomic age. It argued that they marked the end of an epoch in Irish painting and were a foretaste of things to come. From the turn of the century, it commented perceptively, Irish artists had concentrated on painting the landscape and recording its changing moods; but few of the younger generation were now interested in the landscape, they preferred to paint figure compositions. 'The post-war world is allergic to tradition. A chapter is closed', it concluded.[17] In works such as 'Our lady of Bikini' and 'Landscape, rock pool', Middleton and Johnson exposed the 'prickly conscience'[18] of the times which so many tried to ignore although Yeats, in late works like 'On through the silent lands', 1951 (Ulster Museum), had touched the same chord. Younger painters were less sensitive to contemporary events and in their own way recorded a romantic landscape. George Campbell's 'Claddagh Duff, Connemara', c.1947 (Ulster Museum), is Expressionist in execution, but straightforward in concept, as is Dan O'Neill's 'Knockalla Hills, Donegal' (Ulster Museum) of 1951. O'Neill's close friend, Gerard Dillon, painted mainly figure compositions, but frequently, as in 'Aran Islanders', c.1946-49, he captured the romance of the landscape and its people, like Keating and MacGonigal, but without their didactic import.

Most of the previous generation of artists continued to paint in the late 1940s, but Henry and Lamb, sadly, became rather trite. Keating, on the other hand, retained his earlier attitudes, but was overtaken by events. He remained hostile to modern painting and even resigned as president of the R.H.A. in 1962 because he saw his colleagues belatedly reaching an accommodation with Modernism and compromising with what he called 'anarchy'. 'Art is skill', he said as late as 1965, 'modern art will go down the drain',[19]

The search for a distinctively Irish school of art was finally frustrated, yet in a broader sense such a school *did* exist in a form which few recognized. Given the temper of the times, the Irish school which was desired was nothing more than a quasi-sentimental, nationalist offering, which would endlessly repeat the stock motifs of an Irish identity. Fortunately, such desires did not materialize, for just as people are subject to the character of the times in which they live, so too are countries. By the late 1940s, Modernism was in the ascendancy everywhere in the arts and any appeal to tradition was, ultimately, hopeless.

CHAPTER 8

Representation in modern Irish poetry
by
Eamonn Hughes

The introduction to *The Penguin Book of Contemporary British Poetry* claims 'to extend the imaginative franchise'.[1] The anthology functions as a Representation of the Poet's Act, suggesting that somewhere, a poetic equivalent of Westminster, there are those who hold the power to extend the franchise. Seamus Heaney's response to the anthology, *An Open Letter*, is at root a declaration of independence, an expressed desire *not* to be represented at a poetic Westminster. But there are problems with this declaration of independence. Seamus Deane has spoken of how Heaney caresses the intimacies of the Anglo-Irish connection and we live in a world of interdependencies in which such intimacies cannot simply be rejected, constituting as they do our reality. Rejecting them does not return us to a pristine origin; it leaves us instead in a void. The usual questions which arise from such considerations are about how the Irish are (mis)represented. Instead, I want to consider how certain Irish writers represent other cultures, particularly England's.

The second section of Seamus Heaney's *North*, particularly 'Singing School', is a pivotal moment in his career. Although often dismissed,[2] it is Heaney's first sustained interrogation of his intimacy with English culture. His response is to strip his writing of the influences of that culture. His later writing shows this to have been a wrong turning, rejects the attempted nativism of 'Singing School', and returns to English culture with a new and dialectical purpose: nor is Heaney alone in this.

Paul Muldoon's volumes end with long poems influenced by the Irish language traditions of voyage and vision poetry but referring only to these neutralises him by locating him in a safe, known tradition. It implies a nativist endorsement of the methods of a modern writer. Other, equally weighty influences on Muldoon's writing, for example, the narrative songs of Bob Dylan or the detective quests of Raymond Chandler, must be acknowledged. This is not just to say that there is a need to relocate Irish poetry in a broader context, although this is no small matter. It is rather to stress that the continuous influence of local contexts is dialectically balanced by influences from the wider world. Consequently, Irish poetry is best viewed as an intertextuality which can only be understood through a consideration of both nativist and external influences. '7 Middagh Street', the bravura poem which closes *Meeting the British*[3] (hereafter in the text as *MtB*), is a deliberately intertextual debate on whether poetry can make things happen. The figure of Auden begins the sequence by quoting from Masefield's 'Cargoes', itself previously represented in the volume as a parentally recommended distraction from growing sexual and political knowledge (Profumo, *MtB*, p.8). The sequence ends with Louis (MacNeice) and others proclaiming that '... poetry can make things happen-/not

only can, but must ...' (*MtB*, p. 59). Nevertheless, there are those who hold to the idea
that poetry is separate from the political:

> 'MacNeice? That's a Fenian name.'
> As if to say, 'None of your sort, none of you
>
> will as much as go for a rubber hammer
> never mind chalk a rivet, never mind caulk a seam
> on the quinquereme of Ninevah.'
>
> (*MtB*, p. 60)

These lines pit a monocultural and aestheticist position against the actualities of
Northern Ireland in a rewrite of 'Ulster was British, but with no rights on/ The
English lyric ...'[4] and make clear the fatuity of trying to hold on to the autonomous
text – whether it be 'Ulster' or 'Cargoes' – in an internationalist, multinationalist
and post-imperial world.

Tom Paulin's poetry is also often read in relation to a nativist tradition. In this case
it is the unionist tradition which provides a safe point of reference, on the assumption
that Paulin's attitude to it is a disgust for its shabbinesss and vulgarity as apparently
typified by a poem such as 'Off the Back of a Lorry':

> A zippo lighter
> and a quilted jacket,
> two rednecks troughing
> in a gleamy diner,
> the flinty chipmarks on a white enamel pail,
> Paisley putting pen to paper
> in Crumlin jail ...[5]

However, the poem, like the tradition it describes, relies on American popular
culture – its 'tune' is that of 'These Foolish Things' – which alters its apparent
disgust to exasperated affection. Without a sense of such external presences we are
unable to appreciate the full impact of the poetry. This is especially so in Paulin's
most recent collection, *Fivemiletown*,[6] which deploys a pentecostal range of
tongues as it sets out Paulin's 'defiant version of dinnseanchas'.[7]

There are a number of reasons for considering *North*, (hereafter in the text as *N*.)
especially Part II, in this light. It was among the first and most keenly anticipated
poetical responses to the Northern political situation.[8] It is the first step in the politics
of contemporary poetry in the North and is indicative of the struggle the Northern
poet has to undergo in order to create a representative voice.

North, famously, is divided into two parts. In Part II, Heaney turns from the
synoptic vision of Part I, which is historical and analogical in method, to a more
personal and intertextual approach, particularly in 'Singing School'. Certain
theoretical considerations, which bear on my opening comments, will elucidate
Heaney's method throughout *North*.

Stan Smith has used Julia Kristeva's concepts of 'foreign discourses' and 'intertextuality' to assess Yeats' attitude to inheritance.[9] The issue of inheritance has
a number of determinants, not the least of which is the problematic relationship of
the Irish writer to English language and culture. Traditionally this gives rise to the
lot of the Irish writer; alienated from language, the writer must work with language

in such a way as to redefine the self in language by forcing language to come to terms with experience for which it is not fitted. The concept of 'intertextuality' is thus of central importance to modern Irish writing as the writer's 'fretting' issues in a dialogic procedure within language and his discourse becomes 'carnivalesque'. This, Kristeva defines as 'a social and political protest. There is no equivalence, but rather, identity between challenging official linguistic codes and challenging official law'.[10] The problematic nature of Irish identity required both a challenge to cultural and political preoccupations, and an attempt to comprehend, in both senses of that word, the variety of cultural experience which is available because of the split and joined nature of Irish-English. Irish writing is therefore a literature in which lived experience and linguistic performance are not necessarily matched. However, while much of this applies to contemporary writing, the historical situation for Heaney is different from that of Yeats. Volosinov has distinguished the 'native language ... one's "kith and kin"; we feel about it as we feel about our habitual attire' from the foreign language:

> Only in learning a foreign language does a fully prepared consciousness – fully prepared thanks to one's native language – confront a fully prepared language which it need only accept. People do not 'accept' their native language – it is in their native language that they first reach consciousness.[11]

His point is that active response, rather than passive understanding, is available through the native language. To acknowledge English language and culture as foreign is to be passive, to be represented. To reject English language and culture as foreign may achieve independence but does not alter those representations. To accept English language and culture as now native may be to lose a measure of independence, but it is to gain the right to be active, to represent. This is the central concern of Part II of *North* in which Heaney represents the constituents of the self and its voice.

The first three poems of Part II represent the North as a babble of voices. Throughout this welter, the poet's concern is with the possibilities of freedom and of reshaping language. 'Singing School' continues this representation of other voices with the purpose of representing the self.

The epigraphs to 'Singing School', from the autobiographical works of Wordsworth and Yeats (*N*, p. 62), signal Heaney's examination of the 'tradition of myself'.[12] The self which he presents is obviously from a Catholic background. To say this, however, is not enough. If it were, we should have to agree with O'Brien about the 'bleak conclusiveness'[13] of the volume, because we would be surrendering to the implication that the self, and its voice in these poems, is fixed, consistent, and unitary. Heaney's method in 'Singing School' does not allow that conclusion. The 'foreign discourses' within this sequence are external and determining in one way, but they are equally internal and determined presences; that is to say they exist apart from Heaney, but they are also a part of Heaney's own voice. His experience of language is both personal and social; language exists as both 'langue', the social order of language, and 'parole', the personal voice.[14] Intertextuality is, therefore, a fact of language as a whole, although it can be subject to conscious manipulation as in 'Singing School'. Heaney's voice does not exist apart from the allusions of 'Singing School'. We can recognize the voices of Wordsworth, Yeats, Kavanagh, Deane, Shakespeare, Coleridge, Hopkins, Lorca, Goya – if a painter may be allowed a voice – Michael McLaverty, Mansfield, Chekhov, Joyce, Montague, Mandelstam, and Ovid in this sequence – all voices which are themselves intertextual and informed by history – but if we removed them we would not be left with the 'pure drop' of Heaney.

Each epigraph to 'Singing School' contains an apparent opposition: 'beauty and fear' for Wordsworth, and 'Orange' and 'Fenian' for Yeats. In the autobiographical works from which the oppositions come, the impulse is for both elements to be comprehended. Wordsworth and Yeats are not simply opposed for Heaney – they are not just English and Irish – because Wordsworth was a part of Yeats' cultural 'langue' and both are a part of Heaney's cultural 'langue'. The sequence is concerned with comprehension rather than opposition even if comprehension ultimately fails.

'The Ministry of Fear' (*N*, pp. 63-65) is about Heaney's growth as a poet. Addressed to Seamus Deane, it begins with a reference to Kavanagh,[15] and goes on to school life, education and the learning of a variety of voices, but returns to the 'South Derry rhyme' (*N*, p. 64), which locates his voice. The poem matches Heaney's lived experience against an array of 'foreign discourses'. The language in which he registers experience is the language of a poetic tradition which he is constructing. Gazing into 'new worlds' from his school, he echoes Shakespeare;[16] throwing biscuits away becomes a Wordsworthian 'act of stealth';[17] his first attempts at writing poetry develop, in Kavanagh's terms, into a life (*N*, p. 63). His experiences in school – 'inferiority complexes ...' – and corporal punishment, are both Shakespearean[18] and Joycean[19] (*N*, p. 64). Certain events seemingly cannot be voiced in this way – the growth of sexuality and the encounter with the R.U.C. (*N*, p. 64)[20] – which is consonant with the inability of the English poetic traditions perceived by Heaney to comprehend particular types of experience. He has spoken of the 'insulated and balanced statement ... that corsetted and decorous truthfulness' towards which 'recent English language' poetry has tended.[21] Although certain issues cannot, apparently, be forced into this tradition, Heaney relies on it to represent the facts of his own life. The name he gives the framework in which he grows, 'the ministry of fear', evokes both Coleridge's 'secret ministry' and Wordsworth's 'ministry/more palpable'[22] in such a way as to suggest the importance of this poetic tradition in Heaney's self-representation.

Heaney, as schoolboy, is 'shying as usual' (*N*, p. 64) – still indulging the reticence of his community. This is not a response to the overwhelming force of English culture. That culture represents a means of expressing himself while still remaining true to the traditions of his community. The poem is an effort to comprehend both the silence of the community and this poetic tradition. 'Ulster was British, but with no rights on/ The English lyric...' (*N*, p. 65) is therefore a statement of the situation which Heaney is trying to redress in his very articulation of it.

The poem's 'foreign discourses' can be divided into English and Irish with the Irish voices being apparently more intimate. The latter are just as removed from Heaney as the English ones. Deane, for example, is bewildering. His 'hieroglyphics' are not easily comprehended and his 'svelte dictions' seem almost an embarrassment (*N*, p. 65). Deane's strangeness is balanced by Kavanagh's reminder of the importance of the local, which Heaney both endorses and alters. Heaney's balancing of these two is a mark of his confidence. English poetry, Irish poetry, Catholic schooling, sexuality, and the fear of living in a hostile state are the elements which constitute Heaney's identity in this poem. His confidence rests not in a certainty about how they fit together but in his juxtaposition of them as his identity.

I threw them over the fence one night
In September 1951
When the lights of houses in the Lecky Road
Were amber in the fog. It was an act
of stealth.
Then Belfast, and then Berkeley.
Here's two on's are sophisticated,

(*N*, p. 63)

The movement from an exact time, place and climate, to Belfast and then Berkeley
– the outermost point of travel – provokes an allusion to Lear which implies both
a regret at this sophistication – meaning disguise – and the sense that the wish to cast
off one's 'habitual attire' is a sign of madness.[23] This is all the true voice of the poet,
because it is the voice he has composed from the available components. When Blake
Morrison reads 'The Ministry of Fear' as a sign of Heaney's aspiration to participate
in the English poetic tradition,[24] he imposes his own provincial attitude and does not
admit the complexity of Heaney's relationship, which encompasses both Kavanagh's distinction between the 'craven provincial' and the 'genuine parochial', and
the duality of the self, to that tradition:

> One half of one's sensibility is in a cast of mind that comes from belonging to a
> place, an ancestry, a history, a culture, whatever one wants to call it. But
> consciousness and quarrels with the self are the result of what Lawrence called
> 'the voices of my education'.[25]

Heaney's attitude is not one of being Irish and wanting to be British; nor is it one
of being tainted by Britishness and wanting to be pristinely Irish. Rather, he feels
himself pulled in two ways. His identity and his voice are not unitary because their
determinants are not unitary. This struggle for definition is specifically located in
a preoccupied language.

The language issue is a common feature of any history of colonial dispossession
and the reassertion of national rights:

> For any speaker of it, a given language is at once either more or less his own or
> more or less someone else's, and either more or less cosmopolitan or more or less
> parochial – a borrowing or a heritage, a passport or a citadel.[26]

What makes Heaney's case and that of Irish writers in general, so problematical is
that there is only one language which can practically fulfil all the contradictory roles
of a language-struggle, English. Although English is not itself unitary, the writer
cannot take what he wants from it and leave the rest. The poet's search for a voice
in which to express his own identity, his own 'parole', is made the more complex
by the fact that all the available 'langues' are relativized within the one system. Nor
is the voice wholly determined. It is also determining. The 'literary heritage' of 'The
Ministry of Fear' does not exist as an absolute; it is a heritage which Heaney himself
constructs and it is biddable to his voice. Heaney is aware of this two-way process.
His analysis of poetry as both taking and making, 'a dig for finds that end up being
plants'[27], is a description of how we construct traditions from available materials.
Poetry is both a determined activity and an act of construction. 'The Ministry of
Fear' establishes the complex of factors from which Heaney's voice arises and

which that voice alters. It is the poet's attention to voice, in a world of reticence, which sets him apart from his community and which bestows responsibilities upon him. 'The Ministry of Fear' is located outside common experience because it is attentive to specifically literary concerns, but it has reminders of the world of direct experience. The next two poems turn to experienced rather than linguistic elements of the ministry of fear.

'A Constable Calls' and 'Orange Drums, Tyrone 1966' are both poems of alienation. Throughout the former there is an air of menace and a sense of guilt which is disproportionate to the knowledge of the actual wrong that has been committed. The visit is obviously routine and so too is the fear which nonetheless attaches to it. If 'A Constable Calls' is regarded as a measured response to the R.U.C., rooted in experience, then 'Orange Drums, Tyrone 1966' is most often regarded as being far from measured.

Morrison has called 'Orange Drums ...' (*N*, p. 68) 'hostile caricature', and has noted that Heaney did not include it in his *Selected Poems*, although Morrison's judgement and Heaney's decision are not necessarily related. Morrison has also pointed out the contrast between 'exact' in 'Punishment' (*N*, p. 37-38) and 'grossly' in 'Orange Drums ...'[28]. The contrast is not simply, as he implies, sectarian. 'Exact' is part of an honest effort to account for the way in which a sense of belonging includes collusion in certain communal emotions; it does not imply approval of those emotions but it is an admission of the power of the communal over the individual for which Morrison's liberal conscience does not allow. 'Grossly', primarily a description of a drum, becomes, because of what the drum symbolizes, part of the poet's confrontation of disquieting features within his experience. Both 'grossly' and 'exact' are alike in denoting disquiet.

'Orange Drums ...' is a carefully specific instance of the ministry of fear: Orange drums in 1966 had a sharper edge than they had had in previous years. In 1966 they were a response to the 50th anniversary celebrations in Southern Ireland of Easter 1916, as well as being an expression of Orange triumphalism. As F.S.L. Lyons has said:

> ... The 1916 anniversary convinced staunch Ulster Unionists, if they needed any convincing, that the leopard had not changed his spots and that inside every nationalist there was a ravening republican waiting to get out.[29]

1966 might with some justice be seen as the pivotal year in the development of the present political situation in Northern Ireland. On the one hand Terence O'Neill's 'liberal unionism' seemed to offer hopeful signs, but Ian Paisley had already achieved some prominence. The possibilities of a North-South 'rapprochement' seemed strong, but Catholics were being shot and their businesses burned. The poem is concerned with this balance, no matter how tentatively and unsuccessfully. The fear and hostility in the poem are obvious, but there are three balancing factors which have to be ignored if the poem is to read as a simple expression of bigotry. Firstly, the poem is about a part of Heaney's own experience; it is, like everything else in this sequence, a lesson learnt in his 'singing school'. The voice describing these events is made, in part, by them and cannot deny them. Placing the poem in Heaney's work as a whole confirms that what it describes cannot be merely denied. It is one of his 'craftsman' poems in which there is an explicit or implicit comparison between a craft and poetry making. It would therefore be doubly out of character for Heaney to reject completely the drummer. Finally, the line, 'He is raised up by what he buckles under' (*N*, p. 68), carries the sense of how any craftsman, including Heaney, working within rules and conventions, is better for such discipline. There is a surprising allusion within the line. The only other appearance of a form of the word 'buckle' occurs in 'Fosterage' where G.M. Hopkins is 'his buckled self' (*N*, p. 71), a reference to 'The Windhover' and its central pun on the word 'buckle':

Brute beauty and valour and act, oh, air, pride, plume here
Buckle! AND the fire that breaks from thee then, a billion
Times told lovelier, more dangerous, O my chevalier![30]

Here again rule and convention are seen as both a constriction and a spur to better craftsmanship. The line quoted from 'Orange Drums ...' paraphrases these lines from 'The Windhover' and while the allusion is tentative, it remains central to an understanding of the tensions and difficulties of this poem, as well as to the project of the sequence as a whole.

The sequence has so far moved from the confident intertextuality of 'The Ministry of Fear' to the naked, unallusive voice of 'A Constable Calls' and the awkward, hesitant allusion of 'Orange Drums ...' in such a way that it seems as if the voice which Heaney is constructing is unable to represent all aspects of the self. The 'voices of his education' have little to offer when he wishes to bring certain parts of his lived experience into his writing; the same gap appeared in 'The Ministry of Fear' when Heaney dealt with intimate or Northern Irish experiences. This monologism, as opposed to the intertextual dialogue, suggests that the project of 'The Ministry of Fear' might fail. Alternatively, the second and third poems of the sequence can be seen as precisely those aspects of the lived experience which must be accommodated by 'the voices of education', if those voices are to retain their value, and if Heaney's own voice is not to be irremediably split. In this light, the confidence of 'The Ministry of Fear' becomes an overly easy cultural ecumenism which fails to take account of the project's inherent difficulties and tensions.

'Summer 1969' addresses itself to this issue. In a kind of exile, sweating through the 'life of Joyce' (*N*, p. 69), Heaney is guiltily preoccupied with events in Belfast. The question at the heart of the poem is 'How should the poet respond?'. In what way should he try to 'touch the people', and how should he try to represent these events? Lorca is suggested as a possible model but it is Goya who dominates this poem. If the 'life of Joyce' and the superficial indifference of the first stanza suggest and then discount exile as a possible response, the second stanza acts as a pivot and the references to Goya indicate two possible responses.

Those responses are mediated by an echo of Yeats' 'Municipal Gallery Revisited'.[31] In each case, the poet looks at paintings as a way of representing his circumstances. Heaney, in partial exile, cannot share Yeats' tranquility. The first painting to which he refers, Goya's 'Shootings of the Third of May' (*N*, p. 69), offers engagement as a response. In both the painting and Heaney's description of it, sympathy is with the rebel rather than the military firing squad. This is an attitude Heaney had taken previously,[32] but its dangers become apparent as he turns his attention to Goya's 'Black Paintings': 'Saturn devouring his son' – 'Saturn/ Jewelled in the blood of his own children'; 'Quarrel by cudgelling' – '... that holmgang/ Where two berserks club each other to death/ For honour's sake, greaved in a bog, and sinking.' (*N*, p. 70) which can only be 'The Colossus (Panic)', although it is not a 'Black painting' nor is it in the same room as them.[33] The order in which Heaney consciously places these paintings offers a gruesome commentary by analogy on Ireland. The old sow eating her farrow is evident in 'Saturn devouring his son'; a mass evacuation flees before the figure of chaos and we are left with 'two berserks' locked in a holmgang, the almost obsolete word connoting the 'anachronistic passions'[34] at large in the North. The poem enables us to construct this analogy between Goya's paintings and Northern Ireland, but it is only by placing the poem back in the sequence that we can evaluate it. The preceding poems in the sequence are almost entirely enmeshed in local actualities. 'Summer 1969' suffers the opposite fate. Here the cosmopolitan dominates and Ireland is represented only by analogy. The poem's importance in the sequence lies in Goya as a model of artistic response:

> He painted with his fists and elbows, flourished
> The stained cape of his heart as history charged.
>   (*N*, p. 70)

The histrionic quality does not match Heaney's reticence and thoughtfulness in other poems in the sequence, but while this openness and vulnerability amounts to engagement it also leads to the madness and despair of the 'Black Paintings'. The analogies that we are enabled to construct are subject to O'Brien's strictures about determinism; the imposition of paradigms which are not responsive to local contingencies is not worthwhile, leading only to the cliched response of 'Whatever you say say nothing'.

This critique of 'Summer 1969' is substantiated by the opening words of the following poem, 'Fosterage':

> 'Description is revelation!' Royal
> Avenue, Belfast, 1962,
> A Saturday afternoon ...
>   (*N*, p. 71)

The opening words, spoken by the poem's dedicatee, Michael McLaverty, are immediately responded to by the poem's exact location in time and space, and more importantly by the fact that the poet is once again on home ground. McLaverty, in Heaney's description of him, possesses 'fidelity to the intimate' while being sensible of 'the great tradition that he works in'[35] and the virtues of patience and a sense of the value of words. He is an exemplary presence: the writer as a congruence of the forces at work in Northern Ireland. What is notable about the poem is that it not only moves the poet back to his own place but also back in time, against the flow of the sequence so far. 1962 is a time of origins: 'me newly cubbed in language' (*N*, p. 71), and the preceding poems are therefore partially revoked. The 'ministry of fear' is not denied, but the focus has shifted to the idea of a second ministry, and a new beginning. Other voices are present in the poem; McLaverty's voice, obviously, but it in turn is a conflation of Hopkins, Mansfield, and Chekhov.[36] Affection for McLaverty and his role as foster-father draws Heaney back into Irish history.

There are undercurrents in the poem, however, which belie this, perhaps sentimental, reading. The 'words ... like obols' (*N*, p. 71) may be highly valued but the simile suggests a death of the self. Nor is McLaverty's teaching straightforward. The advice, 'Go your own way./ Do your own work.', is ironical, especially when followed by references to models more suited to the short-story writer than to the poet. In this way the poem distances the voices within it and suggests that the poet's own voice, while acknowledging its components, must speak for itself. The heart of the poem is the restraint proposed by McLaverty which is opposed to the violence of Goya. This restraint can be just as vulnerable and open as Goya's overstatement.

'Exposure' (*N*, p. 72-73) is the consequence of the previous five poems of the sequence. It presents us with the poet at the moment of writing. As with 'Fosterage' it is located in a specific time and place; 'It is December in Wicklow' (*N*, p. 72). The title bespeaks the poet's sense of vulnerability away from the protection of fosterage and the question the poem poses is 'who is responsible for this exposure?'; is it the poet himself or is it a failure of the cultural traditions evident in the rest of the sequence. Those traditions are here present only as hints and traces: Yeats may be present in the diction; Joyce, Montague and Kinsella in the fire imagery.[37] Neil Corcoran identifies Osip Mandelstam as the primary presence in the poem with a secondary reference to Ovid in exile.[38] The English poetic tradition is replaced by others just as the country replaces the city, the South ironically replaces the eponymous North, and the historical replaces the contemporary:

> I am neither internee nor informer;
> An inner emigré, grown long-haired
> And thoughtful; a wood-kerne
> Escaped from the massacre,
>
> (N, p. 73)

The poet, refusing the opposed contemporary terms 'internee' and 'informer', has adopted the strategy of the 'wood-kerne', whose engagements are followed by strategic withdrawals. The choice of term is important, because this reference back to the Elizabethan period is to an originary moment in the relation of Ireland and England. As Heaney withdraws to the South and engages in dialogue with Irish, Russian and Roman voices,[39] he represents himself in a term derived from Old Irish. The exposure of the poem is, in part, a stripping away of English voices. The poem offers no understanding; its tone is one of regret and puzzlement. By refusing both contemporary terms within which the self might be comprehended, there is a sense of lost opportunity and of a lost self. The suggestion of the death of the self in 'Fosterage' is continued by this poem's winter imagery and its movement from the contemporary to the historical, a time before the self. This leads us to a contradiction in the poem's title; what is being exposed if not the self?

The answer is best provided by the autobiographical impulse underlying the sequence. If the other poems are taken to be 'spots of time' – those epiphanic moments which bring the self into definition – then the 'missed comet' is the failure to comprehend the variety of selves in the other poems. The exposure is then not of the self but of the failure of self-comprehension, indicated by the absence of English voices. This is not to say that there has been a complete failure to carry out the sequence's project. Its context is not only the poems which precede it in *North* but also those which follow it in *Field Work*.[40] The autobiographical impulse has not yet been worked out. Comprehension has not yet been achieved because the representation of the self eventually lacks one of its prime constituents. The project of 'Singing School' is thus continued in *Field Work* and beyond until it can achieve, not that Irish shibboleth of independence but rather a sense of dialectical equality in *Station Island*, with a glance back to the missed comet of 'Exposure':

> ... 'Who cares,'
> he jeered, 'any more? The English language
> belongs to us.
> You are raking at dead fires,

    a waste of time for somebody your age.
    That subject people stuff is a cod's game.[41]

After this, Heaney, previously a digger and delver 'par excellence', becomes a traveller, and in *The Haw Lantern*[42] he makes English both a citadel and a passport to cross frontiers, especially the frontier of writing, and in so doing acquires the right to represent as well as being represented.

CHAPTER 9

'The mirror up to nature': the theatre building as a socio-political cypher*

by

Hugh Maguire

In the post-Nikolaus Pevsner school of architectural history[1] too much emphasis has been laid on the sources of and influences on particular architects, while more informative areas of study which might use the building as a source of comment on political, religious and social developments at any given point have been avoided. Architecture, as the most readily accessible of art forms can provide eloquent comment on a society and the state of its culture. A Baroque edifice, such as the Palazzo Barberini, Rome (1628), with its spatial and sculptural complexity, can express in a tangible way the complexities of associated art forms from the same period in music, painting and literature. Such interrelationship of architecture and other cultural forms is found in all periods. In early eighteenth-century England for example, fondness for nature was expressed in the art of Thomas Gainsborough (1727-88), the poetry of Alexander Pope (1688-1744), and the architecture of the 3rd Earl of Burlington (1694-1753). This inter-relationship of culture and architectural form also surrounds us today with the minimalist lines of James Stirling (b. 1927) finding parallels in other cultural trends such as the designs of the Milan-based Bolidista Movement and the music of Philip Glass.

Throughout the centuries the clearest relationship between architecture and pre-vailing cultural ethos has been found in the design of Christian churches. The diversity of protestant denominations in a city such as Belfast has been reflected in its architecture; in the Roman Catholic Church the liturgical changes of the second Vatican Council provide a dramatic example of the inter-relationship of building and religious ethos. In the period following the Council of Trent (1563) church art and architecture emphasised the involvement of the spectator. A painting such as Giovanni Lanfranco's (1582-1647) *Last Supper* (Dublin, National Gallery of Ireland No. 67) emphasised the welcoming arms of the catholic church through the sacrifice of the Mass. This embracing concept was also found in architecture, most notably at Gianlorenzo Bernini's (1598-1680) Piazza San Pietro, Rome (begun 1656).[2] It was in this period too that the close relationship between architecture and stage scenery came to the fore.[3] Architecture in the Baroque period became a theatrical backdrop, in front of which the rituals of the church and the rituals of everyday life in cities such as Rome or Turin were performed.

* Unfortunately, it has not been possible to reproduce the visual material used to illustrate the paper delivered at the conference.

It is from this period of the Italian Baroque, which also witnessed the development of opera, that modern theatre architecture developed, particularly through the work of the Bibiena family from Bologna. Their work on theatre architecture reflected trends in contemporary society. It would therefore seem that, as with church architecture, theatre architecture can provide an eloquent comment on the prevailing cultural ethos. The complexity of such a relationship cannot be discussed in this brief paper. A glance at Irish theatre architecture may however serve to introduce the relationship between architecture, the drama performed therein and the society forming the audience. If it is accepted that drama ought to reflect society, the architecture of the theatre should itself reflect aspects of the drama and therefore of the society forming the audience to the drama. This results in a situation where theatre architecture can provide comment on, or reflection of the state of drama and its importance in society. Perhaps the clearest example of this is provided by the great antique theatres and arenae of Greece and Rome which bear witness to the importance of theatre and drama in their respective societies.

The period in art history loosely referred to as the Baroque was perhaps the period when architecture attained its most fluid, complex and intellectually intense form. Theatre architecture developed in this period and reflected the concepts of the prevailing artistic ethos. The role of a spectator within a building, and the visual effect of that building, was carefully considered. Theatres, especially Opera Houses, responded to the architectural demands of the time and their horseshoe shape created a space where performers were embraced by the spectators and where spectators, as at the Residenztheater, Munich (1751-43),[4] could literally embrace and admire each other. The tiered seating of the typical opera house reflects the hierarchy of continental society in the seventeenth and eighteenth centuries. In addition, within such theatres considerable architectural attention was given to the accommodation of a monarch or presiding noble personage. The absence of such royal boxes in British theatres reflects prevailing British attitudes to the monarchy, with the monarch on state occasions sitting, not apart from the masses, but in the midst of the wealthy and affluent, the state's power base. This is in contrast to the arrangement in the most provincial of continental theatres such as at the Teatro del Giglio at Lucca erected by Lazzarini in 1819. In general in Great Britain the monarch sits in a stage box, as at Frank Matcham's London Coliseum (1904). In writing of the opening of Her Majesty's Theatre, the Haymarket, London (1897), George Bernard Shaw saw this as an example of the British draining the last commercial drop from their monarchs.[5] This architectural detail provides one example of the different attitude to theatre architecture in Britain. The type of theatre developed by the Bibiena, already referred to, characterized opera houses and large theatres on the continent until after the second world war. The type of theatre erected in these islands followed quite different trends.

What is strikingly different about theatre architecture in Ireland is the absence of continental influence until early this century, and its unity with the prevailing British form. This does not reflect on any cultural assimilation between the two islands, but on the theatre's close relation with England, and its exclusion, not only by language but by tradition and ethos, from the culture of the mass of the people; a situation which prevailed until well into the nineteenth century. Theatre in Ireland until the end of the last century was essentially an English tradition, accommodating the tastes of a colonial population and a vice-regal court. This was not always the case in the broader compass of what constitutes drama and theatre. Throughout the Middle Ages, drama was the prerogative of the church and was used to encourage religious fervour. It is of interest that the medieval mystery plays performed in a city such as Kilkenny followed continental staging techniques, while those in Dublin, by contrast, were closely linked to English tradition. As the extent of English control in Ireland increased, such continental influences on the arts were lessened. The resulting closeness of the English and Irish stage became apparent not only behind the footlights but could also be discerned in the actual style of theatre building in both countries. If all other evidence including texts, staging instructions, and written records disappeared, the similarity of building types would by itself suggest the close relationship of the stages in both countries. It would be possible to see the Dublin stage as an appendage of the London stage; for some it still is.

Dublin audiences thoughout the eighteenth century were keenly aware of the fashions of the London stage. Actors such as Peg Woffington (1718-60)[6] and James Quin (1693-1766) were successful in London, Dublin and the other theatrical centre of the age, the Theatre Royal, Bath (1750). Likewise, English actors were successful in Dublin and Sarah Siddons (1755-1831) visited the city to not unqualified acclaim in 1783. The popularity of English actors was also reflected in a number of artistic creations. The print room at Castletown House in county Kildare incorporated, in the manner of present day Michael Jackson posters, prints of the actor David Garrick (1717-79). One represented 'David Garrick between the Muses of Tragedy and Comedy', with the other portraying him in a scene from Thomas Otway's 'Venice preserved' (1682.)[7]

In addition, Lady Louisa Connolly erected a doric temple in the grounds of Castletown in honour of Sarah Siddons. Thomas Sheridan (1721-88),[8] for long manager of the Smock Alley Theatre, Dublin, was the father of Richard Brinsley Sheridan (1751-1816), who was born in Dublin but spent most of his life in London. The younger Sheridan wrote 'The Rivals' for Covent Garden in 1775, thereby introducing yet another boorish bog trotter of Paddy stupidity in the character of Lucius O'Trigger, a recurring type on the West End stage even today, as in the 1984 revival of Joe Orton's 'Loot' at the Lyric Theatre, Shaftesbury Avenue.[9]

The earliest theatre buildings in Ireland were similar to those of London, the theatre in Smock Alley being the first to have any definitive architectural form. The Aungier Street Theatre, Dublin, was designed by Sir Edward Lovett Pearce (1699-1733), himself a cousin of Sir John Vanbrugh (1664-1726). Vanbrugh, an accomplished dramatist and architect, built the King's Theatre in the Haymarket, London, in 1714. Although we have no visual evidence, it seems both theatres were somewhat similar in appearance. Writing of Vanbrugh's theatre, Colly Cibber (1671-1757) noted how practicalities were sacrificed to architectural magnificence. He remarked of the developers that: 'they had yet discover'd that almost every proper Quality, and convenience of a good Theatre had been sacrificed, or neglected to show the Spectator a vast triumphal Piece of Architecture!'[10] Chetwood's description of Pearce's Aungier Street suggests similar grandeur:

> I think the Architect had more View to the Magnificent, than Theatrical: The Audience Part is ornamented with rich Embellishment, that gives it a separate Countenance, but no Disparagement to the Architect in other Buildings, this might have been more convenient with less Cost. But I believe the Contriver had an Eye more to Ridottos, than the Drama, if so indeed his intentions were answered for in that Shape, it may vie with that in the Haymarket in London.[11]

This similarity was reflected on the stage in productions like John Gay's 'Beggar's Opera' (1728), successful in both Dublin and London. The staging was similar and the stage subject to invasion, as was the custom, by up-market members of the audience – the city beaux, who would join in the production whenever they felt like doing so.[12] Theatre in the more important Irish cities such as Derry, Cork and Limerick followed closely the fashions of Dublin.[13] The architectural components of these buildings have not been recorded visually. But, it would seem from written evidence, they generally followed, if in diluted form, the established Dublin and London norms. The social nature of theatre-going in the eighteenth century can be evidenced, not only from surviving views and engravings, but from surviving theatres such as the Georgian Theatre at Richmond, with its intimate disposition of boxes around the auditorium and communal pit.

The dramatic and architectural similarity between London and Dublin stages continued into the nineteenth century. John L. Toole (1830-1906) began his career in Dublin in 1851. Henry Irving (1838-1905) worked at the Queen's Theatre and received from Trinity College, Dublin, the first honorary degree ever awarded to an actor (1892). The Carl Rosa Opera Company was founded jointly in London and Dublin in 1881. In the field of architecture Samuel Beazley (1786-1851) designed the Theatre Royal, Dublin, in 1821. He was subsequently to remodel the Theatre Royal, Drury Lane, London, in 1822 and build the Lyceum Theatre, London, in 1834. Although Beazley's proposed exterior[14] would suggest a similarity with continental theatres such as the Theatre Royal de l'Odeon, Paris (1818) or the Teatro Nuovo, Verona, the actual failure to execute the façade draws the theatre back into a British sphere of influence. The exterior, described by Samuel Lewis in his Topographical Dictionary of Ireland[15], was in keeping with the shoddy appearance of many British theatre exteriors. The mean appearance of the theatre reflected an attitude to the theatre which prevailed in the first half of the nineteenth century, resulting from a number of factors, not least being the rise of the bourgeoisie and their attitude to drama. The interior was however, completed according to Beazley's plan. The decorative scheme incorporated the symbols of burgeoning nationalism associated with the Romantic movement, the nationalism of Robert Burns in Scotland and Thomas Moore in Ireland. Greek key decoration, typical of Neo-Classical architecture was interlaced with harps and shamrocks, but this was merely the trimmings of nationalism in the same way that the 1952 coronation robes for Queen Elizabeth II incorporated shamrock, thistles and roses.

Theatre-going ceased to be a fashionable pastime in the early nineteenth century, but the theatre's fortunes did improve. The revival stemmed from London, particularly with the work of Squire Bancroft (1841-1926) and Marie Wilton (1839-1921) at the Prince of Wales Theatre, Tottenham Court Road, between 1865 and 1880. In terms of fashion, Dublin took its cue from London while smaller cities, such as Cork, Derry and the fast growing town of Belfast, followed Dublin. Theatres in Irish cities were also closely related through personalities. The lessee of the Theatre Royal, Belfast[16], from 1867 to 1898 was Joseph Frederick Warden (1836-98). He had been the leading actor at the Queen's Theatre, Dublin, for a number of years, and lessee of the Gaiety Theatre, Dublin, for a season. He also erected the Theatre Royal, Derry (1877), and was managing director of the Grand Opera House, Belfast.[17] His Theatres Royal were based on the Gaiety Theatre, Dublin, which was in turn based on the Gaiety Theatre, on the Strand, London (1868). All of these were designed by Charles John Phipps (1835-97), the most eminent theatre architect of his day. Phipps designed for the leading United Kingdom actors and managers of the nineteenth century – people such as Henry Irving, Marie Wilton and Herbert Beerbohm Tree (1853-1917). The consistency of Phipp's approach to theatre design reflected a consistency of approach to the stage on the part of management. From his Theatre Royal, Bath (1863) to Her Majesty's Theatre London (1897), his theatres were characterized by a certain domesticity of treatment. Legitimate stage plays were also generally domestic in subject-matter and staging. Such domestic bliss, assisted by the censorship of the period, dominated the stage in the form of comedies by Thomas W. Robertson (1829-71) and Arthur Wing Pinero (1855-1934). It was also the period of the Savoy operas by William S. Gilbert (1836-1911) and Arthur Sullivan (1842-1900). The domesticity of these works was reflected in the theatre building. Foyers and bars such as those of the Gaiety Theatre, Dublin (1871), were comparable to domestic sitting rooms, and exterior details such as the ground floor arcading, inspired by John Ruskin (1819-1900), comparable to much residential architecture of the period. The taste of the Prince and Princess of Wales was essentially middle class and their 'domestic' taste was also accommodated in London theatres. This was particularly so in their own waiting rooms at theatres such as the Prince's (1884) and the Savoy (1881). The typical West-End theatre was felt by Henry James (1843-1916) to be a continuation of the patron's drawing rooms. The drawing-room attitude was also reflected in the 'cup and saucer' stage presentations and the prejudices of the audience.

The plays presented at the Gaiety Theatre, Dublin, reflected the aspirations of the audience, an audience unsure, for the most part, of its cultural identity, afloat on a sea of post-Union provincialism. The theatre had a limited, if economically successful, outlook. Theatre bills and posters advertised train and tram times for areas physically united to the city of Dublin, but ideologically and psychologically outside not only the city but the country and prevailing opinion. In 1899 the Rathmines and Pembroke Estates were defended by Edward Carson and Colonel Saunderson from having to join the corporation area of Dublin, on the grounds that efficient and loyal unionists would be swamped with corrupt and incompetent nationalists.[18] Audiences from areas such as these were appeased by the general nature of the productions at the theatre. For the most part this consisted of visiting companies from throughout the United Kingdom, such as the D'Oyly Carte Opera,[19] the Lyceum Company and Edwin Booth or Arthur Roberts' London Companies in plays such as 'Dandy Dan the Life Guards man.'[20] The strong pantomime tradition of the Gaiety, with its associated pre-Freudian sexual ambiguity, was an established part of British theatre tradition. In spite of its undoubted popularity, it can have borne little relevance to the lives of the mass of the population, which laboured under problems of agrarian discontent, mass emigration, recurring famine and, in Dublin, over-crowding and poor pay.

A winter production of 'The pickpocket' at the Gaiety, which is undated, provides in its setting a suitable example of the stage reflecting the audience's aspirations, or perhaps more correctly, frustrations, such as the recurring syndrome of 'Why were we not born in Chelsea'?

Act 1   S.1. Frederick Hope's House in Kensington
           S.2. Gardens of the Westcliffe Hotel, Southbourne on Sea.
Act 2.   A Sitting Room in the Westcliffe Hotel.
Act 3.   Entrance Hall of the Westcliffe Hotel.

Attempts by the theatre management, with many exceptions, to continue with a similar diet of pantomime, seasons of Gilbert and Sullivan, and plays by Jeffrey Archer would suggest that little has changed at the Gaiety.

Such middle-class taste was markedly different from other theatres in Dublin such as Dan Lowrey's Music Hall. The differences of ethos were reflected in the decor of the theatre. The music hall proudly displayed a cameo Thomas Moore as a poetic hero over the proscenium.[21] The Queen's Theatre, as the home of melodrama, was extremely popular with Dublin audiences. When the theatre was rebuilt for R.J. Sterling in 1909 it took cognisance, with a vengeance, of the contemporary Celtic revival and growing nationalist sentiment – a trait also evident at the Old Mechanic's Institute.[22] The vibrant 'patriotic' plasterwork decoration, executed by John Ryan in 1909, complemented the stirring melodramatic patriotism realized on stage.[23] It incorporated a riot of Celtic revival fretwork, a figure of Erin and a tara brooch. A random selection of performances up to and including the War of Independence reflected such nationalist sentiment. Plays performed include:

'When Wexford rose' P.J. Bourke, Mar 4, 1913
'Father Murphy', Ira Allen, June 3, 1913
'For Ireland's liberty' P.J. Bourke, May 11, 1914
'For Ireland's sake' May 9, 1917
'Erin Machree' Feb 5, 1917
'Sarsfield' July 3), 1917, by J. Whitbread
'Pike O'Callaghan' Sept 10, 1917
'In dark and evil days' 6 May, 1919
'The Fenians' 9 June, 1919

This architectural, decorative nationalism was not solely a product of Irish logic. Just as the founding of the Gaelic Athletic Association in 1884 and Arthur Griffith's Sinn Féin related to contemporary political movements on the continent, the nationalism of the Irish theatre architecture found parallels in the many theatres throughout Italy named in honour of Giuseppe Verdi (1813-1901), and in cities such as Budapest and Brussels. The Vlaamse Schouwburg, the Flemish speaking national theatre in Brussels, reflected its ethos in Flemish-inspired architecture. This stood in marked contrast to the French-inspired Opera House in the same city, the Théâtre de la Monnaie.

Within Ireland, the Grand Opera House, Belfast (1895), contrasted with trends elsewhere in the country. Its architecture related to London and London's tastes. The Hindu motifs dominating the auditorium reflected the presence of a jewel in the crown, and it is significant that Shakespeare rather than Moore was illustrated as a National poet on a stained-glass panel in the foyer. The theatre provided a gorgeous setting for somewhat vapid inanities. It provided an architectural escapism as valid today as at the end of the nineteenth century, and which was again reflected in stage productions such as the sell-out series of performances by Australian drag artist Barry Humphries (Dame Edna Everidge), 'Back with a vengeance' (1988). The overall ostentation related to contemporary tastes in sham-architecture, trends which were at variance with innovative developments elsewhere. Such ostentation was echoed ten years later in the building of the city hall where, as with much contemporary artchitecture, the artistic element was skin deep. Architecture presented, as with the Bedford Street Warehouse, Belfast, a mere veneer of grandeur. The erection of an elaborate street frontage, with complete failure to consider other facades, had for some time been the norm with British theatre architecture, as at the Grand Theatre, Wolverhampton (1895).

Such sham architectural schemes were in dramatic contrast to the simple architectural treatment of the Abbey Theatre, Dublin, remodelled by Joseph Holloway

(1861-1944) in 1904. Elaborate decoration was almost non-existent. What decoration was created was of the highest quality, such as a stained-glass window from the studio of Sarah H. Purser R.H.A., (1848-1943) and copper work from the Youghal Art Metal Schools. Just as Purser[24] was trying to foster a native school of Irish stained-glass art, the Abbey was trying to create a national theatre, expressive of a native culture. The simplicity of the decoration was paralleled by the naturalism of the acting and stageing. The artistic independence of the theatre, including Lady Gregory's production of Shaw's 'The showing up of Blanco Posnet' (1909) against the wishes of Dublin Castle, found a ready response in the popular imagination of the period.[25] The difference was appreciated by the Italian critic Mario Borsa, as early as 1907. Comparing the Abbey to London, and by association, the conventional theatre of the Gaiety, Dublin, and the Grand Opera House, Belfast, he wrote: 'The wayfarer whose eye is accustomed to the pretentious, flaunting shop windows of the city [London] will pause to observe with sympathetic curiosity the modest production of an art so sincere and so spontaneous'.[26] The sincerity of Borsa's 'lowly and unadorned, but genuinely poetic country playhouse'[27] was recognised by the new Free State government in 1921 when the Abbey became the first subsidised theatre in the English-speaking world. The architectural simplicity of the theatre placed the emphasis on the spoken word. The picture was more important than the frame.[28] The spirit of the new theatre encouraged a new drama-type, which survives and recurs to this day with Druid Theatre Company in Galway, Field Day in Derry and the Lyric Players in Belfast. These companies usually present a pertinent drama where text and staging take precedence. The relevance of many Abbey productions continues, despite the theatre's recent artistic vicissitudes, most notably through the work of Tom Murphy.[29] The relevance can again be witnessed in the sparse handling of Michael Scott's New Abbey Theatre (1966) where visual distractions within the auditorium are kept to a minimum and the picture on stage, both verbal and visual, dominates the evening at the theatre. In its attention to the stage as opposed to the auditorium, the Abbey drew itself away from traditions prevailing within the United Kingdom, where theatre architecture, like the actor, so often represented:

a tale told by an idiot, full of sound and fury,
Signifying nothing.

PART III
SOCIETY IN NORTHERN IRELAND

CHAPTER 10

Good leaders and 'decent' men: an Ulster contradiction
by
Maurna Crozier

This paper seeks to show how an in-depth study of a small area can usefully contribute towards an understanding of issues in the larger society of which it is part.

Observers of the political scene in Northern Ireland often wonder why, in a situation where there are two clearly opposed groups, no leaders of significant stature have emerged to guide their followers towards a solution, (either towards the peace which most claim to want, or towards the civil war which they fear). Any adequate explanation of why Northern Ireland has failed to produce strong leaders would have to include a consideration of historical and political factors, as well as an analysis of cultural imperatives: the detachment of the Anglo-Irish politicians from their constituents, the limited options of rebellion or powerless conformity for nationalists, the paucity of local organizations which might foster leadership, the position of the laity in both the Roman Catholic and protestant churches, restrictive land rights, emigration, and economic exploitation are all obviously relevant. However, in this paper the perspective is focused on cultural explanations.

Using the specifically restricted frame of the local value system of a rural area in Ulster, this paper suggests how the prevalent value system, stressing egalitarianism and local allegiance, both militates against the development of the individual self-assertion which is a necessary part of successful leadership, and provides criteria for criticising those who do achieve prominence, thus effectively limiting their potential for initiating change.

Ballintully*

Ballintully is an area of mixed-enterprise, family-worked farms, averaging 60 acres. Some units combine farming with wage work, mostly servicing other farms as tradesmen. The only regular outside labour is that of machine contractors. There are virtually no hired workers, and no identifiable labouring group. Before mechanization, neighbourly co-operation was crucial for survival, a practice still reflected in the emphasis placed on being good neighbours. Although the reduction in the need for mutual aid has significantly affected community social life, kin connections are still central. There is a high incidence of local marriage: in 1984, 83 per cent of the wives in Ballintully had moved less than ten miles, and 92 per cent less than thirty

---

* Ballintully is a collective name used for an area covered by seven townlands in the foothills of the Mourne Mountains.

miles on marrying. The ties thus engendered are crucial in a daily context for social life, and ultimately for inheritance.

The continuing interdependence of households has contributed to the emphasis placed on equalitarian[1] behaviour, an attitude common to many small-scale economically homogeneous communities, which is attributed by F.G. Bailey[2] to their kinship relationships and by Frederick Barth[3] to economic determinants which inhibit the emergence of status differences based on wealth. Both sets of factors apply in Ballintully. Equalitarianism in Ballintully is underpinned by the shared preoccupation with farming, the continuing need for kin and neighbourly co-operation, supported in this church-going community by the Christian premise that all men should be treated as equals.

The shared commitment to agriculture has many implications for equalitarian values, and works at different levels to relate people closely to one another. At a casual level, farming is a body of shared knowledge which forms the substance of local 'chat' from which no-one is excluded. Since the farms are worked by the owner-families there is no division of work on the basis of rank – everybody does everything unless age prevents it. Casual labour is invariably provided by nephews or cousins, or the sons of other farmers, who do not form an inferior labouring group, the equality between them illustrated by the fact that labourers eat with their employers. No subordination or dependency arises from the occupation of tied houses.

Landownership confers a certain status, but 70 per cent of all householders in Ballintully own some land, and are called 'farmers'. Differences in the size of holding does not alter this labelling, and although success may relate to acreage it is seen as being constantly modified by chance factors, such as health, childlessness and the individual preference and aptitude of heirs, so that inequalities relating to size of farm are not seen as definitive influences on status. The wealthier families have, since the 1960s, developed strategies to prevent great inequalities relating to land ownership from arising between siblings, through modified systems of inheritance. In Ballintully, the ideology defining the obligations to kin upholds the practice of primogeniture, the right of the eldest son to 'the home place' but also recognises obligations to subsequent sons. Since the 1940s men have married at a younger age than their predeccessors, and are not ready to relinquish control of their property when their eldest sons become old enough to take over the responsibility. By pooling the labour of father and eldest son, and including the other sons as they grow up, families in Ballintully have developed a modified system of inheritance, where 'one farm buys the next', so that the initial inheritance, with united effort, is expanded in time to maintain all the sons on independent units.

Ironically, while many of the wealthiest families of the nineteenth century have declined, the poorer families have become the most prosperous. With little land for subdivision by inheritance and no educational ambitions, they continued to have large families, with whose labour they first farmed rented land, which they were eventually wealthy enough to buy. The practice of preferential sales of farms to kinsmen also contributes to the maintenance of an equality of living standards within the kin group. Few farms come onto the open market, which acts as a further restraint on large acquisitions by outsiders which effectively inhibits the incursion of agribusinesses, and maintains a degree of equality in the size of local holdings. Between 1926 and 1981 the population of Ballintully dropped by 42 per cent. The trend was for the least and the most prosperous households to leave, the landless seeking urban employment as mechanization rendered them redundant, and the wealthier families educating their children to work elsewhere. The reduction from the economic boundaries of the community has contributed to the homogeneity and the corresponding notions of equality.

Both the notions of kinship which presuppose an equality and the strategies developed for maintaining it, make people antagonistic to any behaviour which suggests a social hierarchy. The high incidence of local marriage consolidates neighbourhood practices, since wives reinforce customary local practices, rather than introducing those innovations by which social distinctions are so often made. The working clothes of the large farmer and the smallholder, for example, are the same, and table manners, so often seen as an indicator of class difference, do not differ substantially between the wealthier and the poorer households. No one in Ballintully is made to feel inadequate in the daily encounters of the neighbourhood. The confidence which this engenders leads to resentment when locals find themselves in a more public position and feel untypically inferior, a fact which should not be underestimated when considering why such a social environment is a poor seedbed for leadership.

Equalitarianism, then, is a key component of local culture. An occupational hierarchy is largely irrelevant, and status differentials are mitigated both by the equality implicit in kin relationships and the attempts to achieve the parity of holdings and hence equality of opportunity between close kin. It is important, therefore, to consider how this equalitarianism is expressed and what attitudes maintain it in the face of the inevitable conflicts of interest which characterize all small communities.

Local attitudes about equalitarianism are expressed in daily life in the 'modest' behaviour of 'decent' men. In Ballintully a 'real, quiet decent man' is one who is self-deprecating when praised, and who never behaves in the superior or presumptious manner, which is considered particularly reprehensible when people have been 'born in the same townland' or 'reared alongside' as Rosemary Harris also notes.[5] A woman who spent all her adult life caring for an ailing niece, maintained that she was 'doing no more than she should': a man who laboured for days to harvest a widow's corn crop did it because he 'wouldn't want to see her stuck'. Since the modest man should not show any inclination to promote himself, there is criticism of the local of whom it is said: 'the paper's never out but there's a picture of him in it'. While Ballintully people use this influential man to further their interests, he is still considered to have 'no call to think that he's any better than the rest of us'.

Men and women who were born in Ballintully, but who leave and prosper in other places, are praised if their manner is 'just the same as ever it was', and if they show no signs of thinking that they have gained status through their achievements. Success for the individual is attributed to the 'good start' provided by the family, or the 'deal of help' from teachers. In a small community it is easy for people to recall the past poverty or dishonesty of those who assume precedence based on their achievements. The parents of a local solicitor are remembered for 'hardly being able to give a dinner' to the neighbours who used to help with their harvest, and some of his contemporaries still refer to an elderly local doctor by his unflattering school nickname, the use of which has been considered by Richard Breen[6] to be a 'continual moral sanction', aimed, in this case, at deflating any sense of distinction arising from professional eminence.

Dislike of an overt hierarchy is also evident in the patterns of address used in Ballintully, where everyone, with the exception of unrelated married women, is addressed by Christian name, and even married women are referred to by their first name in conversation. Only doctors or teachers are given titles, the distinction being made more because they are outsiders than in recognition of their professional status. Reluctance to mark social distinction by the use of titles is illustrated when men are working for someone with whom they are not on familiar terms. The employer is then referred to as 'himself', as in the phrase: 'ask himself if he wants this hedge cut back'. The justification for the use of Christian names, even between those whose material position is substantially different, was suggested to me by a former millworker, who always called the mill owner by his 'given' name, for he 'knew him since he was a lad when there was no difference between him and me'.

The basic assumption is that all those born in neighbouring townlands should act as if they were equal. One man, now in his sixties, still bears a grudge for a slight against his mother who, calling at a neighbour's house when there was a death in the family, was turned away and told that the house was private. This was an unprecedented departure from the local practice of welcoming all callers to a wake when, as undifferentiated mourners, they have both the obligation and the privilege of paying their respects to the dead. My informant, the insult still rankling after fifty years, said: 'You'd never expect to go and be told the house was private, and them born and reared in the same townland'. For almost a century the community has been one of small landowners who equally faced a good year or a bad one, and between whom there was little difference in material wealth. Specialization has now led to variable levels of prosperity, but those who have made 'a killing' (a substantial profit), and have used it in a 'showy' manner, are criticised for their unnecessarily large cars, their over-dressed appearance or the amount of money they spend on leisure. In general, those who behave as if wealth differences implied social distinction are resented. A young man who was educated privately, unlike any of his contemporaries, was later observed to be 'pulling muck (manure) behind him just like the rest of us'.

Cross-cutting ties of obligation deriving from kinship ensures a consistently modest style of interaction, which serves to ease exchanges during which neighbours may be alternately benefactors and recipients. Any show of upper-handedness, for example, when paying a neighbour for work done, is inappropriate when the next day the neighbour may offer unsolicited help. The 'bare bones'[7] of a cash transaction are covered up by masking comments, such as 'the children won't be long using that up around Christmas', often implying, as here, that the money is merely pin money, rather than the stuff of real economics. Even when money is not an issue, the position of being a recipient is difficult in Ballintully, and people dislike feeling indebted. A farmer, parting from a neighbour who had shared a back-breaking day of potato picking, merely said to him, without any word of thanks: 'well that's the job done for another wee while'. The helper may, typically, have agreed to help sometime, but would have expressed the equality of relationship between himself and the owner of the field, by not specifying exactly when he would be free, or even by leaving before the job was quite done – an infuriating trait to outsiders, but a gesture of independence that in Ballintully expresses the equalitarian ethos subscribed to by all.

The reticence of receiving is also evident in the exchange of presents, which are invariably given via a member of the family who is not the intended recipient. Similarly, gifts are rarely opened in the presence of the donor, and thanks are muted, often appended with a remark such as 'you shouldn't have bothered'. Hostesses, equally, will claim that the work involved in hospitality was 'no trouble', and honouring gestures for visitors are minimal, so that those who do the menial tasks involved in preparing and serving food are, by deflating their performance, effectively denying any drop in status. In fact, there is very little formal hospitality in Ballintully, and, customarily, it only involves kin: since being hospitable is in no way status-enhancing it does not justify the investment of much time and effort, except in the interests of maintaining family loyalty. In addition, a lavish spread might be interpreted as ostentatious, and the hosts seen as trying to indicate some kind of superiority – grossly at odds with the prevailing ethos of equality.

The criticism of self-aggrandisement illustrates the importance of modest behaviour as an interactional style, but there are also other ways by which a 'decent' man is assessed. People in Ballintully judge their neighbours by whether they work hard; whether they support and maintain good relations with their kin; whether they are friendly, helpful and honest as neighbours, and whether they are loyal to their church. Success, or failure, in these spheres is crucial to an individual's reputation in the local area.

People in Ballintully, like those described by Elliott Leyton[8] and Howard Newby[9] have a firm belief in the inherent value of hard work. Families are praised if they are 'a great bunch of workers' and shortcomings in areas relevant to reputation – for example in being sociable – can be mitigated if the person concerned is said to be 'always about his work'. Daytime callers at the farmhouses apologize for their intrusion with comments about 'keeping you from your work'. Both the very old and the young are particularly praised if they work hard. The epitaph on one old lady was that 'she wrought hard till the day she died', and a young boy, returning late from school one day was told brusquely by his mother to 'get in, get off you, get on you and get out!', that is, get out of your school clothes, into your working gear and get outside to do some real work.

Perhaps because the product of hard work and idleness is so visible – well-tended stock and pasture or broken fences and rotting crops – it provides scope for praise or castigation. Failure to farm well is considered to be a indicator of other inadequacies: a local man who put himself up as a political candidate was disqualified by Ballintully people on the grounds that he had ploughed a field two years previously and had failed to plant a crop in the intervening time. In the past, labour was the only resource of the landless and only through incessant hard work could they become farmers in their own right. The work ethic that originated in need is still seen as relevant to the realization of new goals – more stock, better machinery and more land. For those who inherit land, hard work is essential to satisfy the demands of contemporary farming people. The younger marriage age creates new family units to be housed, for few brides will now tolerate living with in-laws, nor do the older, but not yet old, couple wish to be relegated to the traditional west room, so hard work and prosperity is seen as the best way of solving these problems.

The emphasis on family identification, arising from the centrality of kin ties, also tends to reduce individualism in a variety of ways. Personal characteristics, for example, are invariably linked to family traits, traced through previous generations. In social life, families operate as units, going to church and social events in a two or three generational family group. Invitations are extended from one whole household to another, and children are never excluded, nor do they ever form an identifiable group in the district outside their families. The importance of family solidarity is also illustrated in more ritualized ways. When disputes arise, most frequently over inheritance, the practice of avoidance ensures that 'bad feeling' does not become 'hard words they might regret'. The 'decent' man is one who always tries to get along with others, especially kin, so family members make strenuous attempts to heal rifts. When disputants are obliged to meet, perhaps as wedding guests, ritual, such as statutory greetings and formal seating plans, helps to maintain a semblance of decency for public consumption. The solidarity of the extended kin is most conspicuous at wakes and funerals, as Leyton[10] also observed. An example of inter-family avoidance in Ballintully was terminated when, at the death of his son, a man 'sent word for cousin John to come to the wake', an invitation not necessary in normal circumstances, but used here when the grief that united the family was considered greater than the argument which divided the individuals. Ultimately and supremely, each individual is a member of the kin group, and the 'decent' man subsumes his personal feelings for the good of the family.

Beyond the 'decent' individual's identification with and responsibility to his kin are his relationships with his neigbours. The notion that 'it's right to be neighbourly' is thought to be both typical of country people and a particularly local attribute. A 'decent' man in Ballintully is 'sound through and through' and 'so honest he'd pay you the last shilling'. Neighbours provide a network of honest contacts whom local people can rely on not to 'do' (swindle) them – not least because a bad reputation would spread around. There is also an ascending scale of neighbourliness which runs from readiness to spend time having 'a bit of a chat', through short-term help during a crisis, to long-term assistance – for example, in helping to run a farm which has no man on it. But in daily life neighbourliness is based more on an interactional style than on substantial transactions. One day two neighbours were cutting a hedge together when a car passed by and one commented that the driver 'must have broken her arm'. When asked who it was he replied that he did not know, but criticised her unfriendliness, since a broken arm was, surely, the only reason that should have prevented her from waving as she passed by. It is this sense of involvement with neighbours which militates against the emergence of a strident individualism. In this incident the driver was ignoring those qualities of friendly identity which are the mark of a 'decent' man in Ballintully. Decency has a specific meaning relating to an individual's integrity in relationships, but is manifest in friendly, modest behaviour.

It has one further set of referents: an individual's commitment to his church. Although religious affiliation separates households in terms of belief, it does not alienate households, since church allegiance, just like notions about kin and neighbours, is a shared value. In Ballintully an individual or family is thought to be letting the side down, as well as to be lacking in a right view of how life should be conducted, if not connected to any church. Paradoxically, as Harris[11] has also noted, protestant/catholic cleavage makes individuals from different groups particularly neighbourly and there are strenuous efforts made to keep any latent hostility latent. Not only are religious and political issues never discussed between protestants and catholics, but all potentially contentious topics are avoided in order to reduce the chance of arguments or the possibility of giving offence. Atrocities, when they are discussed at all across the sectarian divide in Ballintully, are assessed strictly on humanitarian grounds, and if any element of vindication is thought likely for the 'other' group, then they are not discussed at all. The fact that issues arising in the context of Ireland generally are never debated between neighbours of different religious groups, reinforces religious stereotypes, so that any deviation from what is perceived to be 'catholic' or 'protestant' is seen to be a flaw in allegiance. Paradoxically, since any unacceptable attitude can be attributed to religious bias, this also reinforces prejudicial stereotypes.

Thus, the world outside Ballintully is translated and interpreted in its own terms, and judgements and values which are pertinent in the townlands are applied to the world beyond them. In Ballintully, decency is assessed during daily encounters in which there should be 'no difference between one and the other'. The grounds for these judgements are rooted in the economic, social and political realities of rural life in the past, but continue to be relevant to the closely-knit community. Economic homogeneity and intricate kin networks militate against the emergence of powerful personalities at a local level, and have implications in the wider domain of which it forms part. Communities which lay such emphasis on equalitarian attitudes, do not engender or foster assertive individualism, since there are constraints on the self-aggrandisment that invariably accompanies personal achievement. Candidates for leadership almost immediately transgress the local value system by replacing modesty with self-projection, and by moving beyond the circle of neighbours to seek approval among political peers. Since there are few local structures which project into the wider domain, those seeking political power must, in effect, reject the claims of locality in order to advance. When a local boy is successful neighbours are likely first to attribute his success to his background, and then predict failure by allusions to the past history of his family, or to his inability in other areas of life. Nor, when judging public figures, do people find it easy to believe in the altruism of motives.

Since local allegiance demands that one favours one's kin and neighbours above others, it is always assumed that political leaders do the same, and if not favouring their immediate circle, they will, of course, give priority to their co-religionists. Ultimately, the criteria used for assessing leaders are those values crucial in the local area, industriousness and local allegiance, and by these measurements most leaders, inevitably, fail. Their job in politics – often judged by television appearances which show them involved in ineffective protest or sterile debate – is not perceived as 'real' work at all, and visits to the home neighbourhood are seen as motivated by a need for electoral support rather than local loyalty, a view strengthened by the tendency common to most emergent elite – and noted by Leyton in Aughnaboy – to try and shed the impediment of kin responsibilities.

Leadership

To develop a following in Northern Ireland, leaders must not only be useful at a neighbourhood level but must speak with an authentic local voice, and espouse the religious ideology, which is the badge of identity beyond kin and neighbours. They jeopardize their position if they are declamatory, idealistic, altruistic or innovative, all postures unacceptable at a local level. The most successful leaders – and this paper considers, briefly, John Hume and Ian Paisley as representative of these – emphasise either their effectiveness as politicians who get things done for the electorate,[12] or their unswerving allegiance to a shared ideology. At various periods the secular or the religious voice may have to predominate. If the politician is being 'the voice of the people', representing their interests conscientiously, he must be non-innovative, and must not be seen to be hobnobbing with any hierarchy or to be benefiting materially from his position. If he is using his ideological manifesto, particularly if it is a religious one, he can act on the assumption that God is on his side and, using the church rhetoric which translates so easily into political diatribe, he has the sanction to behave in a manner that would be untenable in a 'normal' person: self-important, bombastic, rude and disputatious. While both Hume and Paisley adopt the 'useful common man' approach, Paisley is obviously the best known exponent of the religious politician's role. Hume, his position as a European politician increasingly distancing him from his earlier 'voice of the people', appeal, has latterly made Seamus Mallon the spokesman for his party's views within Ireland, and hence has become the spokesman on Ireland – to the detriment of his grass-roots following.

Weber's typography for leaders divides them into charismatic, traditional, and rational/legal, the latter being the most commonly accepted contemporary model. Developing from this, Roy Wallis[13] has identified two crucial elements of leadership: the role and the message. This paper suggests that the role of leader in Northern Irish society is problematic and can only be maintained by constant appeal to well-established values. The message, also, must be traditional, for when it appears to be innovative it subverts the role. Local value systems limit the development of effective leadership and constrain those in such positions.

Paisley created his role as leader by modelling himself on traditional evangelicals and Unionists, and maintains it by identifying himself as a man of the people. He stressed comparisons between himself and Knox, Wesley, Whitefield, Cooke, or the Israelite prophets who called the faithful back to righteousness. In politics he followed, literally, the Carson trail, welcoming his old gun-running ship and even adopting his costume. Paisley confirms his local affinities by marching at the head of bands, attending funerals, championing individual causes. He has scorned the cosmopolitan style of Terence O'Neill and John Hume, and is always seen to give priority to local rather than 'outside' interests. This, and his ill-mannered behaviour, especially in Europe, earns him the opprobium of middle-class moderates in Ireland and beyond, but is perceived by his followers as a courageous defence of true principles, which gain validity by being stated bluntly, rather than in the 'velvet tongue' of more devious leaders. The narrow boundaries of Democratic Unionist Party (D.U.P.) ideology has frequently constrained Paisley, as when he had to recall his wavering and incredulous flock, having been misinterpreted as having said that the constitution of the Republic was the only block to a united Ireland, and, in 1976, when he made William Craig and William Beattie the scapegoats of a much-opposed proposition for coalition with constitutional nationalists. Paisley's most offensive gestures are often reserved for the Roman Catholic hierarchy (to whom in private he is apparently quite civil) thus marking the rigorous opposition to ecumenism among his followers.

Hume's credibility as a leader has faced the same challenges as Paisley's, but in so far as he has adopted the rational approach which is acceptable to Irish moderates and European and American observers, he has jeopardized support, obviously among the hardliners, and more crucially among the young. In times of crisis he has had difficulty in standing up for his non-sectarian principles, for fear of alienating his nationalist following, as evidenced by his decision not to contest the second Fermanagh and South Tyrone by-election in 1981, in opposition to Sinn Fein; by his initial lack of support for integrated education in Northern Ireland; by his indeterminate opposition of the anti-divorce and anti-abortion lobbies in the South. When followers might be lost by his assumption of a liberal stand, even one he has maintained in private or abroad, Hume invariably plays safe. While he retains support among moderates, there is evidence that the younger element in the party see him as happier winging between Brussels and New York than focusing on their localized complaints, which are readily taken up by Sinn Fein. Recognizing the grounds for criticism, and trying to defend a leadership role beyond the bounds of usefulness, Hume has said: 'If getting drains fixed is what politics is about, about ninety per cent of people are qualified to be politicians'.[14] His personal success as an Irish politician, instrumental in engineering the Anglo-Irish Agreement and in a European context, assures him a future role, no matter what happens in Northern Ireland, but the fact that his credibility on the ground has diminished as his international status has increased is a problem for the leadership of the Social Democratic and Labour Party (S.D.L.P.). Paradoxically, the equalitarian values which cause catholics to critize him, and which are shared by protestants, make it impossible for them to believe in Hume's lack of bias, not simply on the grounds of his religious origins, but because he has obviously graduated from being the lean idealistic local to being a fêted internationalist, at ease with world politicians.

In a colonial or post-colonial society there are perhaps only two possible positions for the potential leaders of the indigenous peoples: they can rebel, a route not chosen by either Paisley or Hume, except symbolically, or they can acquiesce, at least partially, to the status quo and try to manipulate 'invisibly', rallying support by identifying with their supporters, and working within the boundaries which this imposes. It is in this context that local values are still powerful in Northern Ireland, inhibiting the development of potential leaders at local level by discouraging the individualism which might produce politicians with the courage for bold initiatives, and constraining most 'decent' men from becoming the good leaders the country so patently lacks.

CHAPTER 11

Northern Irish gentry culture: an anomaly
by
Amanda Shanks

The word 'anomaly' means a departure from the rules and in this paper it will be
applied to the minor gentry in Northern Ireland. The way in which the Northern Irish
gentry departs from the rules is by having a culture which is different from that of
other groups in rural Irish society. The anomaly arises because the way their culture
is perceived by outside observers differs from the way they perceive themselves.
Such anomalies are to be found in the nature of their culture and more particularly
in perceptions of the political or leadership role of the gentry, of their wealth relative
to other sections of society, and their notions of class, religion and nationality. A
discussion of these subjects in relation to the gentry will illustrate the fact that rural
culture in Ireland is not united, and that minority groups such as the gentry have
cultural links which stretch beyond the boundaries of Ireland and link it into a more
extensive cultural system.

Members of the minor or untitled gentry of the Route area of Northern Ireland
were the subjects of fieldwork carried out in the early 1980s. At this time, fourteen
gentry families were resident there. The minor gentry are members of the aristocracy which consists of two broad divisions, those who are titled or members of the
peerage and those who do not have titles, a group which includes baronets. Because
it is impossible to define members of the gentry by the number of acres they own
or the amount of wealth they possess, the word 'gentry' here refers to untitled
members of the aristocracy who consider themselves to be, and are accepted by
others, as gentry, and who have an association with a certain area of land and a
family house through a head of family to whom they are somehow related. Any
aspirant to the status of gentleman is judged in terms of his performance of a special
code of gentlemanly behaviour. The concept of the gentleman, or one who follows
the code, is significant because it is this which unites the minor, untitled gentry with
members of the nobility, since they both adhere to it. It is for this reason that it is
possible to generalise about the behaviour of the gentry beyond the boundaries of
the Route area of Northern Ireland and the categories imposed by rank.

One of the most important things about the gentry as a group in Ireland is that their
culture is English. In one way their Englishness is not surprising as gentry families
today are mostly, but not all, the descendants of men from the mainland of Britain
who came to Ireland for one reason or another and settled there on land which they
received for services rendered to the Crown, or to major landowners, who had
themselves been granted land. Perhaps what is surprising is that this Englishness
should still be in evidence some hundreds of years later. It may be because of their

English culture that they have been almost totally ignored by researchers interested in the workings of society.

The base-line to which nearly all studies of society in rural Ireland refer is Conrad Arensberg and S.T. Kimball's famous study[1] of farming folk in county Clare. Arensberg and Kimball have been criticised for ignoring the effects of outside factors, such as the influence of religion and politics. They also omitted to make even a passing mention of the role of the gentry in the countryside. Reading their account one would not realise that such a category existed, let alone had played an important part in shaping rural life. Anthropologists following Arensberg and Kimball have also, for the most part, treated the gentry as if they were non-people and have concentrated on folk culture and on the Northern Irish 'Troubles'. The gentry, however, regard their culture as important in Ireland because they believe themselves to have contributed to the culture of the island as a whole. For example, many of the houses which they built still adorn the countryside and are now being used as country-house hotels or as tourist attractions or institutions of one sort or another. Members of the gentry see themselves as an integral part of Irish rural life, members of the community whose families have played an important role there for some centuries, regardless of how that role may be viewed by other people. On the other hand, the gentry still use their culture to distinguish themselves from other groups in Ireland and although they are a minority, and regarded by many as insignificant, it is necessary that their culture should also be studied to achieve a complete picture of Ireland.

One way in which the gentry may be seen as anomalous is in the political sphere. In the past, members of the gentry were important in both the formal and informal government of Ireland, with members of the peerage playing the most prominent role. In the South, the political role of the gentry ended with partition, but in Northern Ireland they maintained their political significance until the early 1970s. Both titled and untitled families in the province provided members of parliament at Westminster, although not many reached this high rank. The same families also provided members for the local parliament at Stormont. Indeed, the last three prime ministers of the province were all members of aristocratic families. Members of the gentry were usually unionists, supporting the link with Britain.

In the past, members of the gentry also played their part at the local level. Heads of families were usually members of the grand jury, the body which administered the public amenities of each county before elected councils came into being. They retained the social position of grand jurors until that body was finally dispersed in 1974. Many of them served on public and charitable bodies and in this way exerted influence on the communities in which they lived. Nevertheless, Rosemary Harris[2] points out that in county Tyrone members of the middle classes were pushed unprotesting into the role of leaders, whereas most members of the community wished to preserve their individual reputations for 'modesty', and so were prevented from offering themselves. Thirty years ago, leaders were chosen not because they were respected, but because they were believed to be more in touch with the outside world as a result of their social and educational attributes. Today, the gentry are still outside the main sphere of community activities, and possess knowledge about how to deal with situations that do not have their origins in the neighbourhood, although it seems probable that people today are rather more sophisticated than those studied by Harris.

This view is supported by the fact that since the eruption of the troubles in the late 1960s, the electorate has made it clear at the ballot box that they do not regard the gentry as suitable representatives. For example, in the North Antrim election of 1970 the Reverend Ian Paisley won the seat by an overwhelming majority from the sitting gentleman M.P.. This does not correspond to the self-perception of the gentry as leaders, nor the emphasis placed upon leadership by many of the public schools at which their sons are educated. Members of the gentry have had to revise their notions of leadership and to confine them to specific situations – so that a gentleman might see himself as the best person to coordinate a certain activity, such as organising his farm workers, or being an officer in the army. On the other hand, the view that abstinence from power has detrimentally affected the gentry is not correct, since they are now quite happy to channel their energies into running their estates. Members of the peerage, as opposed to the minor gentry, may still use their influence informally, as when they have government ministers to stay in their houses.

Members of the gentry are popularly believed to be rich and to have vast resources at their disposal. Today members of the gentry in north Antrim still live on estates modelled on their English counterparts, although in Northern Ireland these are usually on a smaller scale. Whereas in England estates may be well over 1,000 acres, in north Antrim the size of an estate is usually somewhere between 180 and 500 acres. However, in a couple of cases only the house and its so-called 'pleasure grounds' still remain as family property. It is the house which is the heart of any estate and the most important family possession. Each house is unique in its conception. The grand ones may be architect-designed and often beautifully decorated and furnished with antiques. They may also actually bear the family name, for example, Castleward, named after its builder Mr Ward, the first Viscount Bangor. While financial circumstances may oblige a family to sell off its land bit by bit, it will be most reluctant to dispose of the house, for that retains the special identity of the family. Estate owners and their families have a strong sentimental attachment to their land, and in this they are no different from farmers written about by Arensberg and Kimball[3] and Elliot Leyton.[4]

In 1903 there was an event which might be expected to have had a great effect on the gentry's economic state. This was the passing of the Wyndham Land Act. The Wyndham Act began a process of land purchase which led to most farmers owning the land they worked and most gentleman farmers being left only with what in England would be called the 'Home Farm', that is their houses and the farm land which immediately supported it. Even in north Antrim this led to a considerable reduction in the acreages owned by members of the gentry. For example, an estate of approximately 8,000 acres became reduced to about 400. It might have been supposed that the gentry would be bitter about the loss of their land, but at the same time they tended to see the deal they received as advantageous. The money they received in payment from the government could be used where necessary to pay off mortgages. In addition they were rid of the responsibilities of tenants and any arrears of rent.

Nowadays, the gentry do not look back with regret to the land they sold, although they realise that land keeps its value better than money. They are content so long as they still possess the family house which gives the family its identity and sufficient land to support it – and some of them do not even own the latter. Contrary to popular supposition, the symbolic significance of what they own is more important to them than its quantity. Nevertheless, Mark Bence-Jones believes that landlords received a poor return from the government, given the value of land both before the Famine and after the Land Acts. He also claims that the money which they received was often 'badly invested, or spent as income when it should have been treated as capital'.[5]

Since 1903 the gentry have faced mounting difficulties in supporting their estates. One of these has been inflation which increased the value of their properties and the consequent amount of taxation to be paid on the death of a head of family. Depending on which government is in office taxation can be daunting for estate owners. At present, there is provision for the legal avoidance of death duties providing certain conditions are fulfilled, but should these not be met, the sums involved are considerable and would be a serious drain on the resources of any estate. In addition, the cost of running and maintaining large country houses on much reduced acreages is a problem which many of the gentry have met by adopting new strategies for using the land, particularly now agricultural production is being discouraged. Such strategies include letting the land to neighbouring farmers, starting businesses such as nursery gardens or using the potential resources of the estate. Refurbishing and letting old farm cottages to tenants at commercial rents, rearing pheasants and running shoots, growing soft fruits and vegetables for sale and so on bring in additional income. In some cases such alternative strategies are proving to be successful.

Some claimed that they received their income entirely from their land as a result of their own efforts – for nowadays gentlemen participate actively in the running of their estates. It is not usual for heads of minor gentry families to have other sources of income on which to rely, except for pensions or benefits which they have gained in employment prior to taking over the family estates. They do not hold lucrative positions such as non-executive directorships, as members of the aristocracy may do. It is therefore necessary for them to make the best of the assets which they do possess.

Another way in which they spend their money is on the education of their children. It is considered essential that sons should be educated at public school where they learn many of the gentlemanly values, such as leadership, independence and self-reliance. As these public schools are mostly situated in Great Britain, young gentlemen are also physically separated from the communities in which their estates lie and they grow up in a British ambience. A further aim of this sort of education is to provide the eldest son, who inherits the family property, with the initiative to run the estate. Many eldest sons come to their familial duties without any real experience of estate management. Some receive a training at agricultural college, but many are involved in careers of an entirely different nature and what they know about running their estates has been learned in periodic forays into the farmyard and fields during school holidays, but not through any systematic apprenticeship such as was served by the heir in farming families described in literature.

Public school education is seen as useful, not only for the heir, but for his younger brothers who will need to be capable of making their own way in the world. Public school education is therefore also seen as important because it provides a good education which will be a factor when boys come to face a highly competitive job market. Another thing which can be gained at public school, is a network of contacts which can prove to be very useful. Thus, a public school education, although expensive, is regarded as an essential investment. Eldest sons may receive preferential treatment in that they may be sent to more prestigious schools than their brothers, that is to establishments such as Eton or Harrow, while their brothers may go to less expensive institutions where their parents believe that their interests may be better catered for. Girls, who it is still believed will ultimately marry and be supported by their husbands, are today often educated at the local grammar school in order to save the cost of fees.

Although, relatively speaking, the gentry may be well-to-do, they nevertheless regard themselves as being economically modest. They explain this self-perception by the fact that after the expenditure on the house and estate and on education, they have little surplus cash. Most of their possessions are in trust for the next generation. Although selling land might be thought to be the answer to cash-flow problems, this is usually done with the greatest reluctance since it not only reduces the family's financial resources but, more significantly, it threatens their symbolic identity.

The gentry's perspective on class tends to be anomalous when seen in the light of academic pronouncements on the subject. For academics, class is defined in relation to position in the market, but the gentry subscribe to the more popular view of class as culture. Indeed, the gentry use their culture to distinguish themselves from people of other cultural traditions living in Ireland. In the past they had no compunction in acknowledging that their culture was superior to that of other social categories. As a group, they saw themselves as being at the top of the social scale, and they were united by the concept of the gentleman, whose cultural code could not in their view be bettered.

This cultural code still exists and is the means whereby members of the gentry can immediately recognise one another in a social situation. It also enables them to distinguish themselves from people of other social categories. In the 1950s, Professor Alan Ross[6] proposed the thesis, taken up with enthusiasm by Nancy Mitford,[7] that the British upper classes could be identifed by their speech. They made the distinction between 'U' upper-class speakers and 'non-U' or non upper-class speakers. U-speakers were recognisable by their accents and by their usage. This applies to the Northern Irish gentry who still speak with English upper-class accents, and who adhere to many of the rules of U usage identified by Ross and Mitford. For example, it is still considered non-U by members of the gentry to say 'toilet' for 'lavatory' or 'what' for 'pardon'.

There are other ways by which members of the gentry can recognise one another. For example, the code of manners considered appropriate on every occasion, which dictates how things should be done in gentry circles, from laying a table to addressing an envelope or wearing a signet ring. In addition, the ability to prove a relationship to an established family of gentry is taken as an indicator of class and assigns individuals to social categories of gentry or non-gentry. These categories are reinforced by two things. The first is the pattern of marriages. Sons and daughters of the gentry almost exclusively marry the sons and daughters of other gentry and so the social category is perpetuated. Secondly, the boundaries of the group are defined in the coming together of gentry in groups, mainly at the rituals of entertainment. These rituals include the gatherings which mark the life-crisis events of individuals, that is christenings, weddings, funerals and the like, and also at dinner parties, parties, and so on. The guests at these events are almost exclusively members of the gentry and some members of the middle classes whose code of behaviour is similar enough for them not to stand out. Farmers and their families and other non-gentry neighbours of the gentry are not included in such events.

Although the gentry actively maintain their exclusiveness, it is no longer acceptable that they should follow their tradition, and see themselves as being superior to others. They are therefore obliged to rationalise their views, at least in public. They do this by saying that while they do not see themselves as better than others, they are 'different'. And they believe that good relationships exist between themselves and the members of other social categories. While they may perceive themselves as egalitarian, their actions often belie their words.

The gentry have their own perceptions of religion in Northern Ireland which do not conform to popular categorisations. The majority of the gentry are protestants and belong to the Church of Ireland. But this was no always so. Many gentry families started as presbyterians, but pursuit of their interests made it expedient for them to change to Anglicanism. The attributes of a gentleman thus included membership of the Established Church. The saying of Charles II that no presbyterian can be a gentleman is still sometimes quoted, and today members of the presbyterian church are regarded as being less socially acceptable than members of the Church of Ireland. On the other hand, there are some catholic gentry who are considered to be social equals to the extent that they intermarry with members of other gentry families. Marriages between gentry members of the Church of Ireland and presby-terians are rather less common. While, in the past, heads of gentry families often supported their local Orange Lodges, today members of the gentry do not express anti-catholic sentiments, although they may not understand the catholic point of view. On the other hand, they do not understand the point of view of militant presbyterians either. It seems that given the pattern of occasional intermarriage with catholics rather than with presbyterians, gentry divisions of status override those of religion.

In terms of their 'Irishness' the gentry in Northern Ireland have a confusing time and it is here especially that they might also be considered to be anomalous. There is little doubt that their culture is English. Their English accents and use of English, their adherence to the English code of manners and their membership of the Anglican Church in Ireland, all speak of their orientation towards England. In addition, the Northern Irish gentry are open in their support of the link with Britain. They carry British passports, they regard the Queen as their sovereign, the British government as their government, and London as an important landmark. Many of them say that they would not like to live in an Irish republic, and if the situation in Northern Ireland were to force them to flee, most would set up again in England where they would blend themselves into the upper and upper-middle classes. On the other hand, they regard themselves as Irish because that is where their homes are and where their families have lived for hundreds of years. Although they may perceive themselves to be Irish, members of the gentry are often taken as English – as standoffish and snobbish – characteristics commonly attributed by the Irish to the English. In the South of Ireland, members of the gentry are often called 'Anglo-Irish' a phrase which expresses the ambivalence of their position. But, in spite of their English culture, the gentry of the Route do not think of themselves as Anglo-Irish because the families there are the descendants of Scottish families, and they regard themselves as Scots-Irish. Their perception of their nationality is situational. When in Northern Ireland they regard themselves as British, but when in Britain they claim to be Irish.

The gentry today are an anomaly because they belong to an élite group in a society which does not approve of the principles on which élites are based. They are a social rather than a political élite, for they provide a resource for power rather than a power group itself. However it is surprising that they still exist as an élite, because they no longer exercise power. This does not matter to them since their main goal is the maintenance of their estates and family identity. In addition to their loss of power and their economic situation, the gentry's perception of class is outmoded and their vision of their nationality is ambiguous. For these reasons, the visible decline of the gentry might be expected and indeed a slow decrease in their numbers is occurring, but they have by no means suffered the total eclipse that might have been forecast.

The gentry still exist and are doing quite well. Their success can be attributed to their resilience in the face of adverse circumstances. They adapt their culture to meet new situations. Although the culture of the gentry is essentially English it should not be ignored as alien because it adds another element to the cultural diversity of Ireland. It unites members of the social category who promote it, not only throughout the island of Ireland but further afield. While the culture of the gentry separates them from other Irish countrymen, their feeling for Ireland and the land they own shows that, at heart, they too are Irish countrymen.

PART IV
THE COMPUTER AS A RESOURCE FOR IRISH HISTORY

CHAPTER 12

Numbers to the alphabet of history
by
Brenda Collins

The purpose of this paper is to provide a background description of the contribution of computing to historical research. Some people might doubt the value of its place in the programme. Indeed, the argument was made that no-one had proposed a paper on the use of a card index in pursuit of Irish Studies, so why should the techniques of computing be considered any more important? This is a valid point of view and it makes a stark contrast with a viewpoint expressed in the early 1970s that, up to that time, the availability of photocopying machines had exerted a far greater influence on historical practice than had computers.[1] While both these points may superficially imply a demeaning of the value of computing, the lesson which surely does emerge is that, between 1970, when computing was not felt to have been absorbed into historical practice, and 1988, when its value as a technique or resource can be compared with a card index, there lies a tremendous change in attitudes. Instead of computers being ascribed a mystical quality, they and their resources have now become acceptable and user-friendly at all levels of education and research, from primary schools to higher education.

The application of computing leads to one or more of the following situations: 1) the 'creation' of new types of sources; 2) new types of assumptions about the sources and about their place in the discipline and the theme of the study, be it history, geography, sociology, languages, anthropology or archaeology; and 3) leading from the first two, new types of methods of approach, integrating computer-enriched knowledge with knowledge gained from other sources – most often from printed material but also from manuscripts, interviews and verbal exchanges of information in formal and informal settings. Of course, these three situations are interlinked. New types of sources have arisen because the facility of the computer to act as a 'giant clerk' has called into being the possibility of dealing with items of information on a large scale, certainly impossible for the human mind to contemplate, even with a card index! But having new sources also alters the framework of assumptions about exactly what type of information is most relevant to the study of a particular topic. Moreover, though by no means an exclusive, or even necessary, attribute of computing, this approach often puts an emphasis on counting or quantification. The essence of quantification is that it puts a level of certainty in place of vague possibilities, following the admonitions of George Kitson Clark who wrote, 'do not guess, try to count, and if you cannot count, admit that you are guessing'.[2]

One particular way in which the computer has come into its own and which I hope to illustrate below, is the extent to which it can analyse information where both the

95

range and variability of evidence can be predicted, and can, in fact, answer questions which we may not even have begun to formulate. This very attribute is, of course, also its greatest weakness, for a computer can never supersede the human researcher in the interpretations of contexts.

The research examples which are used here are taken from an ongoing research project whose initiation was financed by the Economic and Social Research Council under the title 'Fertility, religion and social class in early twentieth century Ireland'.[3] Its method was to gather for computer analysis a sample of the household enumeration schedules from the 1911 census of county Londonderry and the city of Derry.

Why did this approach seem to be appropriate? Briefly, the background to this choice of topic lay in the interaction between the 'received' view of historical change and the new possibilities of investigation which were thrown up by the existence of census enumeration material. One of the aspects of social change in the period before the First World War within the British Isles was that families became 'modernized' in demographic terms; married couples began to have fewer children than had been the case in early Victorian times, and also people began to live longer. Both these trends have continued to the present day, but they are deemed by contemporary researchers to have originated with the generations of people who reached adulthood in the period 1880-1914.

The 1911 census required every householder in the whole of the British Isles to furnish details of address, age, occupation and literacy of every member of his household on a form. It also asked some unique questions concerning age at marriage of the householder, numbers of children born to that marriage and child mortality; hence the census of 1911 is known colloquially as the 'fertility census'. Our opportunity to analyse it is also unique in that at present only in Ireland, within the whole of the British Isles, is it possible to research the original material. There are, of course, printed census statistics available from government publications but none of these are sufficiently detailed for a study of the topic outlined above.

The areas of study, county Londonderry and the city of Derry, were chosen because of their intrinsic comparative interest, the city having a well developed manufacturing base of female labour in shirt production which can be set against the agricultural hinterland. In addition, in methodological terms, the county and the city were foils for each other, while together they comprised an appropriate size numerically. Hence, even from the conception of the topic of study, the intention to use a computer forced me, as a historian, to think through what I wanted from a piece of research, and what degree of work might have been required to achieve it.

The remainder of the paper describes the stages in research method from the initial document through to the type of conclusion which may be derived from it, and the prospective paths of enquiry which may lead from it. First, however, it may be useful to discuss an example of analysis connected with the broad theme of comparative family size and structure which illustrates the connection between method, explanation, evidence and context.

Table 1a.   Comparative household size in 1911

	Number of people %		
	1-3	4-5	6 or more
Co. L'Derry	37	29	34
England & Wales	41	32	27

Table 1b.   Household size in Co. L'Derry according to religion of the head of household. 1911.

	Number of people %		
	1-3	4-5	6 or more
Catholic	44	26	30
Protestant	34	30	36

Table 1a shows a distribution of household sizes in county Londonderry in 1911 and compares this distribution with that known for England and Wales.[4] We might not be too surprised to find that just about one third of the households in county Londonderry were of six or more people, though we might find it strange that our commonsense supposition that this might have been due to families rearing more children than a modern-day pattern does not seem to hold true when the distribution for England and Wales is considered. We should be led back to the road of defining exactly what it is that is being asked of the data and in what context the comparison is being made. Just how comparable was the rural county in Ireland with the much more urbanised England and Wales? An extension to exploring the Irish aspect is made in table 1b which distinguishes the county Londonderry households by the religion of the head of the household. Here we see that a larger proportion of the protestant households was of six or more people than was the case among the catholic households, 36 per cent compared with 30 per cent. At the other end of the spectrum, in comparison with protestants, or those in England and Wales, a much higher proportion of catholic households was of three or fewer people. These are results which might not have been predicted at the commencement of research. Yet present-day values and the inclination to see history as a sequential chronicle of change where each event is explicable solely in the terms of what preceded it, do colour our perception of the past. A suitable analogy might be with a contemporary photograph; both this table of information and a family photograph might be interesting, but without knowledge of the context in which each was created we cannot reach any firm conclusions about its significance.

If we want to understand the analytical process we must understand the creation of the historical record. Thus Figure 1 shows the layout and quality of information offered by the census documents. It is necessarily abbreviated, but the range of information available on any one individual is clear – first name and surname, religion, literacy, sex, age, marital status, occupation, birthplace, and for married women only, their length of marriage and numbers of children born and surviving. The particular household shown here is quite large, headed by Ruth Collins, a catholic widow aged sixty, with four unmarried children, one widowed daughter, one married daughter, and five grandchildren. This household is only one of the sample of 337 households in Derry city and it is referenced not only by its internal content but by its spatial location and its structure. Figure 2 shows the relationship which each of these aspects bears to the other, while Figure 3 presents a diagram of the complex family relationships within the household.

This household is quite striking in the complexity of its family relationships, but the experience which it records serves as an illustration of two major themes about life in Derry city at the turn of this century which can also be documented through other historical records. Firstly, the dominance of the shirt industry in the economy and prosperity of Derry city was apparent from as early as the 1840s and continued until after the Second World War. By the early twentieth century the Derry

Figure 1. Example of information on household schedule, 1911 census of Ireland.
(personal names are fictitious)

Name	Relat.	Religion	Literacy	Age	Occup.	Mar.	Birthpl.
Ruth Collins	Head of family	Catholic	Can read	60	No occupn.	Widow	Born in L'Derry
MaryAnn Donegan	Daughtr	Catholic	Read & Write	32	Machinist Shirtmkr	Widow	Born in L'Derry
Georgena Dixon	Daughtr	Catholic	Read & Write	27	Machinist Shirtmkr	Mar	Born in L'Derry

followed by,
Ruth Collins' three adult children
MaryAnn Donegan's four sons
Georgena Dixon's son

Figure 2. Example of coded information linking household to family to people,
based on Figure 1.

```
RECORD SCHEMA 1   HOUSE
01    650    52    31    DERRY LONGMORE ROAD

RECORD SCHEMA 2   FAMILY
02    650    1

RECORD SCHEMA 3   INDIVIDUAL
03    650    1    1    RUTH COLLINS    122    60
      3    43
```

hinterland produced over twenty per cent of the total United Kingdom output of shirts, collars and cuffs. Its success mirrored the rise of the white collar worker in Victorian and Edwardian Britain. The increasing numbers of financial and commercial clerks, civil servants and members of other professions had, as a requirement of their positions, to dress in clean white shirts with clean white collars every day. Secondly, most of the workers in the shirt industry were women and girls. The industry employed both 'indoor' workers on their factory or warehouse premises, and 'outdoor' workers who did the sewing in their own homes. Sewing machines operated by hand wheel or foot treadle, had been in use in the industry since the 1850s, soon after their invention across the Atlantic. Nevertheless there were some aspects of the making-up of shirts which the machines could not cover, and so hand sewing continued as an essential part of the shirt-making process well into the twentieth century. Sewing machines with wheel or treadle action did not require to be attached to a power source and so, even with the machines, women could work at home. Some shirt factory owners rented machines on a hire-purchase system to their workers. Similarly, hand-sewing work continued within the factory setting. Though those who worked in their own homes were more marginal to the overall production, their position was important because they could be treated almost as casual labourers and hired and fired according to the amount of work available. In 1902 it was estimated that there were 18,000 'indoor' employees in the city of Derry and nearly 60,000 'outdoor' workers in the city and the surrounding countryside.

From the census record, it is unclear whether the daughters who worked as shirtmaker machinists were home or factory based but probably, as city dwellers, some of them were 'indoor' workers.[5] Statistical analysis of the data (not reproduced here) shows that most of the workforce were young women, such as MaryAnn Donegan and Georgena Dixon. Indeed, two-thirds of the workforce was aged under thirty. Many of the workers were unmarried daughters and nieces living in their parental or a relative's household. There were very few jobs for men in the shirt industry, (as was true for most city-based textile production throughout the British Isles, whether cotton, jute, linen or wool), and many Derry men were casual labourers or went to Britain for temporary work. The opportunity of working in the shirt industry did mean, however, that young girls were able to earn relatively high wages in Derry city, compared to the alternatives available in domestic or farm service. In an account of working conditions in the industry which was published in 1908, a lady factory inspector reported that 'marrying a skilled shirt worker is, for the casual labourer, the equivalent of what marrying an heiress may be in another station of life',[6] and an oral tradition of the importance of women's wages to the family budget persists in Derry to the present day.

The layers of information which have been described above, from the raw census records, their semi-coded forms, their tables of analysis and the secondary material of government reports, local accounts and manufacturers' records, combine to-gether to provide a very powerful tool for historical research. Yet their combination also confirms what should be apparent to all researchers, that the results of a trial investigation can never be totally predicted. The first example of research, on comparative household size, confounded expectations of the likely pattern – that protestant and catholic households would be similar in size; while the second example, of the age, sex and family position of workers in the shirt industry, confirms evidence from other sources. Certainly, it is not claimed that a computing method is essential to reach this knowledge, but it brings into the arena a range of historical information which could not otherwise be examined. An additional aspect of the construction of this type of research base, and one made increasingly important by financial exigencies, is the possibility of exchange of computerized information between scholars. Exchange can take place at any point on the spectrum from free and reciprocal to full commercial cost, depending on the client and the purpose. Computing in history thus offers an opportunity to disseminate historical awareness of just how the past has moulded the present to a much wider audience than heretofore.

Figure 3.   Structure of household 652. (personal details are fictitious)

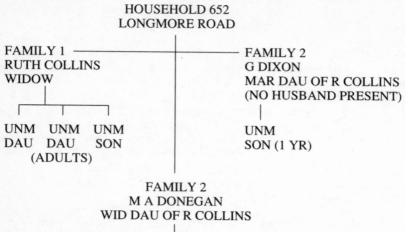

HOUSEHOLD 652
LONGMORE ROAD

FAMILY 1 ———————————————— FAMILY 2
RUTH COLLINS   G DIXON
WIDOW   MAR DAU OF R COLLINS
                                      (NO HUSBAND PRESENT)

UNM   UNM   UNM   UNM
DAU   DAU   SON   SON (1 YR)
       (ADULTS)

FAMILY 2
M A DONEGAN
WID DAU OF R COLLINS

UNM   UNM   UNM   UNM
SON   SON   SON   SON
(9YRS) (7 YRS) (5 YRS) (2 YRS)

CHAPTER 13

The computer as a resource for Irish history: an introduction to the Irish Ordnance Survey Memoirs database

by

Angelique Day

The Ordnance Survey Memoirs are a group of topographical accounts written during the course of the nineteenth-century Ordnance Survey of Ireland, and form part of the large, valuable, but complex archive of papers relating to the history of this unique exercise.[1] The history of the papers is not relevant to the subject under discussion.[2] Suffice to say that the Ordnance Survey Memoirs, for the purpose of the Ordnance Survey database, are confined to those papers in the care of the Royal Irish Academy, Dublin, in fifty two boxes, arranged very much in the original order they were left in the 1860s when they were transferred from the Ordnance Survey, Phoenix Park, Dublin. There are related papers in the same and other locations.

The Ordnance Survey was authorised in 1824 for the purpose of getting accurate maps for more effective local taxation. In other words, they were primarily intended to be used by the valuers for tax, in particular, the county cess tax. The maps were made by members of the Royal Engineers corps, with three companies of sappers and miners, as well as civil assistants whose numbers and importance increased as the survey proceeded. Collection of information relating to physical features represented diagramatically was always encouraged, and indeed specified in Colonel Colby's instructions to officers in 1826. It was, however, the guiding hand of the assistant director, Thomas Larcom, who established the form of report which came to be known as the 'Memoir'. In his pamphlet called 'Heads of Inquiry', printed in 1833, he described topics to be investigated in great detail.[3] The unit of description was to be the parish. There were three main prescribed topics or divisions: Natural Features and Topography (landscape features and place-name material), Artificial Topography, Ancient and Modern (monuments and buildings, as well as enquiry into the purpose of such) and People or Present State (society and culture). It was a very ambitious plan and reports were not always faithfully carried out, nor was equal time given to each county. The resulting Memoirs are very uneven in length and quality, depending on the time of writing and the author responsible. However, the collection of Ordnance Survey memoirs, some 22,000 sheets of manuscript which were not published, contain unique and intriguing documentation, not only because of the wide range of subjects covered, but also because some of the authors, notably the civil assistants, used local informants. As it turned out, the Ordnance Survey Memoirs were written at a crucial time in Irish history, before the devastation of the population and country through the Famine.

The bulk of the reports were written between 1830 and 1840, with considerably more relating to Londonderry parishes where one parish, Templemore, actually reached publication at the time (1837), and Antrim parishes where the surveying teams started earliest. There are fairly substantial accounts for Donegal, Fermanagh and Tyrone: mainly officers' reports. Armagh, Cavan, Down and Monaghan are less thorough, but even amongst these Memoirs there is some fascinating detail. There are fragments for counties Cork, Galway, Leitrim, Louth, Longford, Mayo, Queen's County (Laois), Roscommon, Sligo and Tipperary.

The importance of the Ordnance Survey Memoirs has been acknowledged ever since the furore over the suspension of money and approval for the Scheme in 1840. However, the papers were very infrequently used, except by such notables as Reverend J. O'Laverty, who made a précis of the County Down parishes in his History of the Diocese of Down and Connor. In latter years, Professor E.R.R. Green pioneered their use, as did Dr R. McCutcheon in his *Industrial Archaeology of Ulster*. Dr Brian Trainor pointed the way to making the Memoirs more generally accessible with his transcription of the Ordnance Survey Memoir of the parish of Antrim, with its most useful introduction. Some of the more enterprising local historical societies, with Queen's Archaeology and Extra Mural Studies departments, also followed suit by publishing individual parishes.

Soon after the death of Professor E.R.R. Green, a junior research fellow was appointed to catalogue and trace the collections of Ordnance Survey manuscripts. During the course of this work, it became obvious that a systematic transcription of the Memoirs would provide an invaluable source of information for historians and local historians. At the time, 1982, Dr John Greene was initiating the Belfast Newsletter Index project. He was going to employ an information retrieval program developed at Queen's in the 1960s by Dr Kieran Devine and others. This was 'QUILL', Queen's University for Interrogation of Legal Literature.[4] The QUILL program seemed very suitable for indexing the variable texts of the Ordnance Survey Memoirs. Funding from the Economic and Social Research Council was made available in 1984 when the team consisted of three, including Dr Kay Muhr, now working with the Place Names Project. Since that time to the present, 1988, the team, through various vicissitudes, notably one year's delay in funding, have transcribed Memoirs into a machine-readable form for counties Antrim, Armagh, Cavan, Down, Fermanagh, Monaghan and Tyrone: approximately 12,000 sheets of manuscript text. These texts have been indexed for rapid retrieval using QUILL. At present there are over 13,500 documents on the database. We estimate the total size of the database once Londonderry and Donegal are finished, to be 30 to 40 megabytes, of both text and indexed text.

1.   QUILL

This information retrieval program was developed at Queen's in the 1960s to facilitate lawyers in their search for relevant case material. The other projects utilising QUILL, the Belfast Newsletter Index and the Hiberno-Latin Dictionary project, have used printed sources and, in the case of the Newsletter Index, provided references to the text, not the text itself. QUILL is flexible and comparatively easy to implement for different sorts of material. It was an appropriate system to use for the Ordnance Survey Memoirs because full texts of prose could be run through the system. This means that preparation for transcriptions as well as structuring for QUILL can be carried out simultaneously.

All texts to be indexed by QUILL have to be structured in documents recognisable by QUILL. A document consists of delimited text and descriptor fields. Any word in the text or descriptor field of a QUILL document, except for the thirteen or so most common words in the English Language, are indexed and are, therefore, potentially 'search' words. There are two units for recall: the sentence within the document and the document. There are six descriptor fields: F1, parish or county name; F2, title, author, date; F3, documents reference (inclusive, not page by page); F4, broad subject heading taken from the Heads of Inquiry, like Natural Features, Modern Topography; F5, specific subject heading, often a paragraph heading taken from the Memoirs and F6, informants who are listed in the Fair Sheets.

All the descriptor fields, or a selection of them, may be retrieved, together with text, either in sentences or in the QUILL document (the delimited text) in which they occur. Possibilities of information recall are shaped by the form in which the original material is structured. A huge amount of time is required for the initial stages of preparation.

2. General problems

Problems of setting up and maintaining a database

We may distinguish between two stages of the development of databases: the primary, or initial work, in making records machine-readable or accessible from a computer; and the secondary stage, the use and dissemination of material from the database, or the exploitation of the database, and the continued maintenance of it.

The problems of adequately financing databases such as the Ordnance Survey Memoirs database are perhaps obvious. The type of work, detailed attention to texts, editing into appropriate units and constant checking of finished work, requires the skill and concentration of trained personnel. Although the scale of the work could not be accomplished without a computer, there is no substitute for the trained minds and eyes of the team. The team has run successfully with three or four members, but the full requirements for staff have never been met owing to shortage of funds.

The need for long-term financing is most important to allow for long-term planning and to see the basic or primary work of creating the database through. This of course is the type of finance most difficult to obtain.

The two stages of work in the initiation of a database are the primary transcription and editing of work, to get the records into machine-readable and recallable form, and the secondary work of looking after, updating and possibly selling products of the database. In the prevailing financial climate, emphasis is put on the secondary stage of database development. The idea that databases can generate funds for their own support and attendance, in other words, that they can be self-maintaining, is particularly attractive to funding bodies. This emphasis is often oblivious to the real importance and cost of the primary preparation. For the secondary stage, very different requirements and techniques are needed to the ones required to set up and work the database. It is important to clarify questions of ownership of the material and maintenance of the database. In the case of the Ordnance Survey Memoirs database, it has been difficult to reach any firm decisions about ultimate responsibility and ownership.

This is not a unique situation. These problems are being raised and answered in different ways according to local circumstances. This is partly because such databases are comparatively new in this country, and indeed in the British Isles.

National or international guidelines are in the making. There are examples of institutions initiating databases bearing all these questions in mind; for instance, the Emigration database in Omagh Folk Park has been launched with definite intentions about running the database as an income producing project. They are an example of institutions which will not do the primary work on sources, but will acquire machine-readable records from other databases and concentrate on selling information. This raises the question of how to establish procedures between databases and the exchange of material, since clearly the primary work has to be paid for if great use is to be made from it by other institutions. At the same time, the advantage of machine-readable records is their comparative ease of reference and transference to other systems and locations. Decisions regarding the exploitation of databases might perhaps be reached by referring to the American experience.

3. Specific Problems – Problems of using the database

Procedures for allowing different searchers to use the database can be established only once all the material is processed, and there are no overhauls or updates going on. For instance, we have been re-running the indexing program this spring and summer, which effectively puts the database out of bounds to the outside user.

The next problem is that of educating users to make searches of the database. Written into QUILL are certain prompting facilities which help the novice. The search can be on two levels. A subject can be sought within a document, or within a sentence. The former is a much broader search than the latter because there is more chance of encountering instances of search words throughout a whole document than in one sentence. As indicated, searches have to be made using the vocabulary of the texts themselves. Theoretically, it is possible to relate terms so as to search for synonyms of words used by the Memoir writers; thus although 'folklore' does not occur within the Memoir writers' vocabulary and 'tradition' is the term employed, it is possible to declare equivalent the terms 'folklore' and 'tradition'. There is a separate problem with terms which indicate modern concepts, for instance, 'erosion'. This is not a subject which was consciously treated by the Memoir writers. To look for information relating to this, different search strategies would have to be employed, including that of scanning for equivalent terms in the word lists.

It is possible to search for a number of terms and link them in various ways according to the principles of Boolean logic. First, the terms can be entered without alteration or indication; the command 'Search Document, erosion coast' would mean that a search be made of all documents containing those words and would be produced for inspection. Where the first word in such a combination does not occur at all, the program moves on to the second, in this example, 'coast', and lists the number of times this term occurs in documents. If the operator 'OR' was introduced this would broaden the search to 'erosion' or 'coast', or both. It is possible to narrow down the context of words, particularly where homonyms may occur, by specifically excluding a term when undertaking a search. Consider for instance the term 'combination', meaning a mixture of substances or an association of working men. It is possible to identify the 'combination' which is political by introducing the negative parameter, 'NOT', for example, 'Search Sentence, combination NOT clay'.

It is also posssible to specify the order in which words occur: thus the command, 'Search Sentence, gentle bush', would mean to search for a sentence in which the term 'gentle' preceded the term 'bush'; if unspecified (without the speech marks) the terms could be searched for in any order. It is important to remember that singular and plural terms are distinguished.

There is another very useful facility which searches for words through stems. This is particularly helpful where a great many spelling variants may be preserved, as for instance in the Newsletter Index where all the eighteenth-century spellings were retained. In the case of the Memoirs, variant spellings of ordinary words have been included in angle brackets on first occurrence, and place name spellings have been retained as found. The command, LW1 (list wordstem), also throws up different forms of verb or noun or adjective and so is a very useful tool for choosing a word to search under. A search under the wordstem 'pot' would throw up pot, pots, potteries, potting, potted and so on.

The problems that remain are those relating to preparation and editing. There are still inconsistencies in the spelling of compound terms like 'school-house', or schoolhouse', 'mill house' or 'mill-house'. There are still some proof-reading mistakes in the database. With time, vigilance and, most importantly, the provision of some means of updating and correcting the database, these inconsistencies can be ironed out.

Conclusion

Although a good deal of work has been accomplished, there remains a considerable amount of basic transcription work to complete. The true value of the database will only be realised once all the texts are transcribed and indexed. The value of the initial work can also be realised by actually publishing the texts of parish Memoirs in book format, as the most important audience is still the readers in various localities and abroad, rather than machine-users. We are planning to launch a publication programme to bring out individual parish texts. The material so far transcribed is on public access in the Search Room of the Public Record Office of Northern Ireland; it is also available in the main library at Queen's, and in some of the main libaries of the Library and Education Boards.

The possibility of individuals or institutions at home and abroad using and searching the database must not be underestimated. Although terminals are not plentiful even in most institutions, we must anticipate the possibility of more widespread access. Therefore it is important to begin the work of publicising the material and educating users. The most important method of educating is by demonstration, but publication of methods and techniques will also be important. The new generations of scholars will be much more aware of and confident in the use of machines and machine searches for information. While the potential power of such a research tool can be glimpsed at now, with such factors as speed in consultation of sources, consultation from a geographical distance, ease of comparison, greater analytic power on the plus side, it must be recognised that there are reservations, if not drawbacks, which include the need for instruction in the use of different databases and their conventions, and the actual cost of consulting such records, given the labour-intensive work in preparation and the expense of maintaining databases.

This is not to cast a gloomy eye at the future role of the computer in the publication of sources for studies in all fields. The computer must be seen in perspective however. There is no magic about it; there is much hard work for the data-processor and the data-user. Although, having stated that very obvious fact, there is no doubt that the introduction of machine methods in storage and manipulation of texts and images is the most exciting advance since Gutenberg's invention of printing with movable type in the fifteenth century.

To illustrate the search power of the QUILL program we have prepared some examples.

(1)   Illustrations of methods of coping with homonyms.
TITLE: Combination NOT clay
    1. DOCUMENTS 12357
F1 Parish of *Carrickmacross, County *Monaghan
F2 Fair Sheets by %George %Scott with index
F4 Social Economy
F5 Police
TEXT
7 constabulary men are stationed in the town [*Carrickmacross]. No stipendiary magistrate, the magistrates much respected, no troops in the town. Houses are not generally insured, houses principally of stone, a few of brick. No combination exists.
    2. DOCUMENT 12329
F1 Parish of *Ematris, County *Monaghan
F2 Statistical Report by Lieutenant P.% Taylor, 31st March 1835
F4 Social Economy
F5 Local Government
TEXT
The Petty Sessions are held in the town of *Rockcorry on evey alternate Wednesday. 4 magistrates, all residing within the parish, are generally in attendance: Mr T.C. %Stewart %Corry p11, Mr %Richard %Mayne, Mr %Charles %Dawson, and Mr %John %McNally. Very few outrages have been committed within the parish for several years, and its character is quiet and orderly. A small detachment of police is stationed in *Rockcorry, consisting of 1 constable and 4 sub-constables. No illicit distillation is carried on, neither does combination of any kind exist. Tithe is duly paid.

(2)   Illustration of different fields in documents.
TITLE: Cabinet makers OR Cabinet maker
    1. DOCUMENT 9542 [unique document number]
F1 Parish of *Enniskillen, County *Fermanagh [County and Parish Name}
F2 Statistical Report by Lieut %John %Chaytor, 18 October 1834 {Title, author, date of account]
F3 Box 27 I 1 pp1-171 with some pages omitted [inclusive document reference]
F4 Social Economy [broad subject heading]
F5 Trades and Occupations [specific subject heading]
TEXT
List of traders and occupations showing the number of persons established in each: linen merchant 1, cloth merchant 15, milliners 5, haberdashers 3, stationer 1, spirit dealers 6, spirit retailers 75, distiller 1, brewer 1, malster 1, wine merchant 1, wine retailer 15, grocers 56, ironmongers 4, builders 4, cabinet makers 3, upholsterer 1, coach maker 1, carpenters 4, wheelwrights 4, bricklayers 6, plasterers 2, masons 6, cutler 1, gunsmiths 2, whitesmiths 3, blacksmiths 6, tinsmiths 2, nailers 6, sawyers

4, plumber 1, watchmakers 4, limner 1, painters 4, bookbinder 1, bakers 16, confectionery 6, saddlers 4, tobacconists 3, tannery 2, boot and shoe makers 3, brogue makers 3, tailers 6, coopers 2, butchers 14, tallow chandlers 3, hatter 1, straw hat and bonnet makers 4, ropemakers 1, pawnbrokers 3, auctioneers 2, hair dresser 1, barbers 3, old clothes brokers 4, printers 4, mantuamakers [manuscript blank], marble cutters 2, turner 1, dyer 1, chimney sweep 1, p169.

2. DOCUMENT 9462
F1 Parish of *Enniskillen, County *Fermanagh
F2 Statistical Report by Lieut %John %Chaytor, 18 October 1834
Box 27 I 1 pp1-171
F4 Natural Features and Natural State
F5 Bogs
TEXT
In the western divisions of the parish there are several small patches of bog, in all about 65 acres, but neither of such magnitude as to demand particular attention. In most of them there are a few fir, oak and yew trees of small dimensions occasionally to be met with. In general they seem to lie indiscriminately, though upon close inspection the prevailing direction, which is at best but doubtful, would seem to be from north west to south east. The yew when found in a good state of preservation is by far the most valuable. It has of late been worked into a superior description of furniture by Mr %Bell, cabinet maker. It is a most durable and close grained wood, and susceptible for beautiful polish. It is highly prized by the nobility and gentry of the kingdom, and in some cases it has found its way to *England and *Scotland. Mr %Bell has had considerable experience in searching for yew in the various bogs of the country. He states that it is almost invariably to be found about the bog edges, and when it occurs in bogs in which islands are, it is sure to be found near the edges of the islands, or when found in bog lakes as is sometimes the case (instance Lough *Yoan), it is generally found near the lake shore with top inwards.

(3)   Illustration of word stem search, dictionary of terms in text and number of times word occurs.
LW1, pot
FREQUENCY
58	POT
1	POT-LID
2	POT-WALLOPING
1	POTATOES
119	POTATO
10	POTATOE
1	POTATOED
1541	POTATOES
1	POTATOS
2	POTENCY
1	POTEST
1	POTOTO
1	PORTRAITS
7	POTS
3	POTTAGE
2	POTTAIL

```
 1  POTEEN
 1  POTTER
 2  POTTER'S
 9  POTTERIES
 3  POTTERS
 1  POTTERS'
10  POTTERY
 1  POTTINGERS
 1  POTWALLER
 1  POTWALLOPER
 4  POTWALLOPING
```

The Place-Name Research Project, Department of the Environment for Northern Ireland and the Celtic Department, Queen's University Belfast

by

Kay Muhr

In the autumn of 1987, money became available for a full-scale investigation into the place-names of Northern Ireland. In the words of the first press release, 19 October 1987,

> The Department of the Environment for Northern Ireland is funding Queen's University Belfast, to research the origin of all names of settlements and physical features in Northern Ireland appearing on the Ordnance Survey 1:50,000 scale map; to indicate their meaning and to note any historical or other relevant information. The project will enable an authenticated Irish language version to be provided for most of these names. This research, which is likely to last for 5 years, will broaden and extend the study of place-names in the province which has been going on in Queen's. It is in line with comparable work being carried out in the rest of the United Kingdom and in most European countries. It will be an exemplary, historical and cultural work which will reveal the complexities of place-names and their linguistic, geographical, social and historical aspects.

Five people were chosen to carry out this task, directed by Professor Gerard Stockman, Department of Celtic, Queen's University Belfast. His team consists of Robert Hannan, BA, MA Celtic; Art Hughes, BA, PhD Celtic; Éilís McDaniel, BA Celtic, MSc Computer Science; Kay Muhr, MA, PhD Celtic; Mícheál Ó Mainnín, BA, MA Celtic. All the scholars of the team have primary qualifications in language, and indeed knowledge of the relevant language is the primary qualification for elucidating a place-name. However, place-name study is much wider than this, involving the geography, archaeology and history of an area, the lore and language of its people, and the documents in which this information may be transmitted to us.

Some help with initial training was received from the Place-name Office of the Ordnance Survey in Phoenix Park, Dublin. This office is currently working on administrative names, that is, baronies, (civil) parishes and townlands. This system of nomenclature is very old: most townland names in Ulster antedate the Plantation, and turn up in seventeenth-century records of government grants or taxes, while parish or other ecclesiastical names may also turn up in the records of the Norman administration. The method (if not the practice) is clear-cut: to take the form of the name standardised by the first Ordnance Survey of Ireland and trace backward through the records, using townland maps as a guide to what names should be contiguous. However, fewer than three-quarters of townland names appear on the 1:50,000 map (actual figure 64 per cent in County Down), and names of parishes and baronies (longer obsolete as administrative divisions) to a lesser extent. Nevertheless, baronies and parishes provide useful subdivisions within each county for grouping names, though townlands, parishes, baronies and counties do not fit tidily within each other: a townland may lie in two different parishes or two different baronies, a parish may lie in different baronies or even counties.

The Ordnance Survey of Northern Ireland supplied the project with a full set (18 sheets) of the 1:50,000 map covering the six counties of Antrim, Armagh, Down, Derry, Fermanagh and Tyrone; also a gazetteer with grid references to the 1 inch map which this map supersedes. Unfortunately, the working list of place-names on the 1:50,000 had to be excerpted from the map! Two series of townland index maps (one superimposed on the one-inch map) are used. Finally the project acquired the full series of 6" or 1:10,000 Irish Grid series for the six counties, and the 1974 Local Government District series which indexes townlands on to these. Although not required for the task in hand, minor names have also to be studied, as they can provide useful information towards elucidating larger district names (for example, when a named ringfort gives its name to the surrounding townland). Finally, early maps, such as those of Sir William Petty's Down Survey in the seventeenth century, can give valuable information on former spellings and layout of names.

The task which faced Petty is a salutary indication of our own. As he says in his *Political anatomy of Ireland*,

Ireland is now divided into provinces, counties, baronies, parishes and farm-lands ... but formerly it was not so, but the country was called by the names of the lords who governed the people. For as a territory bounded by bogs is greater or lesser as the bog is more dry and passable, or otherwise: so the country of a grandee or tierne in Ireland became greater or lesser as his forces waxed or waned ... And when these grandees came to make peace and parts one with another, the limits of their land agreements were no lines geometrically drawn, but if the rain fell one way then the land whereon it fell did belong to A, if the other way to B, etc. As to their town-lands, plow-lands, colps, gneeves, bullibos, ballibetaghs ... etc, they are all at this day become unequal both in quantity and value, having been drawn upon grounds which were obsolete and antiquated ... But now all the lands are geometrically divided, and that without abolishing the ancient denomi-nations and divisions above mentioned. So that it is yet wanting to prevent the various spellings of names not understood, that some both comprehending the names of all public denominations according as they are spelled in the latest grants should be set out by authority to determine the same for the time to come. And that where the land hath other names, or hath been spelled with other conscriptions of letter or syllables, that the same be mentioned with an alias. Where the public and new authenticated denomination is part of a greater antiquated denomination that it be so expressed, by being called the east, west, south or north part thereof. And if the same denomination comprehend several obsolete or inconsiderable parcels, that the same be expressed likewise. The last clause of the explanatory act enabled men to put new names on their respective lands, instead of those uncouth unintelligible ones yet upon them. And it would not be amiss if the significant part of the Irish names were interpreted, where they are not nor cannot be abolished.[1]

However most of the place-names retained their Irish-language form; and all the types of name described by Petty can still be found.

The written sources for place-names in Irish can be divided either by language or by chronology. At all periods, from the seventh century to the present day, literature in Irish has taken a great interest in places, their names and their legends. One compilation, the *Dindshenchus*, deals specifically with the origin of placenames, but the interest is legendary rather than etymological, and only important places are mentioned, not small land divisions. In general, references to place-names in native literature are sporadic, not systematic.

Ecclesiastical sources, in Irish and Latin, range from saints' lives (in which foundations etc. may be listed), to the administrative records of the church. After the twelfth century there are charters and episcopal registers listing lands owned by the church, parish organisation etc., which provide considerable evidence of place-names, though not usually in their native spelling.

Civil administrative sources, in Latin and English, become especially name-rich in Sir William Petty's period, the seventeenth-century Plantation, for example Fiants, Patents, Inquisitions, the Civil Survey, Hearth Money Rolls, 1659 Census, Books of Survey and Distribution and the Act of Settlement. These names are always in a foreign-language spelling, and assessment is complicated by the loss of so many original documents in the Dublin Public Record Office fire of 1922, for which one has now to rely on copies and calendars of variable quality.

The first Ordnance Survey of Ireland, in the 1830s, tried to establish standard English spellings of place-names through evaluation of the various forms in use, research which has remained largely unpublished to the present day. The original name-books, compiled by the surveyors and corrected by the Irish scholar John O'Donovan, are available on microfilm, the originals in the Phoenix Park office. The Ordnance Survey Letters, written in the field by O'Donovan, are also available on microfilm, while the related Ordnance Survey Memoirs, compiled by civil surveyors, are currently being edited and computer-indexed by Angelique Day's project in the Institute of Irish Studies, Queen's University Belfast. The map surveyors often attempted to record local pronunciations as a guide to elucidating the meaning of place-names obscured by non-original spellings, (though the indications are that pronunciation does change through time, often influenced by spelling.) A class of names which does not appear in early sources are those, often English-language settlement names in -town, which probably did not arise until the end of the seventeenth century or later, and for which there may well be no original Irish form.

The Project team have aimed to build up their understanding of, and access to, historical sources for Irish place-names. It seeems sensible to gain expertise in handling the most fruitful sources by dealing with their treatment of each county in turn, and leaving fuller research into names of natural features or late settlements, where necessary, to a later stage in the project. However, since Irish names were most often recorded by non-Irish lay or ecclesiastical administrators, with little understanding of what they were writing down, many corruptions in spelling have to be weeded out.

Problems of Assessment (Illustrations from the baronies of Iveagh / diocese of Dromore)

Spelling
First of all there is the well-known manuscript confusion of r, n, m, and ll; l and uncrossed t; c and o. E, i and y; o and u seem to be written indifferently; likewise

c and k and th and gh. In seventeenth-century handwriting 'long' s is confused with f, while c is confused with s, r, and t. It is difficult to tell which spellings represent misreadings and which phonetic differences, (for instance the absence or presence of gh (x)). Current local pronunciations can still sometimes preserve information not recorded in the modern spelling of place-names.

Variability
The elements of which the name is made up also appear to vary: very frequently 'baile' (to be understood as 'townland') is prefixed arbitrarily, but there are also variations like Tullyrappane/Tawnochrapan (Tullylish parish, obsolete); Islanderry/Ballinderry (Dromore); Ardbrin/Ballylisardbrin (Annaclone); Cappagh/Kilkappie (Annaclone); Listullycurran/Ballytollochorran (Dromore).

Reference
When different names are used for one piece of land, other possibilities are that one is the name for the whole piece, the other a subdivision; or that both pieces were originally equal but that one name has taken in the other. A good example occurs in the area known in the seventeenth century as Clanconnell, now the parishes of Donaghcloney and Tullylish. The 'towns and lands' with accompanying 'hamlets' are listed[2] as granted by James I to Glasney McAgholy Magenis in 1609, including: 'Ballytullyconely with the hamlets of Shian and Dowgane' (Ballydugan td. survives, as also Shane's Hill), 'Ballylurganetawrie with the hamlets of Tullycarny and Morigh' (Lurgantamry, Tullycarn and Monree tds. survive). Some of the barony boundaries go between townlands that are not now contiguous, so that other divisions must have gained in importance subsequently. Later administrative sources tend to quote all possibilities, both variants and variant spelling.

Similar names
As well as the problem of different names for the same place, there is the problem of similar names for different places. Some name formations seem to have been common: Ballykeel (Dromore, Magheralin, Seapatrick parishes), Clare (Tullylish and Magheralin parishes), Ballygowan (Aghaderg and Moira parishes), Clogher (Magheralin and Hillsborough parishes); while others recur at no great distance: Corcreeny (Donaghcloney and Hillsborough parishes), Tullyrain (Tullylish and Magherally parishes). This is where information on local context, the name of the proprietor and the position of the name in the grant, become important considerations.

As an example of potential difficulties in context, the area west of Moira where county Down borders Lough Neagh is called Kilmore, had several subdivisions in the seventeenth century, and is part of the parish of Shankill. South of it in county Armagh, and east of it in county Down, are parishes called Kilmore, (there are many other townlands called Kilmore and in the south west of Ulster there is also Kilmore diocese). Aghaderg parish south of Banbridge, and close to the parish of Kilmore in Armagh, contained an area, now simply a townland, called Shankill. Within Iveagh, townland names that might be confused are Ballymacanallen (Tullylish parish) and Ballymacanally (Magheralin), Tullyorior (Garvaghy) and Tullyear (Seapatrick), Ballymacaratty More and Begg (Donaghmore) and Tullymacarath (Dromore). Some of these are not on the 1:50,000 map and thus not available on the database. It is neccessary however to keep a record of all names once or currently existing in the area under survey, in order to avoid mis-assigning historical references to only those names which appear on the map.

Our findings on each name are being recorded on computer, an IBM PS 30, with hard disc (though we are likely eventually to need 30mb per county, rather than have all the place-name data constantly in memory). The less important material will have to be stored on floppy disc and loaded when required. By January 1988, the database contained the basic list of Northern Ireland place-names from the 1:50,000 sheets in several forms: by map-sheet, by county, by grid-reference, by the alphabet. It was then necessary to divide the data into separate files for the related parts. The chief of these will eventually provide the map-name, original form and notes as edited for publication, another will refer back to the maps, another will set the place-name in the administrative structure (county, barony, parish etc.), while another will hold the collection of historical forms. Linguistic analysis, which is important for dating the origin of a name, will also have to be found a place.

The Project also uses two IBM-compatible Amstrad PC 1640s. With the Amstrads, the members of the Project each input their own data using a screen editor, with the 'fields' (i.e. entry-number, name form, date, sources, and page reference) delimited by commas. A screen editor rather than a word-processing package was chosen for simplicity of transfer to Dbase III+, but this editor has two further useful features, searching and windows. Two windows enable one to have files on two parishes open, where a source includes place-names from both. The 'entry-number' field is essential to link the historical forms with the names on the modern map.

The historical forms for each name are being stored in the database under the entry number for each name with the following fields: source, page number and date. Further information gathered, which may be essential for identifying a name but which would be too voluminous to enter into the database, is the proprietor's name for each territory (when given), and also, when the source gives a list of place-names, the position of each name on the list. Such lists of place-names often reflect geographical proximity, and may recur several times in different sources. These criteria are used by the project members in compiling the lists of citations under each entry number. Because an ancient name may appear several times on the modern map with various additional elements such as Bridge, Hill, House, Lake, River, the database has been set up to interrelate such occurrences (127 names in county Down).

To save space in the database the titles of sources are each entered as a numeric code. Bibliographical details of each source and the corresponding codes are kept up to date on disc and supplied to each project members for speedy consultation while entering data into the computer. So far the project has used mainly primary sources (rather than books or articles about place-names), but already about 400 codes have been allocated. The reason for using numeric codes rather than abbreviations is because the computer can search numbers faster than letters. However, it became apparent that the page-number field could not be entirely numeric: many books distinguish between preface/appendix and text, or between page and section numbers by using both arabic and roman numbering, and one cannot convert everything to (arabic) numerals. The position is similar with regard to the 'date' field: one needs a character to express approximation and this cannot be a numeral. (For example, when it seems that a later survey has used a name list compiled at an earlier period.)

Historical references to names are first excerpted from the most name-rich sources, (mostly sixteenth-seventeenth century, but including earlier sources such as the Taxation of Ireland by Pope Nicholas, 1302-6). Administrative areas such as townlands are quite well documented in these sources, though names of rivers and hills are less frequently mentioned, usually only when the bounds of a territory are delineated. Where there are insufficient forms of a name documented, these have to be supplemented from occasional references in other early sources.

Many of the 2,684 county Down place-names on the 1:50,000 map now have a list of ten or more historical citations. From this point, after assessing the relationship between spelling and phonetics, the group can begin to identify the words originally used in coining the name, and from that its original meaning. The work of determining the original linguistic form of county Down names can then begin, though information on local pronunciation will have to be sought in difficult cases. The computer database has been set up with a special field to count the number of names on which work is complete. The working methods borrowed in part from the Place-name Office of the Ordnance Survey, Phoenix Park, Dublin, and in part evolved from 'learning by doing' seem to have stood the test of the first year. From county Down the Project intends to move on county by county, working next on county Armagh in 1988-89.

PART V
PLACE AND PEOPLE: AN HISTORICAL PERSPECTIVE

CHAPTER 15

A seventeenth-century 'political poem'

by

Michelle O'Riordan

In 1952 the scholar of Gaelic literature, Cecile O'Rahilly, edited poems in Irish from the period 1640-60 called *Five Seventeenth-Century Political Poems*,[1] and indeed that is what these poems appear to be. None of them has a specific title but they are generally known as follows:

1. Donnchadha Mac an Chaoilfhiaclaigh (Munster) 'Do frith monuar an uainsi ar Éirinn ...'
2. (Ulster) 'An Síogaí Romhánach'
3. Dáibhí Cúndún (Munster) 'Is buartha an cás so d'tárlaig Éire'
4. Seán Ó Conaill (Munster) 'Aiste Sheáin Uí Chonaill'/'Tuireamh na hÉireann'
5. Éamonn an Dúna, (Munster)'Mo lá leóin go deo go n-éagad'

Two other poems, not in O'Rahilly's collection, are of a similar style and could be classed with these poems, namely:

6. Séamus Carthún (Leinster ?) 'Deorchaoineadh na hÉireann'[2]
7. 'Do chuala scéal do chéas gach ló mé' (Munster)[3]

The poems are very similar in style, composition and content. They are all written in accentual metre. Each one deals with the disturbances which characterized the Irish political scene during the twenty years between 1640 and 1660. They number among the more well known and important items of Gaelic writing for the period. They also had a vigorous life in the manuscript tradition of the eighteenth and nineteenth centuries and the personal names and feats of valour and glory were often changed to suit the areas and times in which they were being transcribed.[4]

The poems can be broken down into three main parts. Each one opens with a spectacular lamentation, a description of the poet's utter desolation or, in the case of 'An Síogaí Romhánach', the apparition to the poet of a fairy woman who serves to introduce the burden of the poem. The main body of each poem is concerned with an extremely colourful description of the afflictions of Ireland in the course of the Eleven Years' War. Within this section each poet is at liberty to introduce great lists of Munster nobility, who were active in the wars. In 'Do frith monuar...', for instance, the poet contrasts the harmony in Ireland under the legendary kings and which ended with King James VI and I, with the legal chicanery he sees in the new regime. To do this he makes use of lists of legal terms and adapts them to his metre in order to produce an accentual list of rhetorical force. The author of 'An Síogaí Romhánach' eulogizes Eoghan Rua Ó Néill; 'Aiste Dháibhí Cúndún' describes the great defeats known to history and mythology and declares that the state of Ireland in the first half of the 1650s surpassed any of them in conditions of misery and devastation. Ireland's ruin is caused by the abandonment of the Nuncio and Glamorgan by those who accepted the 1646 Peace. In 'Tuireamh na hÉireann', the poet presents a synopsis of the history of mankind from the bible, and weaves in the history of Ireland up to the mid-seventeenth century. This history is based upon a list of battles, great lists of Anglo-Norman families of Leinster and Munster – and especially of the McCarthys of Munster – and a list of legal procedural jargon similar to that used in 'Do frith monuar' and of the same rhetorical effect.

The poem titled, 'Mo lá leóin go deo go n-éagad', is hailed by O'Rahilly as offering:

> no vague lament for the misfortunes of Ireland, but rather a detailed and vivid picture of the actual conditions of the life in Ireland during the period 1652-58.[5]

The ravages of war, described in biblical terms of sword, famine and plague, lists of legal restrictions, transportations and imprisonments, make up the bulk of the poem. Séamus Carthún's poem ('Deorchaoineadh na hÉireann') is particularly concerned to indicate the ruin of the church and the destruction of the nobility without mentioning anyone specifically. The final poem to be considered here is one which compares former power and glory with present destruction and humiliation. Each poem ends with a prayer that Ireland will be delivered from her afflictions, and occasionally with a prayer for the reinstatement of the leaders of whatever faction the author associates himself with. All bewail the unprecedented destruction of Ireland and the undermining of the integrity of her leading classes. All cite Gaelic and Old English lack of virtue in different areas as factors contributing to defeat. All provide some glorifed account of Gaelic pride and success before the latest disaster. Some of the poems are stylistically so similar as to be easily confused, one with another. Their structural and idiomatic similarities can conceal some interesting divergences of opinion and allegiance, evidenced in the individual poems. O'Rahilly prefaces the collection with the remark that the five poems in her collection give us '... the bone and marrow of the period 1640-1659'.[6] She suggests that while, as a rule, such material was 'vague and rhetorical'[7], these five poems are different, being 'detailed and informative', and having above all 'documentary' value. Because the language of the poetry is not that of the bardic schools, it is hailed by O'Rahilly as a populist breakthrough:

> The five poems were written by men of the people and not by the professional poets, and written for the people, not for the chosen few. Hence the language of the poems is full of dialect forms and borrowed English words already current in that speech.[8]

Her suggestion as to the literary pretensions of the authors is somewhat superficial:

> In four cases out of five, it is probable that the poem here edited was the sole production of the poet in question and that he had no pretensions to great literary merit. We should not look, then, in these compositions, for the poetic skill or intricacy of metre that may be found in a writer of great output and long experience.[9]

The impression conveyed by this evaluation of the authors is that of an anguished, spontaneous outpouring by 'ordinary' literate men who were driven to literary creativity by the unprecedented horrors of the time.

Much is made by historians of the witness these poems provide to the depredations surrounding the period immediately prior to, and including, the Interregnum.
The low spirits depicted in the poems are variously held to indicate the poets'
realization that Gaelic Ireland had seen her final battle; that God had finally
punished Ireland for her perfidy; that the disunity of her leaders sold out the country
to the enemy; that it was her fate to be finally overtaken thus.

The poem entitled 'An Síogaí Romhánach', usually translated as the 'Roman
Vision', is often used by historians as an expression of the Old Irish position in the
Eleven Years' War. This poem deals with the apparition to a grief-stricken visitor
to Rome, of a fairy woman who declaimed the poem in a transport of grief at the state
of Ireland between 1641-1653. It is the work of a devoted supporter of Eoghan Rua
Ó Néill and possibly written by a Franciscan who supported the Papal Nuncio
faction. O'Rahilly introduces the poem with this brief resumé:

> She [the fairy woman] tells briefly of events in Ireland from the Reformation to
> the execution of Charles I. Then comes the 'important part of the poem': an
> account of the Confederate War and of the exploits of Eoghan Rua Ó Néill.[10]

It is with this single statement: 'then comes the important part of the poem', that
O'Rahilly sets the tone for the analysis to which all of these poems have since been
subjected. This, according to O'Rahilly's evaluation, is where the 'documentary
value' of the poem begins. In O'Rahilly's words, the 'important' part of the poem
comes when the literary editor or the historian recognizes in the poem a personal
name, place name, law, act or crime.

Brian Ó Cuív, in his article 'The Irish language in the Early Modern Period',[11]
substantially agrees with O'Rahilly's evaluation of the accentual poems being
discussed here. And he is even more specific as to their importance as historical
rather than literary documents. Like O'Rahilly, he takes them together to represent
a factually realistic documentation of the feelings of 'the people' at the 'unprecedented sufferings of their fellow Irishmen'. In his analysis, Ó Cuív paraphrases
O'Rahilly's description when he says:

> [they are] vague, rhetorical and figurative in places, but they contain a consider-
> able amount of detailed reference and comment from the Old Irish side on such
> things as the operation of the court of wards, the star chamber, and the king's
> bench to the detriment of the Old Irish interests, the confiscations, the transplan-
> tations, the transportations of the Irish to the West Indies, the confederate wars
> ...[12]

Ó Cuív then exhalts Eoghan Rua Ó Néill to a position of prominence in the literature,
not borne out in the poems to which he refers: '... the exploits of Eoghan Rua Ó Néill,
who more than any man of his time was celebrated in Irish poetry...'[13] In fact Ó Néill
is mentioned in two of the seven poems under consideration here. 'An Síogaí
Romhánach' is practically devoted to him, and the poem attributed to Éamonn an
DEuna, 'Mo lá leóin go deo go n-éagad', of Munster provenance, mentions him in
one line – '... is Eoghan na gCath mac Airt Uí Néill t'fhior'.[14] Ó Cuív also attributes
relevance of some weight to other aspects of these poems taken in isolation – the
technical legal terms used in the poems indicates the spread of the English language
and is a reminder of the necessity of its mastery among Irishmen, '... who would
otherwise be at a disadvantage where legal processes were concerned ...'[15] The use
of terms like 'bodaigh an bhéarla' and 'brúscar an bhéarla' are taken to refer solely

to 'the influx of planters'.[16] Likewise, the historian, Nicholas Canny, in *Reformation to Restoration*, treats of these poems 'en masse', without individual reference or quotation. They are heaped together as one, the authors of which are said by Canny to have, without exception, applauded the Nuncio's sentence of excommunication and espoused what he sees as the catholic cause.[17]

This kind of analysis is no advance on that put forward by O'Rahilly in the 1950s. That, in itself, is no indictment – the merry-go-round of debunking and rebunking can be counter-productive. However, this particular kind of interpretation leads to a 'cul de sac' which fails to provide an adequate assessment of either the literary worth or historical relevance of such material. Historians have taken literateurs at their word where these poems are concerned, and literateurs have done the same for historians. The 'cul de sac' inhibits examination of these poems in any context other than that of the reaction of the Old Irish to the turmoil of the mid-seventeenth century. There is one exception; that is the work recently published by Tadhg Ó Dúshláine on the influence of continental baroque on Gaelic literature in the seventeenth century.[18] He emphasizes the influence of the devotional literature of the European Renaissance and Baroque on secular and devotional literature in Irish at that period. He draws particular parallels between the treatment of Ireland's wrongs by the poets and that by Agrippa d'Aubigné in 'Les Tragiques',[19] on the persecution of the Huguenots in France in the 1570s. He points out that the sack of Rome in 1527 brought forth great poems of lamentation from Bishop Stfileo,[20] who made use of the conceits of biblical plagues and famines to represent the turning of God's face away from his people. Rome has drawn this disaster upon herself, she is the Whore of Babylon, only repentance and God's forgiveness can return her to her former status. This poem and d'Aubigné's epic were among the most well-known examples of a form which was extremely popular throughout Europe in the late sixteenth century and reached a peak during the wars of religion.

Ó Dúshláine points out the similarity between the political poems in Ireland in the mid-seventeenth century, which were written under the literary influences of Europe and especially of the new devotional didactic techniques of the Counter-Reformation colleges, and the poetry written in the late Renaissance and early Baroque period in Europe. This makes for great areas of shared reference within a single literary genre. There is no need to suggest that the poets did not have a native idiom in which to articulate this kind of destruction, the interesting thing is the synthesis they were enabled to evolve by using traditional and continental motifs to indicate the turmoil. In his analysis of two devotional works, *Trí Bhior-ghaoithe an Bháis*, and *Eochair-sgaith an Aifrinn*, and a cursory analysis of the continental influence on the political poems of the seventeenth century, Ó Dúshláine makes it very clear that a vast area of reference and context was left out of the interpretations offered by Ó Cuív and O'Rahilly. I would like to draw attention to a third source of comparison.

O'Rahilly, who consulted Hardiman's edition of the 'Roman Vision', makes no mention of a very helpful footnote in his version in *Irish Minstrelsy*, which was published in 1831, which draws the readers' attention to an English seventeenth-century work:

> The poet Cowley's 'Discourse by way of Vision', concerning the government of Oliver Cromwell, will convey to the English reader an idea of the poetic machinery adopted by the Irish bards in many of their effusions, and of which the present poem affords an example.[21]

Hardiman was right to suggest Cowley as a likely source of comparison. Abraham Cowley was probably nearly contemporary with our 'seventeenth-century political poets'. He was born in London in 1618 and his first collection of poetry came out in 1633. In 1636 he went to Cambridge, graduating with a Master of Arts degree in 1643. In 1646 his satire, 'The Puritan and the Papist' was published. He spent ten years abroad working as secretary to Lord Jermyn who was in France on behalf of Henrietta Maria. He was arrested and detained for some time in 1655, being bailed for £1,000. He died in 1667, and lies at Westminster Abbey near Chaucer and Spenser. In 1679 his 'Poem on the Late Civil War' was finally published.[22]

He was a particular friend of Lord Falkland and includes a minor elegy on him within the 'Civil War' poem.[23] Cowley's especial duty, according to a biographical note written by his friend Thomas Sprat, was to maintain the correspondence between Charles I and Henrietta Maria. His biographer mentions the two distinct spheres of his poetic activity; the university and the court.[24] Cowley's writings show the influence of both. He was a classical scholar, a Doctor of Physics and a diplomatic civil servant. Above all, perhaps, he was a royalist and an Anglo-Catholic. Some suspected him of having what they called 'Romish tendencies', which indeed he had, but they remained tendencies. Cowley's writings were very popular immediately after his own period and he achieved some favour with the Augustans; with Addison, Pope, Johnson, Cowper and even Coleridge, Marvell, Milton and Pope were pleased to reveal his influence on their writing in some very near paraphrasis they employed.[25]

Ardent royalist and high-churchman though he was, Cowley was numbered among Milton's three favourite poets. He is immediately distinguishable from our seven poets in that first, we know considerably more about him; not least that his words are of assured authority. Second, he was not a clergyman nor an agent of the Counter-Reformation. Third, he was not a propagandist for the Old Irish position, a supporter of the Nuncio or of Eoghan Rua Ó Néill. Three substantial works of Cowley's deal with the immediate Civil War period in England, namely; 'The Puritan and the Papist', a satire published in 1646; an essay in verse and prose called 'A Discourse by way of Vision concerning the government of Oliver Cromwell', published in 1661; and a 'Poem on the Late Civil War' published in 1679.

Yet Cowley's works are not called upon to bear the burden of royalist opinion in the mid-seventeenth century. Cowley, as a professional civil servant and royalist activist must be credited with near knowledge of puritans, papists, the intricacies of the Civil War, and with the inner workings of Cromwell's regime. It is to be remembered also that he spent ten years from 1644-1654 out of England and so was not a first hand witness of what he so graphically describes in his poems.[24] It might also be remembered that there is no evidence whatsoever to suggest whether the authors of the Irish poems were in or out of the country during the same decade, nor any indication as to whether they witnessed those events for which they provide such documentary evidence. Indeed, the one poem for which some information relating to the author exists is that of Séamus Carthún. Ironically, this Franciscan priest belonged to the anti-Nuncio faction and supported the peace of 1646, and that of 1648 and, while in prison he endeavoured to convert others to his way of thinking. None of this information can be gleaned from his poem.[27]

Those who are assured, however, of the 'documentary' value of the seven Irish poems, and of their reflection of the actual circumstances and feelings of the Old Irish faction, might consider some of the 'evidence' supplied in Cowley's poem, the 'Civil War'. He wrote the bulk of this poem while the cavaliers were enjoying more victories than not, but he continues into the period of their change of fortune which is covered by the third book of the poem. Cowley suppressed this poem when the Commonwealth was established, because, as he said himself: 'It is uncustomary, as to become almost ridiculous, to make laurels for the Conquered ...'[28] and though it was proper to apply his pen for the good of his faction during the war, when it has been lost; '... and the unaccountable will of God has determined the controversie, and that we have submitted to the conditions of the Conqueror, we must lay down pens as well as arms...'[29] It is not surprising that Cowley, like the Irish poets, begins his poem with great colour and clamour:

> What rage does England from itself divide
> More than the seas doe from all the world beside?
> [The Civil War, lines 1-2]

He too begins with a long list of England's former glories, starting with Henry II's subjection of Rory O'Connor in the twelfth century. He exalts the last sixteen years of Charles' reign as a period of glorious happiness. He then launches into a description of the activities of prominent members of the nobility and aristocracy on the various fields of battle. His information seems to have been distilled from accounts in the royalist newspaper, *Mercurius Aulicus*.[30] Naturally, it often differs quite substantially from events as related in the parliamentary paper, *Mercurius Britannicus*. Cowley's special heroes were Charles I, Lucius Cary, Lord Falkland and Henry Spencer, Earl of Sutherland. Predictably, the enemy were all base-born, and it is with the intention to indicate the low birth of the enemy that he claims that:

> ... we must pay,
> One honest man for ten such slaves as they ...
> Streams of black-tainted blood the field besmeare
> But pure wel-colour'd Drops shine here and there ...
> [Civil War, p. 60]

It is with the same intention to distinguish high-born friends from low-born enemies that the poet Éamonn an Dúna makes a specific distinction between the perpetrators of the depredations of the Gaill, when he qualifies Gaill thus:

> Ní Gaill uaisle luaim san méid si,
> atáid gan chúis acht cúrsa an éigin;
> gérbh éigean dóibh don fhórsa géille,
> bíon a bpáirt do ghnáth le Séarlas.
> Acht sluaite Chromuil chuthuig chraosuig
> [*Five Seventeenth Century Political Poems* no. 5, lines 305-309, p. 96]

Cowley concludes the first book of the 'Civil War' with a prayer to God to teach the rebels a lesson. He begins his second book by likening the war to a deluge, plunging down from the north.[31] Essex's difficulties at Oxford in 1642 when all his troops were cast down with illness, is exulted in by Cowley as God's punishment on them. He omits to mention that Charles' troops in Oxford were also similarly smitten.[32] He devotes over one hundred lines to a description of the former rebels and traitors who filled the rank and file of Satan's legions in hell gladly awaiting fresh numbers from among the parliamentarians. And Cowley suggests that:

But of all lands though they send millions in
More bountiful than Albion none hath bin.
[*Civil War*, pp. 100-102]

Charles I has not been the only sovereign to suffer treachery, and the poet is able to present another potted history of rebels through the ages. So low and vulgar are the parliamentarian crowd, filled with mechanics, 'noisy ranting divines', 'greedy tradesmen', 'hot-brained calvinists' and 'firey Knoxes', that Cowley would rather rejoin Rome than be associated with them:

If such foule Waters the famed Lake containe,
Lets rather drink old Tyber's Flood again,
Let our great Thames pay homage as before
Rather than new and worser streams adore.
[*Civil War*, pp. 108-109]

Neither could he bring himself to name the dead rebels:

low wretched names, unfit for noble verse.
[*Civil War*, p. 117]

There are colonels, sailors, drunken Dutchmen, villains, butchers, carriers and weavers. The spleen of the Irish poets, directed against the Cromwellian rabble – 'brúscar an bhéarla' and 'bodaigh an bhéarla' – and not, of course, against noble royalists, could hardly be more pointed than that of the royalist Cowley whose own countrymen they were. The Irish poets did not need to be bound to the nuncio's cause to spew invective at the parliamentarians, no great Old Irish zeal was needed to carry the conceit of the genre in which they wrote. Cowley was no nuncioist. He echoes the hatred of Séamus Carthún and Éamonn an Duna and of the author of 'Do chuala scéal ...' for the sects when he says:

The Independents their two thousand sent
Who into rags the seamless vesture rent
In whose proud churches may at once be seen
more popes than have at Rome since Peter been.
[*Civil War*, p. 109]

And Cowley takes this poetic excuse to indulge in a diatribe against the various heresies and sects since the earliest times of Christianity. In this, he employs the same style as the Irish poets of the great lists of names and cryptic synopsis of the characteristics of those he seeks to castigate. Like the Irish poets, he casually skips over the subtleties and presents a black-and-white picture. In the middle of book three, the fortunes of the royalists begin to flag, and Cowley's work takes on an even more familiar tone:

[God] some conquest to his host did send
…
He mixed at once his Justice and his love
punished our sins, yet did our cause approve.
[*Civil War*, p. 117]

So Cowley, too, discovered that the sins of the royalists occasioned God's wrath and compassed their defeats. The noble leaders could hardly be numbered personally among those so punished, so in order to account for the death of his hero, the Earl of Sutherland, Cowley chooses to suggest that God called him from the squalor of the battlefield, where parliamentarians died brutish deaths. He chose him from out of the royalist army, and spared him the gory and valourless deaths which infighting and sickness inflicted on unnamed hordes of base parliamentarians. The author of 'An Síogaí Romhánach' subscribed to the same consoling belief in accounting for the death of his hero Eoghan Rua Ó Néill; no Cromwellian compassed his demise, rather God saw fit to carry him to heaven:

> Act gidh crádh liom a thásg san d'éisteacht
> liom níu cás a bhás ar aonchor
> 's nach le Gallaibh do gearradh a shaoghal
> acht is Dia lér mhian a shaoradh
> is gairm go neamh i measg na naomh air.
> [*Five seventeenth-century political poems*, No. 2, p. 26-27]

Cowley devotes a couple of hundred lines to the death of Falkland, and continues the conceit of God's righteous wrath, imploring him to end the fighting, since the loss of Falkland alone should expiate royalist sins:

> Yet gracious God stop here thine hand
> And let this losse excuse our perishing land
> ...
> Think on our sufferings, and sheath then again
> Our sinnes are great, but Falkland too is slaine.
> [*Civil War*, p. 124]

At this stage, Charles I had not yet been beheaded.

Having supressed his 'Civil War' during the period of the Commonwealth, Cowley found a single individual upon whom to place the blame for the chaos of the Civil War and the barbarity of the Interregnum after Oliver Cromwell's death. Like the author of 'An Síogaí Romhánach'; he is visited as in a dream. But his experience is with a malign spirit who attempts to justify Cromwell. Cowley employs this conceit to damn Cromwell in most unrelenting terms. The 'Discourse' is a mixture of poetry and prose, and the verse parts follow a structure similar to that of the 'Civil War' and of the Irish poems, in that he contrasts the formerly happy state of England with the distress and upheaval of the war and its aftermath. Again, God is called upon to save the unhappy country from shipwreck. The use of 'shipwreck' as a metaphor for the destruction of the state and the nobility is one with which readers of Dáibhí Ó Bruadair are familiar:

> Yet Mighty God, yet, yet, we humbly crave,
> This floating Isle from shipwreck save.
> ['Discourse', p. 345]

Cowley speaks of Cromwell's claim to reform religion, only to 'rob it even to the very skin',[33] of his usurpation of three kingdoms 'without any shadow of the least pretensions and to govern them as unjustly as he got them.[34] In as far as the Irish poets described the damage and devastation of Ireland during the wars – and Carthún describes a scene of utter desolation and ruin – so too did Cowley describe plagues worse than those of Egypt, rivers of blood, storms and hail-shot, ulcers, sores, darkness, decimated herds, a proliferation of sects, vermin and greedy troops.[35] The castigation of the parliamentarian forces as particularly avaricious is interesting in this context, since Canny sees mention of this in Irish poems as being in contrast to the legendary generosity and spendthrift ways of the Gaelic chiefs.

It is, perhaps, in the two final verses of the 'Discourse' that Cowley's work indicates the universality of the themes and conceits that characterized contemporary learned polemical poetry. Dáibhí Cúndún in the poem, 'Is buartha an cás so ...' in which he presents a huge list of historical catastrophes, none of which is comparable to those experienced by Ireland in the throes of the Eleven Years' War, concludes by saying that he would rather lie senseless and motionless with closed eyes and no thoughts, while Ireland suffered her present anguish, until God's grace saw fit to release her from this punishment. Ó Cuív, Canny and O'Rahilly are pleased to let this kind of literary polemical rhetoric carry the burden of the Old Irish/Counter-Reformation inspired reaction to the destruction of the Gaelic world in this period. What, therefore, can be said of Cowley's verses, who in this poetic extravagance, wished England sunk beneath the sea, and declared that the earlier conquests made of her by Romans, Normans, and Danes were as nought compared with this latest shame:

> Come eleventh Plague, rather than this should be
> Come sink us rather in the Sea
> Come rather pestilence and reap us down;
> Come God's sword rather than our own
> let rather Roman come again
> or Saxon, Norman, or the Dane.
>   ['Discourse' p. 353]

Just as each of the Irish poems called for the repentance of Ireland to assuage God's wrath and effect a return to the status quo, so Cowley too:

> Let some denouncing Jonas first be sent
> to try if England can repent ...
>   ['Discourse'.p. 353]

So the question can be posed, do the Irish poems reflect the last heartfelt dying complaints of the Old Irish, are they didactic diatribes for the Counter-Reformation or are they royalist polemical tracts. The same three questions are equally applicable to Cowley. He was certainly not a Counter-Reformation apologist, nor was he a propagandist for the Old Irish postition. While no definitive answer is possible for these questions, a definitive answer is not the immediate object of the question, but rather the re-examination of this material outside the perimeters imposed on it by a historiography determined to tie loose ends at any cost.

It is appropriate to suggest that the frames of reference in which the seven Irish poems have been studied are straight-jackets which distort them, rather than frames which display them to advantage. Tadhg Ó Dushláine's work which concentrates on the biblical imagery and the influence of the continental schools of rhetoric and invention, is of immense importance in re-shaping the context of the Irish poems.

It highlights the clerical character of the learning displayed in them and effectively demolishes their superficial attribution to the mythical 'men of the people'. Cowley's poems illustrate that at the literary polemical level, the more overtly 'political' parts of these poems – references to battles, Cromwell, parliamentarians – and the whole world of English, Irish and Scots politics which came together so tragically in those two decades, are a pastiche, employed by men who brought their individual cultural flavours to a common style of articulation, while they articulated a common distress at similar historical experiences, which had vastly different individual consequences, for the men and their countries.

CHAPTER 16

Irish travellers in the Norse world

by

Rosemary Power

The Norse presence in Ireland between the eighth and eleventh centuries has received a fair amount of attention in recent years, in particular since the excavations at Wood Quay in Dublin. The Vikings, pirates who harried the coasts of Ireland, and other parts of Europe, have always enjoyed a certain popularity, while the activities of the Norse as traders and settlers have increasingly become a focus of academic attention. In Ireland the Norse were known as 'Gaill', foreigners, until that name became attributed to the Norman invaders of 1169. The Norse had been assimilated into Irish society well before this date, though as 'Ostmen' they were to retain a separate legal identity as late as the fourteenth century. The presence of the Norse is well recorded in sources from Ireland and neighbouring lands, and by the Norse themselves. Records were initially in oral tradition, or were carved in stone or wood. In the late twelfth and thirteenth centuries, the oral traditions came to be used as a basis for written works, when the inhabitants of one Nordic land in particular, Iceland, began to produce the 'sagas' or histories, and similar accounts, of their own ancestors, of the Orkney earls, and of the kings of Norway. The historical value of the sagas has been much debated, though their literary value has been frequently acclaimed. Those sagas which relate events of the Viking Age are the equivalent of fairly good 'historical novels', while those relating events that took place nearer to the time of writing conform more closely to our concepts of history, though everything is, of course, recorded from the Norse perspective.

There are a number of references in the sagas to events taking place in Ireland, and even more references to events taking place in the Hebrides, which the Norse recognized as culturally, though not politically, related to Ireland. In addition, the sagas contain accounts of Irish or Hebridean people who for various reasons found themselves in those lands of the north Atlantic which came to be settled by the Norse.

The Norse began to settle Iceland in the late eighth century, not long after they had settled the Faroe Islands. Some of the leaders belonged to families of second or third generation Irish or Western Isles settlers who had inter-married with the local people. In the leaders' households were wives, small farmers and slaves, many of whom were of Gaelic origin. This can be seen from the personal names recorded in the main account of the settlement, the *Book of Settlements*,[1] written in Iceland in the late twelfth century and based on earlier works.

Norse explorers of the 860s found the south-east coast of Iceland already inhabited by small numbers of Irish monks. The *Book of Icelanders*, a short account of the settlement, originally written shortly after 1120, explains that before Iceland

127

was settled by the Norse, '... there were Christians here whom the Norse call *papar*, but they went away because they did not wish to live here with heathens, and they left behind Irish books and bells and croziers: from this it can be understood that they were Irishmen'.[2] The work of the Irish cleric, Dicuil, who wrote in about 825, corroborates this. He describes what are clearly the Faroe Islands, on which he says Irish monks had lived for about a hundred years, but which were in his own time deserted due to the depredations of the Vikings. He then turns his attention to Thule, the name given by ancient writers to a Northern land, and used by the English scholar, Bede, for Iceland. Of Thule, Dicuil says

> It is now thirty years since priests who lived on that island from the first day of February to the first day of August told me that not only at the summer solstice, but in the days on either side of it, the setting sun hides itself at the evening hour as if behind a little hill, so that no darkness occurs during that very brief period of time, but whatever task a man wishes to perform, even to picking the lice out of his shirt, he can manage it precisely as in broad daylight. And had they been on a high mountain, the sun would at no time have been hidden from them.[3]

Dicuil is clearly referring to the south coast of Iceland, and it is in the south-east of the country that names containing the element 'papa-', from the Norse name for the monks, can still be found.[4] Archaeological evidence from the Faroe Islands gives further proof of the presence of Irish hermits before the arrival of the Vikings. No archaeological evidence has been discovered in Iceland itself. However, while there is no doubt of the presence of monks in Iceland before the Norse settlement, there is no evidence to support a belief held among some in Iceland today that there was a regular Irish settlement on the island which was wiped out or enslaved by the Norse. This belief, though not widespread, provides an interesting parallel to recent attempts to create a fanciful history of the 'Cruithin' as 'original' inhabitants of the north-east of Ireland.

The first permanent Norse settlers in Iceland are said to have been two foster-brothers, Ingólfr and Hjörleifr, who arrived in the autumn of 870. Ingólfr wintered on the south coast, and in the spring sent out search parties to find the pillars of his high seat which, in ritual fashion, he had thrown overboard on his approach to land. They were found where Reykjavík now stands, and there he settled, at one of the island's few good harbours.

Hjörleifr was less fortunate. When his ship approached land that autumn it had been driven west of Ingólfr's. When the crew ran out of water, ten Irish slaves on board kneaded together flour and butter to quench their thirst, calling the dough 'minthak' (Irish 'menadach'). They acted needlessly, for the rain came, and they were able to collect water from the sails. The dough started to go mouldy and was thrown overboard. It was later washed ashore at a place subsequently named after it. The ship came to land and the crew wintered on the south coast. In the spring Hjörleifr decided to sow some crops, and had his slaves harnessed to the plough. The slaves killed him and his male followers, and fled to the islands off the south-west coast. When Ingólfr heard of his foster-brother's death, he pursued the slaves and slew them on the islands, which have since been known as the *Vestmannaeyjar*, the Isles of the Westmen, that is, of the Irish.[5]

It is hard to determine the degree of truth in a tale like this. The islands may have got their name because Irish monks lived there, or because Irish who came with the Norse settled there. However, the story indicates that Irish people who had experience of survival at sea came with the Norse, willingly or otherwise. One of the slaves was named Dufthakr, in Irish, Dubhthach.

Other settlers followed, of whom we are told that they were Irish, or who had followers with Irish names, or who were followers of Christianity, which often indicates Gaelic influence. This latter group was of considerable interest to Icelandic historians who were writing well into the Christian period, and who were pleased to have evidence of Christian practice by people of social standing during the Norse settlement. At this stage it seems to have been a personal matter, and did not indicate the influence of mainstream European civilisation.

While the majority of settlers were heathen, there were some of mixed persuasion, like Helgi the Lean, whose mother was Rafarta, daughter of Kjarval, king of the Irish, sometimes identified with Cearbhall of Ossory. Helgi himself was raised in Ireland and the Hebrides. He believed in Christ, but invoked Thor on sea voyages and in tight corners. However, he called his new home in Iceland, *Kristnes*, Christ-ness.[6] His sister-in-law, Audr the Deeply-Wealthy, was a more decided follower of Christianity. The widow of Óláfr the White, a Norse king of Dublin, she sailed with an entourage to Iceland from the Hebrides, and married off two daughters on the way. On arriving, she sailed slowly north-west around the coast, looking for a suitable place to settle. Once she had found a satisfactory place, she made claim to large tracts of land which she divided amongst her followers. She raised a farm of her own and lived in state. When she died she was, at her own request, buried below the shore-line because 'she would not lie in the earth with heathens'. Among the Christians in her entourage must be numbered a slave named Myrgjöl, (Irish Muirgheal – Sea-White), the daughter, we are told, of an Irish king, and her son Erpr, whose father was a Scots earl, and to whom Audr gave his freedom.

A less aristocratic settler than Audr, who was also eager to preserve his religion in his new country, was Ørlygr Hrappsson, who in spite of his Norse name was, we are told by the saga-writer, Irish on both sides of his family. He had a Hebridean foster-father, a Bishop Patrekr (Patrick), who is not known in other sources. Before Ørlygr left for Iceland, Patrekr gave him consecrated earth to place under the corner-pillar of his new church, a missal, and a consecrated church bell. Patrekr also described the place in which Ørlygr should settle, though when Ørlygr drew near land he threw his high-seat pillars overboard in good Norse fashion. While at sea Ørlygr was caught in a storm, and, calling on Bishop Patrekr, he promised to name after him the place where he landed. He duly landed at the head of a fjord on the west coast which he named Patreksfjördr, and spent the winter there. In the spring he set out again and found and settled on the land described to him by Bishop Patrekr. We are told that Ørlygr and his family followed the Irish saint Columcille, who in some manuscripts is given his Irish name, while others use the Latin form, Columba.[8] It is impossible to determine whether Patreksfjördr is indeed named after an otherwise unknown bishop, or whether an early settler named it after Ireland's national saint. We are told, however, that the missal and bell which Patrekr is said to have given Ørlygr still existed in the later thirteenth century. The missal, like other missals in medieval Iceland, was written in what are called 'Irish letters', though this may mean no more than in insular script, the script which was, under English influence, initially used in Icelandic works. It would also have been known from works imported during the Middle Ages.

Not far from the devout Christian Ørlygr, settled a devout heathen Thórólfr, who built a temple beneath the holy mountain, Helgafell, on Snaefellsnes, on which sanctuary was given to beast and human, and towards which no one might look unwashed.[9] There seems to have been no friction.

There is a story in the *Book of Settlements* of an Irish monk, Ásólfr, who came to live in Iceland during the period of Norse settlement, though, as he is named as having descendants, he may have arrived as a settler and later took to an eremitical life. However, in the *Book of Settlements*, his arrival is modelled on the arrival at an earlier date of the *papar*. He is said to have been the son of a couple named Edna (Eithne) and Kónall (Conall). He came to Iceland and settled in a lonely place. He would have no dealings with heathens, and would not accept food from them. He was fed miraculously on fish from a nearby stream. When word of this got around he was driven away. The fish disappeared from the stream while the waterfall beside Ásólfr's new home was discovered to be full of fish. Again Ásólfr had to move, but then settled in peace. His memory must have remained alive in Iceland during the 130 years it was largely heathen, for after the conversion to Christianity a church was built at his grave. There is no reference to a local cult of him surviving or being created, however, in spite of the need for local saints in the newly converted land.

One version of the *Book of Settlements* gives an account of the dedication of his church, which indicates that, in death, Ásólfr was as vindictive as any living Irish saint or Norse ghost. He came in a dream to a dairymaid on the farm by his grave to complain that she wiped her feet on his gravemound. On his command she told the farmer, Halldórr, of her dream. He dismissed it as nonsense. Ásólfr then appeared in a dream to a certain monk who consequently went to Halldórr, bought the gravemound, dug up the bones and took them away with him. The next night Ásólfr appeared in a dream to Halldórr and threatened to tear his eyes out if he did not buy back the bones for the price he had received. Halldórr duly did so, had a shrine made and the bones placed on the altar of the church. Ásólfr troubled him no more.[10] We are told too that Ásólfr's uncle, Jörundr, the brother of Edna, also settled in Iceland, and that he became a hermit in his old age.[11]

In spite of these, and other references indicating the influence of Irish Christianity in Iceland at the beginning of the Norse settlement, we are told that the actual practice of Christianity died out. It seems likely that its influence remained, however, perhaps because of the experience of Icelandic traders abroad, for in the year 1000 it became the country's religion by the decision of the parliament. The decision was made without violence and provided for heathens to practice their religion in private. Few seem to have availed of the provisions made and they were revoked after a few years without arousing rancour. In the early eleventh century a number of wandering bishops reached Iceland, at least one of whom was Irish.

Slaves were a major item of the farming and trading economy. Many of the slaves seem to have been captured as adults, for it seems that the children of slaves were often exposed at birth rather than reared. We hear too of a number of slaves who had been born free and were discontented at their changed status. In Iceland slaves were often freed and given land to farm, and slavery died out in the eleventh century, probably for economic reasons.

One of the stories in *Laxdaela saga* tells of how a man named Höskuldr bought a woman slave in Denmark, paying a high price for her although she appeared to be dumb. In Iceland he had a child with her, and one day discovered her secretly talking with her son. She was, she admitted, Melkorka, the daughter of an Irish king, M'yrkjartan (Muirchertach). The strained relations between her and Höskuldr's wife worsened after this revelation and Höskuldr provided her with a farm of her own, and, we can assume, her freedom. Melkorka stayed in Iceland, but her son, Óláfr, travelled to Ireland as an adult. He was storm-driven to a strange part of the coast, far from the towns and harbours where foreigners could land in peace. An attempt was made by the local people to take the ship from the Norsemen, but when Óláfr and another man addressed them in Irish, they agreed to bring the matter to the king, who was, conveniently, Óláfr's grandfather. Óláfr made himself known, fought in local wars for his grandfather, and returned to Iceland laden with honour.[12] While there is no Irish corroboration of the existence of Melkorka or Óláfr, there was an Irish Muirchertach at the time that Óláfr is thought to have visited Ireland, the 950s. This was Muirchertach son of Congalach, the heir-designate of Tara, slain by his brother, Domnall, king of Brega in 964. Their father, Congalach, king of Knowth, was high-king of Ireland until his death in 956. If the identification is correct, it would mean that at the time of her abduction Melkorka was the granddaughter rather than the daughter of an Irish king. An alternative identification of her father is with Muirchertach Leathercloaks, king of Cenél nÉogain, who died in 943, but if the saga's chronology is correct, he lived too early to have been the person in question.[13]

There are a number of other stories concerning Gaelic settlers, and a considerable number of the people named in the *Book of Settlements* and the sagas possessed Gaelic names. These sources have as yet been little used by Irish linguists or social historians. The names include N´jall (Niall), Kjartan (Ceartán), Kormákr (Cormac), Kjarval (Cearbhall) and Brjánn or Brjám (Brian). In addition, a small number of Gaelic words found their way into Icelandic. Like the personal names, in most cases they correspond better to Classical than to Old Irish forms. As well as *papar*, Old Irish singular *popa*, the name given to the hermits, two other words come from Latin originals: *bagall*, Irish *bachall*, Latin *baculum*, crozier; and *bjannak*, Irish *beannacht*, Latin *benedictio*, blessing. There is also *kapall*, Irish *capall*, horse. A few words are domestic: as well as *minthak*, Old Irish *menadach*, the dough used for quenching thirst at sea, we have *brekan*, Old Irish *breccán*, later *breacán*, striped cloth; *lámr*, Irish *lámh*, hand, in Iceland also paw; *skjadak*, from Irish *sceathach*, *sceitheach*, an adjective meaning nauseating, in Iceland, sour beer; *tarfr*, Irish *tarbh*, bull, in Iceland, steer; *thúst*, *súst*, Irish *suíste*, flail. A possible borrowing is in *fjargvidrast*, to become furious, where the first element may be the Irish *fearg*, anger. The relationship between Icelandic *slavak*, a type of chickweed, and Irish *sleabhac*, an edible seaweed, is unclear. A few loanwords are found only in Norse poetry: *lind*, Irish *lind*, *linn*, pool; *korki*, Irish *coirce*, oats; *dine*, Irish *tine*, fire; *bjöd*, Irish *bith*, *bioth*, land, world. In a thirteenth-century Norwegian description of Ireland we find *gelt*, from Irish *gelt/geilt*, mad. In Iceland the expression *verda ad gjalti* (dative), to become mad, remains current. Faroese too, which was largely unwritten until the nineteenth century, has retained a number of Gaelic words and expressions. In Iceland there are in addition several place-names which contain Gaelic personal names.[14]

More difficult to pin-point is the Gaelic influence on the folklore and literature of Iceland. There are a few stories which are apparently derived from tales transmitted to Iceland, probably during the Viking Age. These perhaps include versions of 'The King of the Cats is dead' (AT 113A) and some stories of the enchantment of one person by another. A few tales concerning a delightful otherworld may also show Gaelic influence, though in these, as in other Norse tales, the otherworld is placed to the north of Scandinavia. To the west, the Icelanders knew, lay other, geographically identifiable, lands.

These lands were Greenland and the coast of North America. The south-west coast of Greenland was settled from Iceland at the end of the tenth century. The land was deserted when the Norse arrived, but they found evidence that it had previously been inhabited by a people they identified with the North American natives, but who were in fact Inuit, Eskimoes, of the Dorset culture. Later the Norse were to become increasingly and often violently involved with the Inuit Thule people, who moved south as the climate worsened. There is no evidence that Irish monks reached Greenland, though it would not have been particularly difficult for them to have done so.

The Norse colony was scattered and probably never numbered more than about three thousand, but it survived until about 1515, in spite of a worsening climate, drift ice, lack of timber for ship-building, bad relations with the Thule people, and the loss of contact with the mother country, Norway, in the mid-fourteenth century. In the early years of the Norse settlement, when the prospects were still relatively bright, the Greenlanders attempted to explore and settle the areas of North America which they named Slabland, Forestland and Wineland. These attempts, made in about the year 1000, failed, though the Greenlanders seem to have made sporadic visits there for centuries.

Both Greenland and America were discovered by Norse travellers storm-driven beyond their intended destinations, but it was believed, at least by the saga-writers, and probably also by the people of the Viking Age, that the Irish were in America first. In the *Book of Settlements* we find the following account of an Icelander named Ari Másson.

> He was storm-driven to the Land of White Men; some call it Ireland the Great; it lies west in the ocean near Wineland the Good; it is said to be six days sailing west of Ireland. Ari was not allowed to leave and was baptised there. This story was first told by Hrafn the Limerick's-farer, who had been a long time in Limerick in Ireland. So too said Thorkell Gellisson, that Icelanders who had heard it from Earl Thorfinnr in the Orkneys, said that Ari had been converted in the Land of White Men, and did not get to leave, and yet was well treated there.[15]

While we may suspect that Hrafn the Limerick's-farer had listened to stories of Saint Brendan during his long sojourn in Ireland, the author of the *Book of Settlements* accepted his account, and provided an additional reference in the report said to emanate from Earl Thorfinnr. The author follows his usual practice of giving the sailing time needed to reach one land from another. The 'Land of White Men' is one of the names given in Irish to the otherworld, while 'Ireland the Great' corresponds to 'Sweden the Great', the name the Norse gave to the half-known regions which are now part of northern Russia.

Two short sagas describe the settlement of Greenland and the exploration of North America. In one of these, the *Saga of Eirik the Red*[15], the visiting Norse are told by the native Americans that near their own country is another, inhabited by men 'who wore white clothes, and carried before them staffs to which were attached cloths, and they shouted loudly; and people think that this was the Land of White Men, or Ireland the Great'.

In another saga, *Eyrbyggja saga*, a notable Icelander known as Björn Breidvïkin-gakappi disappeared while abroad. Many years later, a certain Gudleifr, who came from the same part of Iceland, went trading in Dublin. On his way home, sailing west of Ireland, he was blown far out to sea. His ship finally came to an unknown land.

The local inhabitants, who, the Norse believed, spoke Irish, took them captive. A debate seemed to ensue as to whether to kill or enslave the captives. Their leader arrived. He addressed the captives in Norse, and when he found where Gudleifr came from, he questioned him closely about events in his part of Iceland. The leader refused to name himself, because, he said, he did not want his relatives to try to visit him, as the country had poor harbours, and the rulers included many other chieftains hostile to foreigners and more powerful than himself. He gave the Norse certain items which later indicated that he was the lost Björn Breidvíkingakappi. He then let them leave, and they arrived back in Ireland later that autumn.[17]

In the first two of these accounts of the Irish in America the influence may be detected of the *Navigatio Sancti Brendani*, which was translated into the vernacular in Iceland during the twelfth century.[18] The *Eyrbyggja saga* account appears to represent a local Icelandic version of the tradition. No doubt the memory of the *papar* in Iceland, combined with other tales heard in Ireland and along the western seaboard of Europe, also provided a basis for the legends. In Iceland itself tales of new lands to the west are found, for example in the annals of 1285. Four year later the Norwegian king sent a man named Hrólfr to Iceland to gather men for an expedition there, but it seems that this never took place.[19] There are tales of a *Frisland*, to the south of Iceland, throughout the medieval period.

These later references do not concern the Irish. Interest in these islands waned after 1265, when Norway ceded the Hebrides and the Isle of Man to Scotland. The English visitors to Iceland after this date may have had Irish companions, but they were not recognized as such. The main period of contact was during the Viking Age, and after 1265, Ireland, always peripheral to the Norse, faded out of the popular imagination. Only a mild interest remained, which has revived in the last century, due to increased travel and the growth of an academic profession.

CHAPTER 17

New horizons in Hiberno-English studies
by
Patricia Kelly

A marked tendency in many areas of Irish Studies in recent times has been a growing uneasiness with an exclusively Irish perspective in research. This is reflected in a recently-published introduction to the field, which explicitly rejects a preoccupation with 'the "uniqueness" of the Irish experience', and aims rather to interpret that experience in a European or global framework.[1] The field of Hiberno-English (HE) studies, having as its subject matter the non-standard varieties of English spoken on this island, might however at first sight seem unamenable to such revisionism, and open to the criticism of insularity or even parochialism. This was once a valid charge, as can be seen by a glance at the bibliography to P.L. Henry's *An Anglo-Irish Dialect of County Roscommon* (Dublin), 1957): it contains no more than thirty-one works on HE, and over half of these are mere collections of very local words, the majority by Irish authors. Thirty years on, however, the province of enquiry of HE studies extends beyond the confines of this island. It also now attracts researchers not just from Ireland, but from Great Britain, Europe and North America, and articles on HE appear in prestigious periodicals such as the British *Journal of Linguistics* and the American *Language*. New lines of investigation are calling some long-held views into question and opening up perspectives for future research. This paper aims to survey some of these recent developments, and especially to show how they relate to the international discipline of linguistics, both descriptive and theoretical.

1. Descriptive Methods

Henry's 1957 study was a milestone in the development of the field, but at the time of publication was peripheral to both Irish and English schools of linguistics. In Ireland, linguistic research was focused almost exclusively on Irish, and Henry's description of the phonology, morphology and syntax of a small geographical area had more in common with the long tradition of dialect studies in Irish than with any similar investigations into English dialects. In England, the prestige of Standard English hampered the development of dialectology, whereas in Irish the lack of a standard furthered it. The main methodological component in Henry's work was German dialectology, in which he had been trained by Eugen Dieth in Zurich in the late 1940s. Again, it was to Irish that this methodology was first applied on a large scale in Ireland, in Heinrich Wagner's *Linguistics Atlas and Survey of Irish Dialects* (Dublin, 1958-1969).

It was not until the mid 1970s that a comparable survey of Irish English was begun: fieldwork on the Belfast-based Tape-recorded Survey of Hiberno-English Speech (TRS) is still in progress, but the first analyses of results appeared as early as 1981.[2] While the TRS has its origins in traditional English dialectology,[3] which had an historical and rural bias, its comparatively recent application to Ireland has made it possible to incorporate methods which cater for the interests of two modern developments in synchronic descriptive linguistics: sociolinguistics and the currently flourishing field of studies in regional and social varieties of English. Henry's *Anglo-Irish Dialect* can now be seen to have been a pioneer in the latter field. As an in-depth local investigation, it has had only two successors, in studies of the phonology of the urban dialects of Dublin and Belfast,[4] but the acceptance of Hiberno-English as a major 'variety' was marked by the inclusion of a contribution on 'The English language in Ireland' in a recent collection of articles on varieties of English throughout the world.[5] The upsurge of interest in varieties of English has given rise to a new linguistics journal devoted wholly to this topic, *English World-Wide*, the first volume of which contained an article on Hiberno-English phonology.[6]

A fundamental requirement in modern linguistic methodology is the access to reliable linguistic data. Until Henry's *Anglo-Irish Dialect*, descriptions of HE syntax had been based largely on unsystematic personal observations or on literary texts, particularly on the works of the writers of the Anglo-Irish revival.[7] Although J.P. Sullivan has pleaded for 'the validity of literary dialect',[8] today most scholars are careful to argue from tokens of genuine spoken language gained through fieldwork. Thus it is a surprise to find a recent article[9] quoting from the plays of Synge and Yeats as representative examples of southern Hiberno-English speech.

2.   Theoretical Models

The first symposium on Hiberno-English, held in Dublin in 1985, reflected the growing interest in the field, with a wide range of topics, covered by participants from Ireland, Britain, Europe and North America. More importantly, the *Proceedings* of the symposium[10] show that the advances in descriptive methods discussed above are being matched by parallel advances in the use of theoretical models. These include studies in syntax within the Chomskyan Government and Binding framework,[11] the application of discourse analysis techniques to oral narratives,[12] and an investigation of the contribution of lexical phonology to the question of phonological variation,[13] to mention just a few. Even more substantial expressions of the integration of HE studies and modern theoretical linguistics than this impressive collection of twenty papers are two full-length books on aspects of HE phonology and syntax. John Harris's *Phonological Variation and Change* (Cambridge, 1985) applies the techniques of socio-historical linguistics as developed by Suzanne Romaine[14] to the history of the northern HE sound system and Markku Filppula's *Some aspects of Hiberno-English in a Functional Sentence Perspective* (Joensuu, 1986) analyses clefting and topicalization (e.g. HE *twas always the fiddle I heard him playing*[15]) in the framework of the Prague school theory of information distribution in sentences.

3.   Diachronic Concerns

The above-mentioned monographs both have a large diachronic component.

Filppula, whose topic is a construction said to be especially common in southern HE, pursues the two-fold aim of describing the construction and also demonstrating that it is due to the influence of Irish syntax. The question of the possible Irish origins of much that is non-standard in HE syntax is one which has always attracted attention. The most extreme stance on the Irish interference hypothesis is that of Bliss (1984): 'in grammar, syntax and idiom the peculiarities of southern Hiberno-English depend exclusively on the Irish language'.[16] Among the structures frequently adduced as evidence for an Irish substratum are such verbal expressions as *I have a letter written* and *She does be here every day*, for which Standard English would have *I have written a letter* and *She is here every day*, respectively. The HE constructions have traditionally been taken to be calques on the Irish, as in *Tá litir scríofa agam* and *Bíonn sí anseo gach lá*. Recent articles, however, have pointed out that the role of English in the formation of these structures has been underestimated, there being constructions in Early Modern English which could have served as models. These new findings are reflected in increasingly cautious formulations on the degree of input from Irish that HE evinces: compare 'I take it as beyond dispute that much of what sets Hiberno-English (HE) apart from Standard English is due to the influence of Irish'[17] and 'It is commonly accepted ... that at least some of the distinctive qualities of the English language in Ireland arise from contact with Irish'.[18]

This suggests a locus for future diachronic studies in HE syntax: the retention of earlier English forms which have elsewhere become obsolete. The possible EModE component is, however, not easy to assess, as this period is severely underresearched; its neglect has recently caused one scholar to dub it 'the Cinderella of English historical linguistics'.[19]

Further research in this area, if it supports the argument for continuity from Early Modern English, may also have consequences for our understanding of the history of the English language in Ireland. Again, the *locus classicus* for the traditional view is Bliss (1979), who argues, largely from historical and anecdotal sources, that by 1600 medieval HE was virtually extinct outside the towns, Fingall, and the baronies of Forth and Bargy. Thus, except in Ulster, he states, 'the English spoken in most parts of Ireland today is descended from the English of Cromwell's planters'.[20] This interpretation of the sociolinguistic history of late medieval and early modern Ireland has however been challenged by recent historical research, which suggests that, on the contrary, 'indigenous Hiberno-English was ... a vital and expanding language throughout the sixteenth century'.[21] Although English did become much more widespread from the Cromwellian period on, 'this was the culmination of a long process rather than the result of a sudden change, and much of the English spoken thereafter is likely to have been a direct descendant of the native Hiberno-English dialect rather than "the English of Cromwell's planters"'.[22]

This new historical perspective raises the question of a possible linguistic continuity even from the medieval period. Since the work of Heuser (1904)[23] and Hogan (1927)[24], little research has been done on medieval Hiberno-English, but a reappraisal of the material is warranted by the discovery of a considerable number of new Middle English texts of Irish provenance, bringing the total number to forty-five.[25] Future work on these texts, on non-standard Early Modern English, and on modern HE, particularly the urban varieties, will provide a broader data-base for a reexamination of the traditional hypothesis – that modern HE has its roots no further back than the mid-seventeenth century – from a linguistic viewpoint.

Whatever date we set for the linguistic ancestors of the modern HE dialects, that they had their origins in Britain is beyond dispute. Thus the geographical scope of historical HE research cannot be limited to Ireland, but must always include the neighbouring island. This extra-Hibernian dimension to the diachronic study of HE has, of course, always been acknowledged. A further geographical extension will be discussed below (5).

4.   Paradigm Shift

The above discussion has indicated the possibility of multiple origins for features of modern HE, and the importance of such extra-linguistic factors as history and geography. These aspects are not well catered for in traditional historical linguistics, which stresses the role of internal factors (e.g. phonological environment and analogy) in linguistic variation and change, and thus emphasizes the autonomy of individual languages or language families. This monogenetic approach cannot, however, account for the development of hybrids such as Hiberno-English, in which two genetically distant languages have been involved. These products of the contact between two or more languages have come in for increasing attention in the last thirty years, giving rise to a thriving new branch of linguistics, the study of languages in contact. That this paradigm is particularly appropriate for the analysis of the Irish linguistic experience was recognized by Myles Dillon: 'Ireland is a privileged area for the study of languages in contact'.[26] The first explicit application of the contact framework to Hiberno-English was by Bliss in 1972.[27]

A contact situation facilitates influences in both directions between the languages involved, and thus an adequate treatment of contact phenomena will include bi-directional studies. Interesting examples of two-way traffic in the lexicon are given by Barry (1982) in a list of 'English words borrowed into Irish at an early date and given an Irish pronunciation' which are then borrowed back into HE in the Irish form.[28] The starting point for such traffic can also be in Irish: Ó Dochartaigh discusses the case of an Irish word entering English and being borrowed back into Irish in its HE form.[29] With regard to syntax, it is worth noting that though interferences from Irish on HE are often discussed, there has been little work done on the influence of English syntax on Irish (*Béarlachas*). And yet, in the case of the perfective construction referred to above, viz. HE *I have a letter written* / Ir. *Tá litir scríofa agam*, it could be argued that the transfer is from English to Irish and not vice versa.[30]

The contact framework as applied to Ireland implies the inclusion of Britain, as the languages involved are to a great extent the same.[31] The overlapping encompasses more than the varieties of English or Scots introduced into Ireland. For instance, the two major influences on English viz., Scandinavian and Norman French, were also spoken in Ireland. English first came into contact with Irish in Scotland, and Scottish influences in the north of Ireland include not just Lowland Scots but also Scottish-Gaelic. English may have undergone changes through contact with British Celtic which because of their late attestation might be ascribed to Irish influence. Indeed Henry[32] has suggested that what seventeenth-century English writers present as Hiberno-English is more likely to be a heavily Celticized mainland West Coast English.

The recognition of Britain and Ireland as a geographical unit for contact studies was incorporated in a recent conference on 'Language contact in the British Isles', held on the Isle of Man in September 1988: eight papers dealt with language contact in Ireland, four of them specifically with Hiberno-English.

Irish and English have been in contact in Ireland since the twelfth century. Although the possibility of influence from Irish on medieval Hiberno-English is allowed,[33] no attempts have been made to establish English influence on Irish for the early period. Hitherto only Norman-French has been investigated as a source of lexical borrowings in the Classical Irish literary standard (1200-1650).[34] Again, the case for a reappraisal of the sociolinguistic scenario this implies has first been formulated by an historian: 'From the thirteenth century onwards, Irish began the process of heavy borrowing *from English*[35] that continues to this day, though at the time Anglo-Norman contributed its share ... As the use of this dialect of French declined, the void was filled by English'.[36] If 'the mental stance of the country as a whole was focused on England',[37] a degree of language contact can surely be assumed. The potential of the contact approach for a study of the early centuries of the linguistic interaction between Irish and English has yet to be exploited.

5.   Language Contact in the Diaspora

The previous two sections pointed out the necessity for extending the geographical scope of HE studies to Britain. Another necessary extension is to all countries with substantial Irish immigration, where language contact or dialect contact situations may have found expression in an HE component in the varieties of English spoken there.[38] The most interesting case is that of North America, as there is a remarkable parallel between the verbal systems of HE and Vernacular Black English (VBE) in the use of special habitual aspect markers: compare HE *He bees/does be sick* (i.e. frequently, regularly) v. *He is sick* (i.e. now) with VBE *He be busy* (i.e. habitually) v. *He busy* (i.e. at the moment). A traditional view[39] might explain the VBE form as the result of diffusion from HE, probably originating in the contact between Irish and African slaves in the Caribbean in the early seventeenth century. A more recent treatment[40] of this feature sees VBE 'habitual *be*' as deriving ultimately from a Caribbean creole *d(a) de*, which in a process of increasing approximation to Standard English ('decreolization') gives *does de > does be >(does) be > be*.

The marking of habitual aspect is not confined to English-based creoles, but seems to be common to creoles in general. Thus it may not necessarily be derived from any particular substrate or superstrate language. An alternative hypothesis, currently much debated, is to interpret this and other features shared by genetically unrelated creoles as a reflex of a linguistic universal which is activated in the situations of abrupt large-scale language contact which give rise to pidgins and creoles.[41] This raises new questions about the origins of the habituative in HE itself. A creole hypothesis for HE is supported by recent historical research, which emphasizes that the colonization of Ireland was just the first stage in England's westward expansion:[42] some of the conditions under which the New World creoles developed may have been anticipated in Ireland. And linguistic evidence for creolization in HE has in fact been adduced from seventeenth-century literary texts purporting to represent the spoken HE of the time.[43]

An adequate treatment of this complex subject is beyond the scope of this paper, but perhaps enough has been said to show that HE plays an important role in one of the major issues in theoretical linguistics today.

6. Theoretical Contribution

The discussion so far has focused mainly on the contribution of linguistic theory to the interpretation of HE data. However, in one area at least research in HE has itself contributed to theory. The sociolinguistic studies of Belfast vernacular carried out in the 1970s by James and Lesley Milroy addressed, *inter alia*, what has been called the 'actuation problem' in phonological change, viz. the problem of determining the social conditions under which linguistic change occurs. By applying the anthropological concept of the 'network' and distinguishing between 'innovators' and 'early adoptors', they have been able to shed light on the sociolinguistic process involved in the diffusion of sound change.[44] The impact of the Milroys' work on linguistics in the 1980s has been assessed as follows by Peter Trudgill: '[it] has provided a stimulus for considerable amounts of the best research in the area of language and society which has appeared in subsequent years, especially perhaps in Britain'.[45]

7.   Conclusion

This paper has argued that in the past two decades, HE studies have discarded the parish-pump perspective to become a lively field firmly anchored within modern international linguistic thinking. However, this is a development which has been fuelled largely from the outside. Within Ireland, Hiberno-English still awaits recognition as an important area of research. One can only concur with Kallen (1988), who deplores 'the isolation of Hiberno-English from the mainstream of academic work in language or the sociology of language at the theoretical or applied level in Ireland'. Likewise there can be no dispute about his claim that the field has 'unrealized potential for further growth',[46] some of which has been indicated in this survey.

NOTES

Chapter 1
The conflict in Northern Ireland: institutional and constitutional dimensions
J. TODD

1. C.D. McGimpsey, 'Reconciliation in Northern Ireland. The future: the contribution of politicians', in Social Study Conference, *Reconciliation in Northern Ireland* (Dublin, 1987), p.41.
2. For example, John Hume's statement at Westminster that unionists 'couldn't stomach equality'. *Irish Times* (5.3.86).
3. For example, John Whyte, 'Why is the Northern Ireland problem so intractable?', *Parliamentary Affairs* xxxiv, 4 (autumn 1981), pp 423–4.
4. See Frank Millar's interview with James Molyneaux, 'Molyneaux's alternative to the Hume approach', *Irish Times* (14.2.89). Also Peter Smith, 'Opportunity lost: A unionist view of the Report of the Forum for a New Ireland' (12.11.84), p.16.
5. David Trimble, 'Initiatives for consensus: a unionist perspective', in Charles Townshend (ed) *Consensus in Ireland: Approaches and Recessions* (Oxford, 1988), p.88; The Unionist Task Force Report; Harold McCusker, reported *Irish Times* (6.3.87).
6. Molyneaux interview, *Irish Times* (14.2.89).
7. Ulster Political Research Group, 'Common Sense' (1987); Unionist Task Force report; John Darby, 'Initiatives for consensus: powersharing', in Townshend (ed), *Consensus* pp 55–6.
8. Unionist Task Force Report; Trimble, 'Initiatives', pp 78,92.
9. See Ken Maginnis's calls for 'selective' internment, for example interview with D. Purcell, *Sunday Tribune* (11.9.89); Frank Wright, *Northern Ireland: A Comparative Analysis* (Dublin, 1987), pp 20-7; Adrian Guelke, *Northern Ireland: The International Perspective* (Dublin, 1988), pp 21–39.
10. See Frank Millar's interview with Peter Robinson, *Irish Times* (20.3.89). While Molyneaux's approach differs, he also requires the Republic to recognise the legitimate status of Northern Ireland. Also Trimble, 'Initiatives', p.80.
11. Darby, 'Initiatives', pp 55–6.
12. For example, Raymond Ferguson, *Fortnight* 259 (February 1988), p.9 and *Irish Times* (12.9.86, 13.9.86, 10.12.87). Ken Maginnis at the Young Fine Gael conference, reported *Irish Times* (13.2.89).
13. See Frank Millar's interview with John Hume, *Irish Times* (13.1.89).
14. Whyte, 'Northern Ireland Problem', pp 426–7.
15. See Hume's studied ambiguity on the constitutional issue in Hume interview, *Irish Times* (13.1.89).
16. SDLP comment of 13 June 1988 on Sinn Fein Document of 2nd May 1988 pp 8,9, *Irish Times* (19.9.88). John Hume, *Irish Times* (21.11.88). Also Hume's speech to 1987 SDLP conference.
17. See the discussion of unionists' 'natural veto' in SDLP comment on SF, *Irish Times* (19.9.88).
18. See Eddie McGrady's talk at the conference 'Northern Ireland - finding a way forward' at the Corrymeela Centre, Ballycastle, 8.10.88. Reported *Irish News* (10.10.88).

19. 'Northern Ireland: a strategy for peace', policy document adopted by the 10th Annual Conference of the SDLP, November 1980, point 5.
20. Hume's speech to SDLP conference, 1988; Wright, *Northern Ireland* pp 20–7; Adrian Guelke, *Northern Ireland* pp 21–39.
21. Their constitutional aspirations, while somewhat ambivalent, are still important. The survey and poll data shows that while less than 30 per cent of Northern Catholics opt for a united Ireland as an immediate policy preference, less than 10 per cent never want to see a united Ireland. The percentage preferring a united Ireland varies over time, increasing as it appears more possible, and as more detail on its nature is given in the questions.

Chapter 2
Some comparative aspects of Irish and English nationalism in the late nineteenth century J. LOUGHLIN

1. British imperialists in the late nineteenth century were also inhibited from using terms like 'nationalism' that Irish nationalists had made their own. See S.R.B. Smith, 'British Nationalism, Imperialism and the City of London 1880-1900' (Unpublished Ph.D. thesis, Queen Mary College, University of London, 1985), p.11.
2. Carlton Hayes, *Nationalism: a Religion* (New York, 1960), pp 2, 9–10.
3. C.C. O'Brien, *Parnell and his Party 1880-1890* (2nd ed., Oxford, 1974), pp 5–6.
4. On nationalist ideology see James Loughlin, *Gladstone, Home Rule and the Ulster question 1882-1893* (Dublin, 1986), chapter one.
5. Michael McDonagh, *The Home Rule Movement* (Dublin, 1920), p.13.
6. See for example, Hugh Cunningham, 'The Language of Patriotism 1750-1914' in *History Workshop*, 12 (Autumn, 1981), pp 8–33; Martin Weiner, *English Culture and the Decline of the Industrial Spirit* (3rd impression, London, 1987); Robert Colls and Philip Dodds (eds), *Englishness: Politics and Culture 1880-1920* (London, 1986); Gerard Newman, *The Rise of English Nationalism* 1750-1830 (London, 1986); Smith, op. cit.
7. Cunningham, 'Language of Patriotism', pp 8–25.
8. Hayes, *Nationalism*, pp 38–42.
9. Newman, *English Nationalism*, pp 77, 189–91.
10. See for example, Benjamn Disraeli, *Vindication of the English Constitution* (London, 1835), passim.
11. Loughlin, *Gladstone*, pp 48–9.
12. See *Hansard 3*, ccxxxiv, 1752–3 (14 June, 1877); G.A. Best, 'Popular Protestantism in Victorian Britain', in Robert Robson (ed), *Ideas and Institutions of Victorian Britain* (London, 1867), pp 137–8. For the persistence into the twentieth century of the view that Catholicism was inconsistent with English national character see W.R. Inge, *England* (6th ed., London, 1938), pp 80–1.
13. A.C. Dicey, *England's Case against Home Rule* (London, 1886), pp 79, 90.
14. Hugh Berrington, 'Partisanship and dissidence in the nineteenth century House of Commons' in J.D. Lees and Richard Kimber (eds.), *Political Parties in Modern Britain* (London, 1972), pp 113–29.
15. Martin Pugh, *The Tories and the People 1880–1935* (Oxford, 1985), p.90.
16. Benedict Anderson, *Imagined communities: Reflections on the Origins and spread of Nationalism* (London, 1983).
17. Weiner, *English Culture*, chapters one and two.
18. See Jean Blondel. *Voters, Parties and Leaders: the Social Fabric of British Politics* (Harmondsworth, 1963), pp 24–6.
19. Joseph Lee, *The Modernisation of Irish Society 1848–1918* (Dublin, 1973), pp 97–8.
20. M.O. Sale, 'The problem of Wales' in *National Review*, 62 (Nov. 1913), pp 507–18.
21. See Loughlin, *Gladstone*, chapter five.

22. Ibid., chapter one; Alan O'Day, *The English face of Irish Nationalism: Parnellite Nationalism 1880-1886* (Dublin, 1977), pp 29–30.

23. Loughlin, *Gladstone*, pp 64–5, 187–8.

24. McDonagh, *Home Rule Movement*, pp 26–7.

25. Wilfrid Scawen Blunt, *The Land War in Ireland* (London, 1912), p.311.

26. See Loughlin, *Gladstone*, p.22.

Chapter 3
Revolution and radicalism in County Dublin, 1921-31 C. MURPHY

1. T.W. Freeman, *Ireland: Its Physical, Historical, Social and Economic Geography* (London, 1950), p.189; Dan Bradley, *Farm labourers: Irish Struggle, 1900–76* (Belfast, 1988), pp 10–11: labourers made up about 1/3 of Dublin's workforce; Inspector General and Co. Inspector, R.I.C., monthly confidential reports, Feb. 1898-Dec 1921 (Public Record Office, CO 904/68–120; National Library of Ireland, pp 8320–8557).

2. B.M. Walker (ed.), *Parliamentary Election Results in Ireland, 1801–1922*, New History of Ireland ancillary publications, iv (Dublin, 1978).

3. Co. Inspector, Apr-Sep 1914 (P.R.O., CO 904/93-94; N.L.I., pp 8536–7).

4. 230 volunteers enlisted between December 1914 and December 1915, Breandan MacGiolla Choille (ed.), *Intelligence Notes, 1913–16* (Dublin, 1966), p.179.

5. Inspector General and Co. Inspector, Jun. 1914–Jan. 1916 (P.R.O., CO 904/93-9; N.L.I., pp 8536–40).

6. Inspector General, Jul. 1915 (P.R.O., CO 904/97; N.L.I., p.8539); Sinn Fein movement, police reports, 1916–17 (P.R.O., CO 904/23/3/a; N.L.I., p.8174).

7. Co. Inspector, Jul. 1917 (P.R.O., CO 904/103; N.L.I., p.8544).

8. Inspector General, Oct. 1917 (P.R.O., CO 904/104; N.L.I., p.8544).

9. Inspector General and Co. Inspector, Sep-Oct. 1917 (P.R.O., CO 904/104; N.L.I., p.8544).

10. Inspector General, Dec. 1918 (P.R.O., CO 904/107; N.L.I., p.8547).

11. Inspector General, Jan. 1919 (P.R.O., CO 904/108; N.L.I. p.8548).

12. Inspector General and Co. Inspector, Feb. 1920–Sep 1921 (P.R.O., CO 904/111–20; N.L.I., p.8551–55); Military reports, railway transport officers, 1920–22 (P.R.O., CO 904/157/2; N.L.I., p.8178); Outrage returns, Apr. 1920-Dec. 1921 (P.R.O., CO 904/148–50; N.L.I., p.8559).

13. Dermot Keogh, *The Rise of the Irish working class, the Dublin Trade Union Movement and Labour Leaderships, 1890–1914*, cited in Bradley, *Farm Labourers*, p.33.

14. Bradley, *Farm Labourers*, pp 33–4.

15. ibid., p.34.

16. Co. Inspector, May 1916 (P.R.O., CO 904/100; N.L.I., p.8541).

17. Bradley, *Farm Labourers*, p.34.

18. Inspector General, Jan. 1919 (P.R.O., CO 904/108; N.L.I., p.8548).

19. ibid.

20. Co. Inspector, Jan. 1919 (P.R.O., CO 904/108; N.L.I., p.8548).

Chapter 4
'Quotas': affirmative action, reverse discrimination M. GOLDRING

1. R.J. Cormack & R.D. Osborne, *Religion and Employment in Northern Ireland*, (Belfast, 1983); A.C. Hepburn, 'Employment and religion in Belfast 1901–1951', in Cormack & Osborne, (ed), *Religion and Employment*; C. McCrudden, 'The experience of the Legal Enforcement of the Fair Employment (NI) Act 1976'; SDLP: 'Equal and Just Opportunities for Employment', SDLP document presented to the 16th Annual Conference, Slieve Donard Hotel, Newcastle, 21–13 November 1986; Cormack and Osborne, 'Inequality of misery', *New Society*, 22 November 1985; Policy Studies Institute, Report

on job discrimination, (London, 1987); Robert Miller, 'Evaluation research Ulster style', in *Network*, British Sociological Association, no. 42, October 1988, pp 4–7.

2. For the loyalist criticism of such studies: see Gregory Campbell, *Discrimination, the Truth*, 1987. 28 pp.; John Morrison, on the FEA, *Sunday News*, 24 January 1988.

3. 'Religious Equality of Opportunity in Employment, Guide to Effective Practice', Department of Economic Development, Northern Ireland, September 1987.

4. SDLP 'Equal and Just Opportunities for Employment', op. cit.

5. Signed by Sean McBride, Dr John Robb, Inez McCormack (NUPE), Fr. Brian Brady, Belfast. On the discussion, see Austin McGill, *Fortnight*. Michael Farrell; 'The McBride's Principles'. *The Listener*, 24 September 1987, Peter Archer, MP and Stuart Bell, MP, Labour Party spokespersons on Northern Ireland, July 1986; 'Labour Party Statement on Discrimination', Conference on Employment discrimination and its context in Northern Ireland', Camden, 28 November 1987.

Chapter 5
Typical case or deviant? Nationalism in Ireland in a European perspective
J. COAKLEY

1. This view informs the dominant tradition of historical writing on Irish nationalism, though not necessarily expressed explicitly; see the standard histories of modern Ireland and also those works which address the issue of Irish nationalism more directly, such as Owen Dudley Edwards, "Ireland" in Owen Dudley Edwards et al, *Celtic Nationalism* (London, 1968), pp 1–209; Robert Kee, *The Green Flag: A History of Irish Nationalism* (London, 1972); and Sean Cronin, *Irish Nationalism: A History of its Roots and Ideology* (Dublin, 1980). Social scientists tend to be more theoretical in approaching the issue, and to be more disposed to accept comparative evidence; see, for instance, Tom Garvin, *The Evolution of Irish Nationalist Politics* (Dublin, 1981) and D. George Boyce, *Nationalism in Ireland* (Dublin, 1982), both the output of politics departments. The geographer D.G. Pringle uses relatively little comparative evidence in his original and wide-ranging study, *One Island, Two Nations? A Political Geographical Analysis of the National Conflict in Ireland* (Letchworth, Herts, 1985); at the opposite pole is perhaps the most explicitly comparative study, by political scientist Frank Wright, *Northern Ireland: A Comparative Analysis* (Dublin, 1987). These examples are intended as illustrative of the breadth of approach to this topic rather than as being bibliographically exhaustive.

2. Stein Rokkan and Derek Urwin, *Economy, Territory, Identity: Politics of West European Peripheries* (London, 1983).

3. This characteristic of nationalism has long been noted; see for instance, Joshua A. Fishman, *Language and Nationalism: Two Integrative Essays* (Rowley, MA 1972).

4. On this concept, see Michael Hechter, *Internal Colonialism: The Celtic Fringe in British National Development, 1536-1966* (London, 1975), especially pp 30–43.

5. For an extensive treatment of the phasing of nationalist movements see Miroslav Hroch, *Social Conditions of National Revival in Europe: A Comparative Analysis of the Social Composition of Patriotic Groups Among the Smaller European Nations* (Cambridge, 1985).

6. On the Protestant minority, see Patrick Buckland, *Irish Unionism: One: The Anglo-Irish and The New Ireland 1885-1922* (Dublin, 1972) and J.C. Beckett, *The Anglo-Irish Tradition* (London, 1976).

Chapter 6
'Quiet Desperation': variations on a theme in the writings of Daniel Corkery, Michael McLaverty and John McGahern S. KING

All letters, except where otherwise stated, are in the possession of the McLaverty family.

1. H.D. Thoreau, *Walden or Life in the Woods* (New York, pbk, 1960), p.10. Quoted by Daniel Corkery as epigraph to *The Threshold of Quiet* (Dublin, 1917).

2. Corkery, *The Threshold of Quiet* (3rd impression, 1919). p.4.
3. Michael McLaverty, 'Irish fiction', unpublished lecture to Young Ulster Society, 27 February 1940.
4. John McGahern to Michael McLaverty, 13 January 1959.
5. McLaverty to McGahern, 23 January 1959.
6. Michael McLaverty, *In This Thy Day* (New York, 1945), p.213.
7. McLaverty to John Pudney, 31 December 1949.
8. Daniel Corkery to McLaverty, 21 May 1949.
9. McLaverty to Cecil Scott, May 1953.
10. McLaverty to Scott, 19 June 1953.
11. McLaverty to Scott, 2 November 1953.
12. Corkery to McLaverty, January 1954; *Truth in the Night* (New York, 1951, London, 1952).
13. Corkery to McLaverty, August 1954.
14. McLaverty to Corkery, 9 August 1954.
15. *The Choice* (New York and London, 1958).
16. McLaverty to McGahern, 23 March 1961.
17. McGahern to McLaverty, 25 March 1961.
18. McLaverty to McGahern, 27 September 1962; *The Barracks* (London, 1963, New York, 1964).
19. McGahern to McLaverty, 30 September 1962.
20. McLaverty to McGahern, 23 May 1965; *The Dark* (London, 1965).
21. *The Pornographer* (London, 1979).
22. *The Threshold of Quiet* op. cit., p.310.

Chapter 7
Irish landscape painting in a political setting, 1922-48 B. KENNEDY

1. *Irish Statesman*, 20 June 1925.
2. Cyril Barrett, 'Irish nationalism and art 1800-1921' , in *Studies*, winter 1975, p.398.
3. John Hewitt, *Art in Ulster: 1* (Belfast, 1977), p.83.
4. Stephen Rynne, *The Leader*, 28 April 1945, pp 10, 12.
5. Sean Keating, letter of 8 July 1975 (Ulster Museum archives: Keating 589).
6. Anne Crookshank & the Knight of Glin, *The Painters of Ireland c.1660–1920* (London, 1978), p.273.
7. For a discussion on this point see Dymphna Halpin, '"The Breaker-Out": Jack B. Yeats (1871–1957): a study of his change in style', unpublished M. Litt. thesis, Trinity College, Dublin, 1984, p.30.
8. R.S.W., 'Distinguished Irishmen, 23: Jack B. Yeats and his art', *Daily Express*, 12 October 1929.
9. Count Plunkett, 'President's Address', *Journal*, Academy of Christian Art, vol. i (n.d., but c.1937), p.7.
10. *Irish Times*, 7 May 1932.
11. L.S. Gogan was Keeper of Art and Industry at the National Museum, Dublin.
12. 'At the Royal Hibernian Academy', *The Leader*, vol. lxxvi, 30 April 1938, pp 186–7.
13. 'The Dublin painters', *Irish Statesman*, 27 October 1923.
14. 'The new Irish salon', *Irish Statesman*, 16 February 1924.
15. John Dowling, 'Surrealism', *Ireland To-Day*, vol. i, no.2, February 1937, pp 60, 62.
16. Mainie Jellett, 'The R.H.A. and youth', *Commentary*, May 1942, pp 5,7.
17. 'Art in Ireland', *Irish Tatler & Sketch*, October 1947, p.14.
18. The phrase is H.R.F. Keating's, in 'The art of Nevill Johnson', *Icarus*, vol. ii, May 1952, p.89.
19. Keating, interviewed, *News Letter*, Belfast, 1 May 1965.

Chapter 8
Representation in modern Irish poetry E. HUGHES

1. Blake Morrison and Andrew Motion, 'Introduction', *The Penguin Book of Contemporary British Poetry* (Harmondsworth, Middlesex, 1982), p.20.
2. The two most recent studies of Heaney – Neil Corcoran, *Seamus Heaney* (London, 1986), and Elmer Andrews, *The Poetry of Seamus Heaney* (London, 1988) – follow the usual pattern of concentrating discussion of Part II on 'Exposure'.
3. Paul Muldoon, *Meeting the British* (London, 1987).
4. Seamus Heaney, *North* (London, 1975), p.65.
5. Tom Paulin, *Liberty Tree* (London, 1983), p.33.
6. Tom Paulin, *Fivemiletown* (London, 1987).
7. George Watson, 'An uncomfortable, spikey poet', in *Irish Literary Supplement*, 7 no.2, (Fall 1988), p.33.
8. Blake Morrison, *Seamus Heaney* (London, 1982), Ch.4. See also Simon Curtis, 'Seamus Heaney's *North*', *Critical Quarterly* 18, no.1, (Spring 1976) pp 80–3, 83. Edna Longley, 'Fire and air', *The Honest Ulsterman* 50 (Winter 1975), pp 179–83, 182. Douglas Dunn, 'Manana is now', *Encounter* 45 (Nov. 1975), pp 76–81, 76, 77. Conor Cruise O'Brien, 'A slow north-east wind', *The Listener* (25 Sept. 1975), pp 404–5.
9. Stan Smith, 'Writing a will, Yeats's ancestral voices in "The Tower" and "Meditations in time of Civil War"', *Irish University Review* 13, no. 1, (Spring 1983), pp 14–37.
10. Julia Kristeva, 'Word, dialogue and novel', in her *Desire in Language* (Oxford, 1980), p.65.
11. V.N. Volisinov, *Marxism and the Philosophy of Language* (trans. Ladislav Matejka and I.R. Titunik), (Cambridge, Mass., 1986), pp 73–81; the direct quotations are on pp 75, 81 and 73 respectively.
12. W.B. Yeats, *The Autobiography of William Butler Yeats* (New York, 1964), p. 312.
13. Conor Cruise O'Brien, 'A slow north-east wind', p.404.
14. Ferdinand de Saussure, *Course in General Linguistics* (trans. Wade Baskin, intro. Jonathan Culler), (London, 1974), p.9. See also Culler's 'Introduction', pp xvii-xviii and Blake Morrison, *Seamus Heaney* p.15, n.2 for Heaney's own sense of this issue.
15. Patrick Kavanagh, 'Epic', *Collected Poems* (London, 1972), p. 136. Allusions will be identified in the footnotes where appropriate.
16. William Shakespeare, *The Tempest* V, i, p.182.
17. William Wordsworth, *The Prelude, A Parallel Text* (ed. J.C. Maxwell), (Harmondsworth, 1972), 1805 version, Book 1, pp 388–9. Heaney's epigraph is identifiably from the 1805 text, Book 1, pp 305–9, so I shall refer only to it.
18. William Shakespeare, *The Tempest* V, i, p.148.
19. James Joyce, *A Portrait of the Artist as a Young Man* (London, 1968), pp 51–2 – the 'pandy bat' incident.
20. The incident with the R.U.C., and with the priest at school, recall Joyce's two masters, Church and State, and there is an echo of Yeats' 'The years like great black oxen tread the world', 'The Countess Cathleen', 1892 text, in *The Variorum Edition of the Plays* (ed Russell K. Alspach), (London, 1966), p.158 in the description of the police 'like black cattle'. Although only hints it is significant that the writers whom Heaney calls on here are both Irish. Sexual and political knowledge are precisely those areas of self comprehension to be repressed by reading Masefield's 'Cargoes' in *Meeting the British*.
21. Seamus Deane, 'Unhappy at home, an interview with Seamus Heaney', *The Crane Bag* 1 (Spring 1977), pp 61–7, 63. See also Blake Morrison, *Seamus Heaney* p. 44, n.42.
22. Samuel Taylor Coleridge, 'Frost at Midnight', 72, in *Poetical Works*, (ed. E.H. Coleridge), (London, 1969), p.242. William Wordsworth, *The Prelude*, Book 1, pp 370–1. There is a slight Orwellian allusion here.
23. Shakespeare, *King Lear* III, iv, p.105. Michael Longley uses the same quotation as epigraph to 'Options' which pre-dates 'Singing School' and is similarly about the variety of voices available to a poet; *Poems 1953–1983* (Harmondsworth, 1986), pp 106–7.

24. Blake Morrision, *Seamus Heaney* pp 66–7.
25. Patrick Kavanagh, *Collected Prose* (London, 1967), pp 282–3, and Seamus Heaney, *Preoccupations, Selected Prose, 1968–1978* (London, 1980), pp 29, 35; Lawrence, of course, being a 'voice of education'.
26. Clifford Geertz, *The Interpretation of Cultures, Selected Essays* (London, 1975), p.242.
27. Seamus Heaney, *Preoccupations* p.41.
28. Blake Morrison, *Seamus Heaney* p.66.
29. F.S.L. Lyons, *Ireland since the Famine* (London, 1973), p.761.
30. G.M. Hopkins, *Poems and Prose* (selected and introduced by W.H. Gardner), (Harmondsworth, 1953), p.30.
31. W.B. Yeats, *The Poems: A New Edition* (ed R.J. Finneran), (London, 1983), pp 319–21. This poem's presence is felt throughout *North*.
32. Seamus Heaney, 'Old Derry's walls', *The Listener* (24 October 1968), pp 521–3.
33. See Antonio J. Oneiva, *A New Complete Guide to the Prado Gallery* (trans, P.M. O'Neill, new edn, rev. Miriam Finkelman), (Madrid, 1966), p.182. See also Hugh Thomas, *Goya: The Third of May, 1808* (London, 1972); F.D. Klingender, *Goya in a Democratic Tradition* (intro, Herbert Read), (London, 1948); G.A. Williams, *Goya and the Impossible Revolution* (London, 1976), for accounts of the historical and political background to Goya's work which enables Heaney's analogy.
34. Seamus Heaney, 'Delirium of the brave', *The Listener* (27 Nov. 1969), pp 757–9.
35. Seamus Heaney, 'Introduction' in Michael McLaverty, *The Collected Short Stories* (Dublin, 1978), p.7.
36. *Ibid*, p.7 where 'that note of exile' is to be found in Chekhov.
37. See *A Portrait* pp 189–90, John Montague, *The Rough Field* 3rd edn, (Dublin 1979), p.19 and Thomas Kinsella, 'Death Bed', *New Poems 1973* (Dublin 1973).
38. Neil Corcoran, *Seamus Heaney* pp 124–6; and see Seamus Heaney, *The Government of the Tongue* (London, 1989), p.72.
39. An echo of Yeats' 'Politics', with its rejection of Roman, Russian, and Spanish politics; Yeats, *The Poems* p.348.
40. Seamus Heaney, *Field Work* (London, 1979).
41. Seamus Heaney, *Station Island* (London, 1984).
42. Seamus Heaney, *The Haw Lantern* (London, 1987).

Chapter 9
'The mirror up to nature': the theatre building as a socio-political cypher
H. MAGUIRE

1. Nikolaus Pevsner, eminent architectural historian, editor of the *Pelican History of Art and Architecture* and author of works such as *the Englishness of English Art* (London, 1956) and *An Outline of European Architecture* (1943).
2. J.R. Martin, *Baroque* (New York, 1977), p.151.
3. Compare: Pietra da Cortona's 'Santa Maria della Pace' (1656–57) See, Martin: *Baroque* pp 195–6.
4. Designed by Françoise Cuvilliés (1695–1768).
5. George Bernard Shaw, 'The Saturday Review, May 1, 1987' in George Rowell, *Victorian Dramatic Criticism* (London, 1971), p.197.
6. J. Fitzgerald Molloy, *The Life and Adventures of Peg Woffington*, (London, 1884)
7. The former based on a painting by Sir Joshua Reynolds (1723–1792), the latter on a painting by Johann Zoffany (1725–1810).
8. Esther K. Sheldon, *Thomas Sheridan of Smock Alley* (Princeton, 1967).
9. Contrast: *Theatre Ireland* Sept./Nov. 188, No.16; R.A. Cave 'Killing the Stage Irishman' pp 15–16.
10. Colly Cibber, *An Apology for the Life of Mr Colly Cibber, Comedian* (London, 1740), p.183.
11. W.R. Chetwood, *History of the Dublin Stage* (Dublin, 1749), p.71.

12. Compare William Hogarth (1697–1764) 'The Beggars Opera' c.1729 (coll. Tate Gallery, London).

13. Compare: Charles Benson, '"Wild Oats" in New Ross: Theatre in an Irish Country Town, 1789–95' *Long Room* nos. 2 & 3, Spring-Autumn, 1981, pp 13–18.

14. Original watercolour view of proposed facade in the collection of the Royal Irish Academy, Engraved for G.N. Wright *An Historical Guide to the City of Dublin* (London 2nd. ed. 1825), plate p.147.

15. Samuel Lewis, *Topographical Dictionary of Ireland* (London, 1837), 2 vols., vol.1, p.541.

16. Designed by C.J. Phipps in 1891 following a fire in the earlier building. See too: B.M. Walker and Hugh Dixon, *In Belfast Town 1864–1880* (Belfast, 1984), p.9.

17. See: Era 1 March, 1898 p.13. Grand Opera House, ignored by C.E. Brett, *Buildings of Belfast 1700–1914* (London, 1967). Mentioned by Paul Larmour, *Belfast An Illustrated Architectural Guide* (Belfast, 1987), No.134, p.57, colour ill. plate xii. Note change of attitude to Victorian theatre architecture.

18. Mary Daly, 'Dublin life' in Tom Kennedy (ed), *Victorian Dublin* (Dublin, 1980), pp 7–89, p.87.

19. An 1876 G. & S. tour prior to the forming of the D'Oyly Carte Co. included 'The Duke's Daughter' and 'Trial by Jury'.

20. By Basil Hood and Walter Slaughter.

21. Subsequent changes and rebuilding of the theatre as the Empire Palace in 1896 were more in keeping with prevailing British concepts of Empire and grandeur.

22. Compare: J.B. Yeats, *Willie Reilly at the Old Mechanics Theatre* watercolour, (Dublin, coll. Abbey Theatre).

23. See: Thomas Mac Anna, 'Nationalism from the Abbey stage' in *Theatre and Nationalism in Twentieth century Ireland* (London, 1971), pp 89–101, p.91. See too: Seamus de Burca, *The Queen's Royal Theatre 1829–1969* (Dublin, 1983) illus. of auditorium, p.2. Compare plays presented by J.W. Whitbread pre. 1906, pp 20–1. Also typical later nationalist plays; *Father Murphy* by Ira Allen, June 3rd, 1912: *For Ireland's Sake* Jan. 9th, 1917; *The Croppy Boy* by Alfred Foley, 3rd May, 1920. Posters and playbills for plays pp 48–68.

24. Crookshank and The Knight of Glin *The Painters of Ireland c.1660-1900* (London, 1978), pp 65–6.

25. The Lord Chamberlain to whom all stage plays presented in Great Britain had to be submitted had no jurisdiction in Ireland, but Dublin Castle could intervene in other areas such as its banning of the poster for P.J. Bourke's 'In Dark and Evil Days' (1914) which depicted French and British fleets in Loch Swilly.

26. Mario Borsa, *The English Stage Today* (1908) Translated from the Italian, originally published 1907. 'The Irish National Theatre', pp 86–314, p.86.

27. Borsa, *The English Stage*, p.86.

28. John McDonagh, in reference to the Hardwicke Street Theatre, quoted in W.J. Feeney *Drama in Hardwicke Street, A History of the Irish Theatre Company* (Cranbury, New Jersey, 1984), p.87.

29. Fintan O'Toole, *The Politics of Magic, The Work and Times of Tom Murphy* (Dublin, 1987).

Chapter 10
Good leaders and 'decent men': an Ulster contradiction M. CROZIER

1. A.P. Cohen, *Belonging: Identity and Social Organization in British Rural Cultures* (Manchester, 1982), p.17. I follow Cohen in using the term 'equalitarianism'; that is 'the intentional masking or muting of social differentiation' rather than egalitarianism – equality as a moral principle, since I am considering the behaviour associated with the strategies involved in relationships in a face-to-face society.

2. F.G. Bailey, *Gifts and Poison* (Oxford, 1971), p.41.

3. Frederick Barth, 'Capital, investment and the social structure of a pastoral nomad group in South Persia', in Le Clair, E. and H. Schneider, *Economic Anthropology: Readings in Theory and Analysis* (New York, 1968), p.420.
4. Rosemary Harris, *Prejudice and Tolerance in Ulster: a Study of Neighbours and 'Strangers' in a Border Community* (Manchester, 1972).
5. Harris, *Prejudice and Tolerance* p.124.
6. Richard Breen, 'Naming practices in western Ireland' in *Man* 17 (1982), p.23.
7. John Blacking et al., *Situational Determinants of Recruitment in Four Northern Ireland Communities* (SSRC: British Library 1978), p.23.
8. Elliott Leyton, *The One Blood; Kinship and Class in an Irish Village* (Newfoundland: Institute of Social and Economic Research, Memorial University, Newfoundland Social and Economic Research Papers, 15 1975), p.11.
9. Howard Newby, *Green and Pleasant Land? Change in Rural England* (London, 1979).
10. Leyton, *The One Blood* p.11.
11. Harris, *Prejudice and Tolerance* p.198.
12. Barry White, *John Hume: Statesman of the Troubles* (Belfast 1984), p.214.
13. Roy Wallis & Steve Bruce, *'No Surrender!': Paisleyism and the Politics of Ethnic Identity in Northern Ireland* (Belfast, 1986)
14. White, *John Hume*, p.276.

Chapter 11
Northern Irish gentry culture: an anomaly A. SHANKS

1. Conrad Arensberg and S.T. Kimball, *Family and Community in Ireland* (Cambridge, Mass., 1940).
2. Rosemary Harris, 'The selection of leaders in Ballybeg', in *Sociological Review* N.S. 8 (1961), pp 137–49.
3. Arensberg and Kimball, *Family and Community*, p.133.
4. Elliott Leyton, 'Spheres of inheritance in Aughnaboy', in *American Anthropologist*, 72 (1970), pp 1378–88.
5. Mark Bence-Jones, *Burke's Guide to Irish Country Houses* (London, 1978), p. xxviii.
6. A.S.C. Ross, 'Linguistic class indicators in present day English', in *Neuphilologische Mitteilungen* (1954).
7. Nancy Mitford, (ed.) *Noblesse Oblige: An Enquiry into the Identifiable Characteristics of the English Aristocracy* (London, 1956).

Chapter 12
Numbers to the alphabet of history B. COLLINS

Note. The paper title is taken from M. Bragg, *The Hired Man* (London, 1984), p.16.

1. H.J. Hanham, 'Clio's Weapons', *Daedalus* (Spring 1971), pp 509–19.
2. G. Kitson Clark, *The Making of Victorian England* (London, 1962), p.4, as quoted by W.O. Aydelotte, *Quantification in History* (Reading, Mass., 1971), p.42.
3. The research grant, reference number GOO 23 2224, was awarded by the E.S.R.C. during 1986.
4. Figures for England and Wales are to be found in P. Laslett, 'Household size in England and Wales since the sixteenth century' in P. Laslett and R. Wall (ed.), *Household and Family in Past Time* (Cambridge, 1977) p.142.
5. Further information on the shirt industry is contained in Brenda Collins 'Sewing and Social Structure: the flowerers of Scotland and Ireland' in R. Mitchison and P. Roebuck (ed.), *Economy and Society in Scotland and Ireland 1500–1939* (Edinburgh, 1988), pp 242–54, and in 'The organisation of sewing outwork in nineteenth century Ulster' in M. Berg, (ed.) *Markets and Manufactures in Early Industrial Europe*, (forthcoming).
6. M.H. Irwin, *Homework in Ireland* (Glasgow, 1909), p.24.

Chapter 13
The computer as a resource for Irish history: an introduction to the Irish Ordnance Survey Memoirs database A. DAY

1. John Andrews; *A paper landscape, The Ordnance Survey in Nineteenth Century Ireland* (Oxford, 1975).
2. A. Day: Habits of the People; 'Traditional life in Ireland, 1830–40, as recorded in the Ordnance Survey Memoirs' in *Ulster Folklife* vol. 30, (1984).
3. Larcom Papers: National Library of Ireland, 7550.
4. Dr K. Devine and Professor F.J. Smith: QUILL, an online Text Retrieval System, Department of Computer Science, Queen's University, Belfast, CS 026, (April, 1983).

Chapter 14
The Place-Name Project, Department of the Environment for Northern Ireland and the Celtic Department, Queen's University Belfast K. MUHR

1. Printed in A. Thom, *A collection of Tracts & Treatises illustrative of Ireland*, (1861) vol. I pp 72–3.
2. *Calendar of Patent Rolls of James I*, Irish Record Commission (pre-1830, reprinted 1966 PROI), p.193a

Chapter 15
A seventeenth century 'political poem' M. O'RIORDAN

1. Cecile O'Rahilly (ed.), *Five Seventeenth-Century Political Poems* (Dublin, 1952).
2. Cuthbert Mhág Craith (ed.), *Dán na mBráthár Mionúr* (Dublin, 1967), poem no. 49, p.251.
3. de Brún, Ó Buachalla, Ó Concheannainn (eds.), *Nua-Dhuanaire 1* (Dublin, 1975).
4. O'Rahilly, *Five Seventeenth-Century Political Poems*; see variant readings throughout, especially, for instance, notes on pp 147–51.
5. O'Rahilly, *Five Seventeenth-Century Political Poems*, p.85
6. *O'Rahilly, Five Seventeenth-Century Political Poems, p.vii.*
7. *O'Rahilly, Five Seventeenth-Century Political Poems, p. vii.*
8. O'Rahilly, *Five Seventeenth-Century Political Poems*, p. viii.
9. O'Rahilly, *Five Seventeenth-Century Political Poems*, p. viii.
10. O'Rahilly, *Five Seventeenth-Century Political Poems*, pp 16–17.
11. Ó Cuív, 'The Irish language in the early modern period', in T.W. Moody, F.X. Martin, F.J. Byrne (eds.), *New History of Ireland*, Vol. III, (Oxford, 1976), pp 509–46.
12. Ó Cuív, 'The Irish Language', p.541.
13. Ó Cuív, 'The Irish Language', p.541.
14. O'Rahilly, *Five Seventeenth-Century Political Poems*, no. 5, lines 401–4, p.99.
15. Ó Cuív, 'The Irish Language', p.541.
16. Ó Cuív, 'The Irish Language', p.541.
17. Nicholas Canny, *Reformation to Restoration* (Dublin, 1987), pp 211–2.
18. Tadgh Ó Dúshláine, *An Eoraip agus Litríocht na Gaelige 1600–50 – Gnéithe den Bharócachas Eorpach i Litríocht na Gaelige* (Dublin, 1987).
19. Ó Dúshláine, *An Eoraip agus Litríocht na Gaelige*, p.180.
20. Ó Dúshláine, *An Eoraip agus Litríocht na Gaelige*, p.181.
21. J. Hardiman, *Irish Minstrelsy II* (Shannon [reprint], 1970), introduction by Maire Mhac a' tSaoi, p.431.
22. L.C. Martin (ed.), Introduction and notes to *Abraham Cowley, Poetry and Prose: with Thomas Sprat's Life, and Observations by Dryden, Addison, Johnson and others* (Oxford [reprint], 1959), pp v-xv.

23. Abraham Cowley, *The Civil War*, ed. Allan Pritchard, (Toronto, 1980), Bk. 2, pp 121–4.
24. Martin, *Abraham Cowley Poetry and Prose*, pp xv-xxxix.
25. Martin, *Abraham Cowley Poetry and Prose*, pp viii-x.
26. Martin, *Abraham Cowley Poetry and Prose*, p.xiii.
27. Mhág Craith, *Dán na mBráthar Mionúr II*, notes to poem 49, pp 236–9.
28. Martin, *Abraham Cowley Poetry and Prose*, p.67.
29. Martin, *Abraham Cowley Poetry and Prose*, p.67.
30. Cowley, *The Civil War*, p.120, n. 29–30.
31. 'Civil War', p.94.
32. 'Civil War', p.94.
33. 'Discourse', p.349.
34. 'Discourse', p.349.
35. 'Discourse', pp 352-3.

Chapter 16
Irish travellers in the Norse World R. POWER

1. Jakob Benediktsson (ed.) *Íslendingabók, Landnámabók*, Íslenzk Fornrit I (Reykjavík, 1968), pp 29–397. *Landnámabók* is translated by Hermann Pálsson and Paul Edwards, *The Book of Settlements* (Winnipeg, 1972).
2. *Íslendingabók, Landnámabók*, pp 1–28; reference on p.5. There are translations by Halldór Hermannson, The B*ook of Icelanders, Islandica* 20 (New York, 1930); and in Gwyn Jones, *The Norse Atlantic Saga*, 2nd ed (Oxford, 1986).
3. From *Liber de Mensura Orbis Terrae*. The passage is translated in Gwyn Jones, *A History of the Vikings* (London, 1968), p.270.
4. Einar Ólafur Sveinsson, 'Papar', *Skírnir* (1945), pp 179–203.
5. *Íslendingabók, Landnámabók*, pp 42–5.
6. *Íslendingabók, Landnámabók*, pp 250–3.
7. *Íslendingabók, Landnámabók*, pp 136–42, 146–7.
8. *Íslendingabók, Landnámabók*, pp 52–5.
9. *Íslendingabók, Landnámabók*, p.125; *Eyrbyggja Saga*, Einar Ólafur Sveinsson and Matthías Thórdarson (eds), *Íslenzk Fornrit* IV (Reykjavík, 1935) pp 8–9.
10. *Íslendingabók, Landnámabók*, pp 62–5. See Judith Jesch, 'Early Christians in Icelandic History – A Case-Study', *Nottingham Medieval Studies* 31 (1987), pp 17–36.
11. *Íslendingabók, Landnámabók*, p.61.
12. *Laxdaela saga*, Einar Ólafur Sveinsson (ed), Íslenzk Fornrit V (Reykjavík, 1934), pp 23–8, 49–59. See *Laxdaela saga*, trans. Magnus Magnusson and Hermann Pálsson (Harmondsworth, 1969), pp 64–9. 86–95.
13. See J.I. Young, 'Olaf Peacock's Journey to Ireland', *Acta Philologica Scandinavica* (Copenhagen) 8 (1933–4) pp 94–6.
14. See W.A. Craigie, 'Gaelic Words and Names in the Icelandic Sagas', *Zeitschrift für Celtische Philologie* I (1897), pp 439–54; Gabriel Turville-Petre, *Origins of Icelandic Literature* (Oxford, 1953), pp 3–4. I have given, unless stated otherwise, Classical Irish forms.
15. *Ílendingabók, Landnámabók*, p.162.
16. *Eríks saga rauda*, in *Eyrbyggja saga*, pp 193–237, the reference is on p.234. The other relevant saga, *Graenlendinga saga*, is in *Eyrbyggja saga*, pp 239–69. Both are translated in *The Vinland Sagas*, by Magnus Magnusson and Hermann Pálsson (Harmondsworth, 1965); the reference to Ireland the Great is on p.103.
17. *Eyrbyggja saga*, pp 176–80.
18. As *Brendanus saga*, in C.R. Unger (ed), *Heilagra manna sögur*, 2 volumes (Christiania [Oslo], 1877), i, 272–5.
19. *Flateyjarbók*, Flateyjarútgáfan [ed. Sigurdur Nordal], 4 vols. (Akranes [Iceland], 1944–5), iv, 330–2.

Chapter 17
New horizons in Hiberno-English studies P. KELLY

1. See the editors' comments in T. Bartlett, C. Curtin, R. O'Dwyer and G. Ó Tuathaigh (eds.), *Irish Studies: A General Introduction* (Dublin/Ottawa, 1988), pp 5–6.

2. M.V. Barry (ed.), *Aspects of English Dialects in Ireland* (Belfast, 1981).

3. M.V. Barry, 'The methodology of the Tape-Recorded Survey of Hiberno-English speech' in Barry, *Aspects*, pp 18–24.

4. Siegfried Bertz, *Der Dubliner Stadtdialekt* (Freiburg, 1975) and James Milroy, *Regional Accents of English: Belfast* (Belfast, 1981).

5. M.V. Barry, 'The English language in Ireland' in R.W. Bailey and Manfred Görlach (eds.), *English as a World Language* (Ann Arbor, 1983), pp 84–133.

6. James Milroy and John Harris, 'When is a merger not a merger?: the MEAT/MATE problem in a present-day English vernacular' in *English World-Wide* i no. 2 (1980), pp 199–210.

7. Cases in point are: A.G. Van Hamel 'On Anglo-Irish syntax', in *Englische Studien* xlv (1912), pp 272–92 and Jiro Taniguchi, *A Grammatical Analysis of Artistic Representation of Irish English* (Tokyo, [1956]).

8. J.P. Sullivan, 'The validity of literary dialect: evidence from the theatrical portrayal of Hiberno-English forms' in *Language in Society* ix (1980), pp 195–219.

9. J.R. Rickford, 'Social contact and linguistic diffusion: Hiberno-English and New World Black English', in *Language* lxii (1986), p.262.

10. John Harris, David Little, and David Singleton (eds.), *Perspectives on the English Language in Ireland* (Dublin, 1986).

11. Eithne Guilfoyle, 'Hiberno-English: a parametric approach', in *Perspectives*, pp 121–32.

12. Thomas Vogel, 'Verbal planning and narrative structure: the Belfast narrative' in *Perspectives*, pp 245–55.

13. John Harris, 'The lexicon in phonological variation', in *Perspectives*, pp 187–208.

14. Suzanne Romaine, *Socio-Historical Linguistics: Its Status and Methodology* (Cambridge, 1982).

15. The example is from Filppula, op. cit., p.34.

16. A.J. Bliss, 'English in the south of Ireland' in Peter Trudgill (ed.), *Language in the British Isles* (Cambridge, 1984), p.151.

17. John Harris, 'The Hiberno-English "I've it eaten" construction: what is it and where does it come from?' in D.P. Ó Baoill (ed.), *Papers on Irish English* (Dublin, 1985), p.36.

18. J.L. Kallen, 'Bilingualism and the genesis of Hiberno-English syntax', in *Teanga* v (1985), p.98.

19. Manfred Görlach, 'The study of early Modern English variation – the Cinderella of English historical linguistics' in Jacek Fisiak (ed.), *Historical Dialectology: Regional and Social* (Berlin/New York/Amsterdam, 1988), pp 211–28.

20. A.J. Bliss, *Spoken English in Ireland, 1600–1740* (Dublin, 1979), p.20.

21. N.P. Canny, review of Bliss, *Spoken English* in *Studia Hibernica* xx (1980), p.170.

22. Canny, p.171.

23. Wilhelm Heuser, *Die Kildare-Gedichte: die ältesten mittelenglischen Denkmäler in anglo-irischer Überlieferung.* Bonner Beiträge zur Anglistik 14 (Bonn, 1904).

24. J.J. Hogan, *The English Language in Ireland* (Dublin, 1927).

25. A. McIntosh and M.L. Samuels, 'Prolegomena to a study of mediaeval Anglo-Irish', in *Medium Aevum* xxxvii (1968), pp 1–11.

26. Myles Dillon, *Celtica* x (1973), p.16.

27. A.J. Bliss, 'Languages in contact: some problems of Hiberno-English' in *PRIA* lxxii Section C (1972), pp 63–82.

28. Barry, 'The English language in Ireland', p.110.

29. Cathair Ó Dochartaigh, 'Some anomalous vowels' in *Éigse* xix (1982), pp 137–44.

30. The Irish material is discussed by David Greene, 'Perfects and perfectives in Modern Irish' in *Ériu* xxx (1979), pp 130–41. For the origins of the HE construction in Early Modern English, see the reference in footnote 17.

31. For a survey see Gearóid Mac Eoin, 'Linguistic contacts in Ireland' in P. Sture Ureland (ed.), *Die Leistung der Strataforschung und der Kreolistik* (Tübingen, 1983), pp 227–35.
32. P.L. Henry, review of Bliss, *Spoken English* in *Éigse* xviii (1981), pp 325–6.
33. Heuser, *Kildare-Gedichte*, p.49.
34. Henry Risk, 'French loanwords in Irish' in *Études Celtiques* xii (1968-71), pp 585–635 and xiv (1974), pp 67–98.
35. My emphasis.
36. Gearóid Mac Niocaill, 'The legacy of the Middle Ages' in Bartlett et al., *Irish Studies*, p.25.
37. Ibid., p.26.
38. Cf. Peter Trudgill, 'The role of Irish English in the formation of colonial Englishes' in *Perspectives*, pp 3–7.
39. For example, C.N. Bailey, 'Irish English and Caribbean Black English: another joinder' in *American Speech* lvii (1982), pp 237–9.
40. Rickford, 'Social contact and linguistic diffusion, pp 245–89.
41. This position reflects the 'language bio-programm hypothesis' as expounded in Derek Bickerton, *Roots of Language* (Ann Arbor, 1981).
42. K.R. Andrews, N.P. Canny, and P.E.H. Hair (eds.), *The Westward Enterprise: English Activities in Ireland, the Atlantic and America 1480–1650* (Liverpool, 1978).
43. I argued this point in my paper 'The development of Hiberno-English in the seventeenth century' given at the 8th International Symposium on Language Contact in Europe, held in the Isle of Man in September 1988.
44. James Milroy and Lesley Milroy, 'Linguistic change, social network and speaker innovation' in *Journal of Linguistics* xxi no. 2 (1985), pp 339–84.
45. Peter Trudgill, Preface to Lesley Milroy, *Language and Social Networks* (2nd ed. Oxford, 1987), p.vii.
46. J.L. Kallen, 'The English language in Ireland' in *International Journal of the Sociology of Language* lxx (1988), p.137.